C000125806

Women and the Criminal Justice System

"Just over ten years ago the Corston report highlighted that the prison system was largely designed by men for men. The papers included in this volume reflect on women's experiences in the criminal justice system: they consider what has, or has not, been achieved in the period since Corston, the current state of play, and what we need to think about in terms of future strategies. Its focus is on women's involvement in the criminal justice system as a whole, rather than being simply characterized as 'victims' or 'offenders'. Written by both leading experts and those relatively new to the field, it provides a timely and refreshing perspective that will be of great interest to academics and policy makers alike. The insights contained in each of the papers underscore the need for women's experiences to be at the centre of debates on crime and criminal justice policy."

—Jayne Mooney, *John Jay College of Criminal Justice, USA*

Emma Milne · Karen Brennan · Nigel South
Jackie Turton
Editors

Women and the Criminal Justice System

Failing Victims and Offenders?

Editors
Emma Milne
Middlesex University
London, UK

Karen Brennan
University of Essex
Colchester, UK

Nigel South
University of Essex
Colchester, UK

Jackie Turton
University of Essex
Colchester, UK

ISBN 978-3-319-76773-4   ISBN 978-3-319-76774-1   (eBook)
https://doi.org/10.1007/978-3-319-76774-1

Library of Congress Control Number: 2018934664

Printed on acid-free paper

This Palgrave Macmillan imprint is published by the registered company Springer International Publishing AG part of Springer Nature
The registered company address is: Gewerbestrasse 11, 6330 Cham, Switzerland

We would like to dedicate this book to the professionals, volunteers and academics who work to improve the experiences of women as they come in contact with the criminal justice system.

We are grateful to the following for funding contributions that enabled us to run the conference that formed the basis of this book, as well as several follow-on activities: University of Essex ESRC Impact Accelerator funds, CHASE DTP—Consortium for the Humanities and the Arts South-East England, the Centre for Criminology and the School of Law at the University of Essex, the Royal Statistical Society and Palgrave Publishers.

The original version of the book frontmatter was revised: The affiliation of the book editor Emma Milne has been corrected. The erratum to the book frontmatter is available at https://doi.org/10.1007/978-3-319-76774-1_11

Contents

Editors and Contributors

About the Editors

Dr. Emma Milne is Lecturer in Criminology at Middlesex University. She gained her Ph.D. in Sociology from the University of Essex. Her research interests are in feminist criminology and women offenders. The wider context of Emma's work is consideration of social controls and criminal justice regulations on all women, notably in relation to pregnancy, sex and reproduction.

Dr. Karen Brennan is a Lecturer in Law at the University of Essex. Her research interests focus on the criminal law/practice in the context of childbirth and motherhood. Her published work examines the historical, socio-legal and gendered aspects to the criminal justice response to infanticide, and she is currently exploring the potential role of the criminal law on the issue of obstetric violence. She is also interested in the role of compassion in the criminal law and criminal justice practice, particularly in the context of assisted dying.

Nigel South is a Professor in the Department of Sociology and Director of the Centre for Criminology, University of Essex, and a visiting Adjunct Professor at the Crime and Justice Research Centre, Queensland University of Technology. He has published widely on various aspects of criminology and criminal justice including crime, inequalities and citizenship, and on public health and community services. In 2013, he received a Lifetime Achievement Award from the American Society of Criminology, Division on Critical Criminology, and in 2014 was elected a Fellow of the Academy of Social Sciences. Recent books include A. Brisman, E. Carrabine and N. South (eds.) (2017) *The Routledge Companion on Criminological Theory and Concepts*, Routledge.

Jackie Turton is a Professor in the Sociology Department at Essex University. She joined the University after a career in the health service and has taught sociology and criminology since 1996. Jackie is an experienced qualitative researcher and has completed projects for the Home Office, Department of Health and the Royal College of Paediatrics and Child Health linking her research and analysis with policy and practice. Jackie's teaching and research interests have focussed on domestic crime in particular child abuse as well as women as victims and offenders. She has taken part in discussions about female child abusers on Woman's (Radio 4) as well as child abuse more generally on local radio. Her book *Child Abuse Gender and Society (2008)* is a critical reflection of her research in this field.

Jackie has recently been working with a multidisciplinary team developing an evaluation strategy for community projects set up to support women (often victims themselves) who have "repeat losses to care"— children removed because of child protection concerns. Her recent co-authored publications detail the problems and difficulties for this set of women and the issues for evaluating small feminist-led community initiatives. She took on the role of Deputy Dean (Education) for the Faculty of Social Sciences at Essex in August 2016.

Contributors

Dr. Gemma Birkett is a Lecturer in Criminology at City, University of London. Gemma has published in the fields of penal reform, criminal justice policy-making, the courts and courtroom interactions, and gender and crime. Gemma sits on the steering group for the Women, Crime and Criminal Justice (WCCJ) Network of the British Society of Criminology.

Aviah Sarah Day is completing her Ph.D. titled "Partnership and Power: Feminist responses to domestic violence in the Criminal Justice System". She also has several years worth of experience in a range of front-line domestic violence services. In 2018, Aviah will start working with the charity Against Violence and Abuse as Project Manager, working on the House of Lords Commission into domestic violence and substance use. Aviah is also a member of Sisters Uncut—a feminist direct action group fighting cuts to domestic violence services.

Jenny Earle has led the Prison Reform Trust programme to reduce women's imprisonment since September 2012. Before that she was senior legal policy analyst at the Equality and Human Rights Commission, where she specialised in gender equality, led the Commission's work on CEDAW and prepared codes and guidance under the Equality Act 2010. Jenny has led on equality and justice issues in both government and community organisations in the UK and Australia, where she served on a Women in Prison Taskforce. She has been a senior research officer in the Women's Equality Unit, Cabinet Office, and director of the Work and Family Unit in the Australian Government's Department of Employment and Workplace Relations. In March 2018, Jenny was awarded an honorary doctorate by the Open University.

Loraine Gelsthorpe FRSA, FAcSS, is Professor of Criminology and Criminal Justice, and Director of the Institute of Criminology at the University of Cambridge. She has written extensively on women, crime and criminal justice and about youth justice, community penalties, deaths after periods of custody in police stations or prisons, and ethical dimensions of research. She is also Director of the Cambridge

University ESRC Social Sciences Partnership and an Adjunct Professor at the Crime and Justice Research Centre, QUT, Brisbane.

Dr. J. M. Gray is Associate Professor in Forensic Psychology at Middlesex University and leads the M.Sc. Forensic Psychology programme. Her sexual violence research focuses on the influence of rape myths in the Criminal Justice System, especially in the context of rape trials. She has published research into the interpretation of sexual consent and also sexual offending on public transport. She has published and presented research at national and international conferences, and in a range of peer-reviewed journals and edited texts.

Katrin Hohl is a Senior Lecturer in Criminology. She completed her Ph.D. at the London School of Economics and Political Science in 2012 and is now based at City, University of London. Her research centres on policing, in particular the police response to rape, sexual assault and domestic violence.

Dr. M. A. H. Horvath is Associate Professor in Forensic Psychology and Deputy Director of Forensic Psychological Services at Middlesex University. She has extensive research experience having conducted national and local multi-site/team/strand evaluation and research projects in a range of applied forensic and community settings. Projects have focussed on women and children who have experienced sexual and domestic violence. She has published and presented in a range of arenas including international peer-reviewed journals, national and international conferences and edited two books about rape.

Angela Jenner started at the University of Essex in 2009 and graduated in 2012 with a first class B.A. in criminology with social psychology and a prize for "exceptional achievement". She was then awarded a scholarship to go on and complete a masters in sociology. Having since been awarded an ESRC doctoral scholarship, Angie is now also completing her Ph.D. at the University of Essex as part of a collaborative project with Essex Police. Angie has also been a part-time Criminology Lecturer at London Metropolitan University since 2013.

Prof. Elizabeth A. Stanko OBE recently retired (April 2016) from the Mayor's Office for Policing and Crime in London. She worked inside the Metropolitan Police Service's Corporate Development for over a decade, establishing a social research function alongside performance analysis. She was also Professor of Criminology, at Clark University (USA), Brunel University, Cambridge University and Royal Holloway, University of London. She has been awarded a number of academic lifetime achievement awards, including the American Society of Criminology's Vollmer Award (1996), recognising her outstanding influence on criminal justice practice. She was awarded an OBE in 2014 for her services to policing.

Charlotte Triggs OBE acted as the CPS Senior Policy Advisor where she drew on her extensive experience as a specialist rape prosecutor. She was a member of the inspection team for *Without Consent—a report on the joint review of the investigation and prosecution of rape offences* and the Department of Health's Response to Sexual Violence. Charlotte worked closely with Dame Elish Angiolini on her 2015 Independent Review into the Investigation and Prosecution of Rape in London. Now freelance, Charlotte's work includes raising awareness of the reality of sexual abuse by delivering bespoke training.

Ruth Weir read Geography at University College London. After graduating in 2001, she worked as a researcher in the Community Safety Unit at Suffolk County Council. She undertook an M.Sc. in Geographical Information Science 2002–2004 and worked as a GIS specialist in the Research, Development and Statistics Directorate at the Home Office between 2004 and 2006. Prior to commencing her doctoral studies at University of Essex, she worked as a researcher on the Whole Essex Community Budget Domestic Abuse Project. Her Ph.D. is funded by Essex County Council and the ESRC.

List of Tables

1

Women and the Criminal Justice System—Moving Beyond the Silo

Karen Brennan, Emma Milne, Nigel South and Jackie Turton

The experience of women as offenders and victims is different to that of men and their interactions with the criminal justice system are shaped by their gender. Gender is not the only factor impacting individual experiences but women's involvement with criminal justice is

K. Brennan
School of Law, University of Essex,
Colchester, Essex, UK
e-mail: kbrennan@essex.ac.uk

E. Milne (✉)
Department of Criminology and Sociology, Middlesex University,
London, UK
e-mail: e.milne@mdx.ac.uk

N. South · J. Turton
Department of Sociology, University of Essex,
Colchester, Essex, UK
e-mail: n.south@essex.ac.uk

J. Turton
e-mail: turtje@essex.ac.uk

quantitatively and qualitatively different to that of men. In the first instance, women tend to commit less crime than men. According to Ministry of Justice statistics, in 2012/2013 only 15% of people arrested in England and Wales were women, and women made up only 5% of the prison population (Ministry of Justice 2014). Secondly, the offending profile for women is distinct from men's as they commonly commit a different range of offences. They commit more acquisitive crime and they are less involved in serious violence, criminal damage or professional crime (Gelsthorpe and Wright 2015). Finally, evidence suggests that the motivation for crimes committed by women is often different to their male counterparts, furthermore punishment, particularly penal punishment has a disproportionate adverse effect on female offenders (Scraton and Moore 2004). The end result of all these factors is a small number of offenders who are female and are pushed into a mechanism for punishment that was designed for and is dominated by men—the modern prison estate.

These issues and concerns were highlighted by the Corston Report (2007, p. 2) which noted that the prison system is 'largely designed by men for men' suggesting that women have been marginalised within it. As such, prison can be disproportionately harsh for women. Corston concluded that a distinct approach was needed and that, in contrast to the view that 'equal' must mean 'the same' for all people regardless of gender, in the context of the prison, equal treatment for women requires a different focus. Unfortunately, the impact of the Corston Report has been seen by many to be limited. A number of academics and professionals working with women in the field have been critical of responses by the criminal justice system to female offenders over the last ten years (Annison et al. 2015; Birkett, this volume; Earle, this volume). Although the problems surrounding the fate of female offenders have received some political focus—for example, in February 2016 the then Prime Minister, David Cameron (2016) indicated in his speech on prisons that there was 'a strong case' for women with small children to be diverted from prison—the political focus on crime and offenders has diminished significantly since the vote on Brexit in June 2016. For women, the political rhetoric has failed to translate into effective measures (for further discussion see Earle in this volume).

In cases where women are victims of violence, they are far more likely than men to have been attacked by a person with whom they are intimately acquainted. Domestic abuse, including emotional violence, continues to feature in the lives of too many women. Women are twice as likely to be a victim of domestic violence than men. In the year ending March 2016, 7.7% of women, equating to 1.3 million individuals experienced this form of violence, compared to 4.4% of men (CSEW 2017). This paints a bleak picture for the experience of women. On average in England and Wales, two women a week are killed by a violent partner or ex-partner. This constitutes nearly 40% of all female homicide victims (Povey 2015; Wykes and Welsh 2008). When considering women's lives as a whole, rather than just an experience over the last year, 27.1% of women and 13.2% of men have experienced domestic abuse since the age of 16 (CSEW 2016). These numbers illustrate that the experience of violence is very clearly gendered—men are likely to be attacked by a person they do not know, while women are at threat from men with whom they are acquainted, often intimately. A similar pattern of victimisation can be identified in sexual crime more generally; 3.2% of women have experienced sexual assault, compared to 0.7% of men. When considering this figure, we must acknowledge that intimate partner violence and abuse may include sexual violence. Recent research and media revelations have confirmed the pervasiveness of sexual harassment and assault within the workplace and on the street, as illustrated in the social media campaign #MeToo, launched at the end of 2017 (Khomami 2017). The recent study by Walby and Allen (2004) concluded that 45% of women have experienced some form of domestic violence, sexual assault or stalking in their lifetime.

The private and invisible nature of violence against women, including sexual violence, means that these crimes have, in the past, been overlooked. These issues have garnered more attention in recent decades and there have been many efforts to improve protection for victims of domestic and sexual abuse and to produce more effective criminal justice responses. This has included reform of criminal laws and rules of evidence: for example, reform of sexual offences in the Sexual Offences Act 2003, restrictions on the use of sexual history evidence at trial in the Youth Justice and Criminal Evidence Act 1999 and the creation of a new controlling or coercive behaviour offence in the Serious Crimes Act 2015, as well as changes in policies, procedures and practices in different criminal justice agencies, including the police and the CPS. However, notwithstanding growing awareness of the particular vulnerability and difficulties faced by victims of domestic and sexual violence, and some well-intended efforts to respond to this, problems have stubbornly persisted in investigation, prosecution and criminal justice responses to these crimes. Perhaps what this shows is that the law and the criminal justice system will have limited effect if they work in a silo that does not allow for connection with, and understanding of, wider social and cultural factors, which include patriarchal structures, gender norms, 'rape myths' and social inequalities such as the link between gender, poverty and violence (McManus et al. 2016). A more holistic approach is therefore required, in particular, one which takes account of the non-legal factors, particularly those relating to gender, in the criminal justice response to these crimes—crimes which are gendered.

It is hardly surprising then that the subject of 'women and criminal justice' has been, and remains, high on the agenda of feminist research, political discussion and the focus of activists within the voluntary sector. However, the different ways in which women may be involved with the criminal justice system are often treated as very distinct, separating women as victims or women as offenders. It is with this consideration in mind that we brought together academics, professionals and activists to consider the current state of research and practice concerning women as victims and offenders. The conference, held in April 2016 at the Royal Statistical Society in London, was entitled *Women and the Criminal Justice System—Past, Present and Future*. It is from the inspiring papers, discussions and motivations for change that this book developed.

This volume attempts to bridge the gap between the 'woman as victim' and the 'woman as offender' by considering women's involvement in the criminal justice system as a whole—to move beyond the silos of seeing two distinct groups that can sometimes overlap. Furthermore, it aims to put women at the centre of the debate on crime and punishment. Too often in political discussions, academia and media reports, women's involvement in the system is marginalised, ignored or lost in the concerns about male crime. Reports such as Corston's offer evidence that responses to women involved in the criminal justice system are failing on many levels; therefore, we need to find new ways of addressing these issues. The contributors to this book—academics and professionals working with women—make a powerful case that a focus on women in the criminal justice system needs to be seen as a high priority in terms of research, policy and practice, if we are to ensure justice for women.

This book gathers together some of the leading experts in England and Wales to reflect on what has happened in the past, what is going on right now and what needs to be done in future for women as victims and offenders. The book is separated into two parts, reflecting two of the themes that emerged from the conference, namely the position of women as victims and offenders, recognising that these are often not mutually exclusive experiences, and the question of whether the criminal justice system is failing or improving in the light of some recent developments.

In their chapter *Rape Myths in the Criminal Justice System*, Gray and Horvath explore the role of sexist cultural norms pertaining to sexual violence, in other words 'rape myths', in the criminal justice system. These myths lead to a fallacious understanding of sexual violence and affect decisions made at each stage of the criminal process following the reporting of a sexual crime; from decisions made by police officers in investigating an allegation (something which is also touched on in other chapters in this book), though to the jury's decision at trial. In their chapter, Gray and Horvath provide an introduction to the topic of rape myths, focusing in particular on their role at trial and in juror verdicts. They consider what has been done to try to reduce the use of rape myths in court and to diminish the impact of such stereotypical expectations regarding sexual violence on jurors. They argue that a thorough assessment of current interventions is needed and that efforts to challenge rape myths in the courtroom should continue.

The issue of rape myths and the negative impact they have on criminal justice decision-making is also highlighted by Triggs in her chapter, on *False Allegations of Sexual Violence: The Reality*. The categorisation of a report of rape as being false not only means that the complaint is not pursued (something which is problematic if the police or prosecutors are incorrect in their conclusion on this because sexual offenders are then not prosecuted) but also because it can result in the prosecution of the complainant for an offence such as Perverting the Course of Justice or Wasting Police Time. Triggs explores recent developments in how the CPS deals with suspected false rape allegations. For example, a case where a vulnerable woman, the victim of domestic abuse, was prosecuted by the CPS when she withdrew a complaint of rape she had made against her husband, resulted in the production of policy guidelines for prosecutors when deciding whether to prosecute someone on the grounds that they have made a false allegation or have withdrawn a complaint they had made. Triggs shows that the idea that women 'cry rape' without reason is not supported by statistics and that very few false allegations are made. A recent review by the CPS also highlights that even where a false allegation of sexual offending has been made, the motive is often not malicious but is connected with particular vulnerabilities of the accuser. Triggs also points to the difficulties that arise in relation to identifying a false allegation of sexual offending, something which is compounded by stereotypical views of how 'real victims' behave and the absence of a specific offence defining the meaning and scope of a 'false rape allegation'. Although the CPS has engaged in useful reflection on its approach to suspected false allegations, Triggs highlights the problems that will continue to beset this issue particularly in the context of police investigations.

Moving onto the topic of domestic violence, which is similarly plagued with difficulties in terms of producing effective criminal justice responses that protect victims, Day, Jenner and Weir in their chapter *Domestic Abuse: Predicting, Assessing and Responding to Risk in the Criminal Justice System and Beyond* present findings from three research projects, each of which takes a different approach to this issue. The first study examines the issues of underreporting and predictors of risk. The second focuses on the police response to domestic violence, something which has drawn media attention in recent years when women were killed by their partners/former partners after the police failed to take effective action following reports of current or previous violence. This research draws attention to the gaps in service provision to victims. The final project examines specialist courts and the work of independent domestic violence advisors. These projects seek to feed into current approaches to tackling domestic violence, and to improve criminal justice responses, examining ways in which professionals within the system might predict, assess and respond to risk in relation to domestic abuse.

In *Criminalising Neonaticide: Reflections on Law and Practice in England and Wales*, Brennan and Milne consider the unusual case where a woman is suspected of killing her newborn baby following a secret pregnancy and birth. This chapter explores what current research tells us about the circumstances and incidence of what has been termed 'neonaticide'. Following this, the difficulties from a legal perspective, and that arise when seeking to prosecute women for homicide when their babies die after a concealed pregnancy and unassisted birth are considered, particularly, evidential shortcomings which may make it difficult to prove the requirements for criminalisation under English and Welsh homicide laws. There is limited research on current criminal justice practice in these cases, and therefore little is known about the approach taken by the police, prosecutors and the courts in cases involving suspected homicides of newborns. This chapter highlights the complexities of these cases in terms of their circumstances and the vulnerability of women who conceal their pregnancies. The need for further research on the criminal justice responses is highlighted, and the appropriateness of criminalising women and girls in these cases, particularly given their unique circumstances of vulnerability, is questioned.

Milne and Turton, in their chapter *Understanding Violent Women*, consider recent research concerning women's violence, the public and professional responses to violent women, and how researchers have attempted to understand their behaviour. The chapter focuses on two 'extreme' acts of female violence—women who kill and women who sexually abuse children—to explore what we know about female violence and the significance of gender in both the social and legal contexts. The chapter illustrates the importance of understanding women's acts of violence within the context of their gender, as women who commit violent crimes challenge gender role boundaries in significant ways. Milne and Turton argue for the importance of including gender as a variable in any analysis of violent offending, in addition to an intersectional approach. To negate the experience of gender, the narratives surrounding women who are violent are either subsumed into male paradigms or become embedded in professional discourse that inevitably leads to the reproduction of the gendered environments.

The second part of the book moves on to explore issues connected with the question of whether the criminal justice system is improving or failing in its response to female offenders and victims. First, considering the impact of government reforms in 2013 to improve outcomes for women offenders, Gemma Birkett, in her chapter *Sentencing Women in the Transformed Probation Landscape*, examines awareness amongst magistrates of the reforms in the Transforming Rehabilitation strategy. Through her interviews with magistrates, Birkett reveals a lack of awareness of the sentencing developments under the Offender Rehabilitation Act 2014, with many magistrates expressing unease when discussing the new legislation as they were unaware of the specific changes it introduced, and only a few had read official documents relating to the Transforming Rehabilitation agenda. Furthermore, few magistrates who participated in the research had knowledge of the gender-specific strategies that were being developed by Community Rehabilitation Companies in their area. Perhaps most worrying, Birkett's research highlights that most magistrates who participated in the research were clear that they did not treat women differently, considering *equal* treatment to mean the *same* treatment. This situation persists despite official guidance to the contrary. Birkett concludes that it is clear that official bodies (including the Ministry of Justice, NOMS, the Judicial Office and the Magistrates' Association) should work to ensure that sentencers are aware of policy developments.

Linked with earlier chapters by Gray and Horvath, and Triggs, which touch on some of the difficulties encountered in responding to sexual violence, in their chapter *Why training is not improving the police response to sexual violence against women: A glimpse into the 'black box' of police training*, Stanko and Hohl look at the specific issue of police responses to complaints of sexual offences and the seemingly intractable issue of the 'justice gap'. Previous research which has highlighted the crucial role the police play in contributing to rates of attrition (which hover at around 6–7%) has emphasised the need for better police training to help address this issue, the idea being that if police officers have a better and more accurate understanding of the impact of sexual violence on victims, are trained to avoid relying on rape myths, and overall develop a better attitude towards victims, this will improve their decision-making during the investigation stage, leading to fewer cases dropping out of the system. Stanko and Hohl explore the effectiveness of police training to date, aiming to stimulate debate about training and why it has so far been ineffective at improving outcomes. They also reflect on challenges presented by academic and police training collaborations and offer some suggestions on how training might improve decision-making by police officers.

Jenny Earle in her chapter *Why focus on reducing women's imprisonment?* explores the gender-specific factors that lead to women's participation in crime, including the fact that previous victimisation can be a crucial factor in a woman's involvement in criminal offending. She argues that despite the fact that women make up only a very small proportion of the prison population, around five per cent, there must be a specific focus on women's imprisonment. Through the lens of the Prison Reform Trust's national advocacy programme, Earle considers opportunities and barriers to women's justice reform, concluding that women's centres and gender-specific services are the best option for women, and that prison is rarely a necessary, appropriate or proportionate response to women who come into contact with the justice system. Earle calls for the government to put in place the measures necessary to achieve the goal of reducing the number of women imprisoned for relatively minor offences, arguing that it is time for political leadership to follow-through on the rhetoric in support of such policies.

In the final chapter, *Women, Crime and Criminal Justice: Tales of Two Cities*, Gelsthorpe outlines the distance that exists between policy visions relating to women and criminal justice, both positive and optimistic, and the practice, which may offer a gloomier outlook. Criminal justice reforms have often created less noteworthy shadows, in this case, a failure to reduce the number of women within the prison estate, and a higher proportion of women being imprisoned for non-violent offences and for short sentences. Furthermore, there is evidence of police increasingly referring women for formal criminal justice proceedings, rather than referring offending women to Women's Centres on an informal basis. The tale of gloom is even worse for vulnerable women, such as women who have been trafficked. Gelsthorpe concludes that while women may no longer be 'correctional afterthoughts' there is more work to do in ensuring consistency in provision of women's centres, facilitating proper evaluation of the work within, promoting scrutiny of net-widening potential in initiatives, and promoting the use of imprisonment as a last resort, to name but a few areas requiring further attention.

This collection was drawn together in 2017, ten years after the publication of the Corston Report. As several contributors note, while much has been achieved since then, there are also reasons to be less than cheerful about whether Corston has had enduring impact. Indeed our contributors provide reasons for reflection on whether the system is improving in its preparation for working with women, in its training or its capacity for change. The system needs to challenge wider societal normative expectations and values in order to pursue effective criminal justice reform and better outcomes. It needs to be able to recognise the uniqueness of the experiences of women, adopting the message from Corston—'equality' does not require 'sameness' of treatment. There is more that could be said. Our hope is that the work of our contributors will encourage others to continue the conversation and debate.

References

Annison, J., Brayford, J., & Deering, J. (Eds.). (2015). *Women and criminal justice: From the Corston report to transforming rehabilitation*. Bristol: Policy Press.

Cameron, D. (2016, February 8). *Prison reform: Prime Minister's speech* [speech]. Available at: https://www.gov.uk/government/speeches/prison-reform-prime-ministers-speech (Accessed 15 October 2017).

Corston, J. (2007). *The Corston report: A report by Baroness Jean Corston of a review of women with particular vulnerabilities in the criminal justice system*. London: Home Office. Available at: http://www.justice.gov.uk/publications/docs/corston-report-march-2007.pdf (Accessed 21 September 2017).

Crime Survey of England and Wales (CSEW). (2016). *Intimate personal violence and partner abuse*. Available at: https://www.ons.gov.

uk/peoplepopulationandcommunity/crimeandjustice/compendium/focusonviolentcrimeandsexualoffences/yearendingmarch2015/chapter4intimatepersonalviolenceandpartnerabuse (Assessed 4 October 2017).

Crime Survey of England and Wales (CSEW). (2017). *Domestic abuse, sexual assault and stalking* [online]. Available at: https://www.ons.gov.uk/peoplepopulationandcommunity/crimeandjustice/compendium/focusonviolentcrimeandsexualoffences/yearendingmarch2016/domesticabusesexualassaultandstalking (Assessed 4 October 2017).

Gelsthorpe, L., & Wright, S. (2015). The context: Women as lawbreakers. In J. Annison, J. Bradford, & J. Deering (Eds.), *Women and criminal justice: From the Corston report to transforming rehabilitation*. Bristol: Policy Press.

Khomami, N. (2017). '#MeToo: How a hashtag became a rallying cry against sexual harassment'. *The Guardian* (20 October edn.). Available at: https://www.theguardian.com/world/2017/oct/20/women-worldwide-use-hashtag-metoo-against-sexual-harassment (Accessed 6 January 2018).

McManus, S., Scott, S., & Sosenko, F. (2016). Joining the dots: The combined burden of violence, abuse and poverty in the lives of women. London: Agenda. Available at: https://weareagenda.org/wp-content/uploads/2015/11/Joining-The-Dots-Report_Final_b_Exec-Summary.pdf.

Ministry of Justice. (2014). *Statistics on women and the criminal justice system 2013*. Available at: https://www.gov.uk/government/uploads/system/uploads/attachment_data/file/380090/women-cjs-2013.pdf (Accessed 6 January 2018).

Povey, D. (2005). *Crime in England and Wales 2003/2004: Supplementary volume 1: Homicide and gun crime* (Home Office Statistical Bulletin No. 02/05). London: Home Office.

Scraton, P., & Moore, L. (2004). *The hurt inside: The imprisonment of women and girls in Northern Ireland*. Belfast: Northern Ireland Human Rights Commission.

Walby, S., & Allen, J. (2004). *Domestic violence, sexual assault and stalking: Findings from the British crime survey*. London: Home Office.

Wykes, M., & Welsh, K. (2008). *Violence, gender and justice*. London: Sage.

Part I

Women as Victims and Offenders

2

Rape Myths in the Criminal Justice System

J. M. Gray and M. A. H. Horvath

Introduction

It is well known that most victims of rape (85%) do not report their experiences to the police (Ministry of Justice, Home Office, and Office for National Statistics [MOJ, HO, and ONS] 2013). Despite this, the last 30 years has seen a marked increase in the number of rapes reported to the police, as more victims of rape by acquaintances, family members and current or former partners have been encouraged to come forward (MOJ, HO, and ONS 2013). At the same time as the number of rapes reported has increased, there has also been some increase in the proportion of rapes receiving a conviction if they are taken forward by

J. M. Gray (✉) · M. A. H. Horvath
Psychology Department, Middlesex University,
London, UK
e-mail: J.Gray@mdx.ac.uk

M. A. H. Horvath
e-mail: m.horvath@mdx.ac.uk

© The Author(s) 2018
E. Milne et al. (eds.), *Women and the Criminal Justice System*,
https://doi.org/10.1007/978-3-319-76774-1_2

15

the Crown Prosecution Service (CPS), with the CPS conviction rate standing at 57.9% in the year 2015–2016 (CPS 2016). Whilst these patterns show some positive developments in the investigation and prosecution of rape, statistics based on three-yearly averages show that fewer than 7% of rapes reported to the police ultimately result in a conviction (MOJ, HO, and ONS 2013).

This chapter examines the role of rape myths in the above figures, drawing on and highlighting the importance of recent research findings on this issue, and also indicating directions for future work. The chapter starts with an introduction to theory and research relating to rape myths. It then moves on to consider the legal context, focussing on the influence of rape myths on the perception of sexual consent and on juror verdicts. It also considers the attitudes of lawyers and judges, and the way in which these attitudes may shape the conduct of rape trials. Following from this, the chapter addresses the experience of rape complainants in court, before finishing with an evaluation of the various attempts that have been made to reform the prosecution of rape.

Rape Myths

Rape myths are attitudes about rape, rape perpetrators and rape victims that serve to shift the blame for rape onto the victim, whilst minimising the perpetrator's responsibility and denying the seriousness of rape. Developing from earlier rape myth definitions such as those of Burt (1980), Payne et al. (1999), and Gerger et al. (2007, p. 425) define rape myths as 'descriptive or prescriptive beliefs about sexual aggression (i.e. about its scope, causes, context, and consequences) that serve to deny, downplay or justify sexually aggressive behaviour that men commit against women'.

Examples of rape myths include: women say 'no' when they mean 'yes'; a genuine victim of rape will fight back and immediately report their experience to the police; women who get drunk, or wear revealing clothing, or behave flirtatiously are 'asking' to be raped. They therefore set out the cognitive framework within which people understand rape in general, and against which they judge any specific incident

(Bohner et al. 2009; Temkin and Krahé 2008). One particularly pervasive rape myth is often known as the 'real rape' stereotype (Estrich 1987; Stewart et al. 1996). This stereotype is a constellation of a number of different rape myths; its key elements being that the rapist is a stranger, the assault occurs outdoors, the rapist uses force and the victim actively resists. This characterisation describes a very particular set of circumstances, which does not reflect the reality of the majority of rapes (e.g. the vast majority are perpetrated by someone known to the victim (MOJ, HO, and ONS 2013)). It also does not reflect the legal definition of rape as set out in section 1 of the Sexual Offences Act 2003, which does not require any of these features to be present in a rape. The legal definition and requirements are discussed below.

Whilst there are myths that exist in relation to the rape of males, the most frequent rape myths are focussed on females. These myths have been characterised as sexual scripts, which set out the expected form of sexual interactions between men and women (Frith 2009). In this 'script', men are the initiators and pursuers of sex, and women act as the gatekeepers with the associated responsibility for refusing men's sexual advances (Frith 2009). This conceptualisation clearly shows the gendered nature of this stereotypical form of sexual relationships, and associated with this, the way in which rape myths excuse male aggression and blame women for rape if they can be seen as not having adequately communicated their refusal of sex. We will return to this idea later.

From the perspective of social-cognitive psychology, it has been suggested that rape myths function as 'schemas', which provide model rape scenarios against which a particular rape claim is judged (Bohner et al. 2009; Temkin and Krahé 2008). Schema-based processing of rape means that cases that fit with commonly held expectations, such as those contained in the 'real rape' stereotype (Stewart et al. 1996), are more readily accepted as being non-consensual and hence judged to be rape. Conversely, those cases that run counter to schematic representations of 'real rape', such as when the complainant has consumed alcohol, flirted with the defendant or was in a relationship with him, are likely to be approached more sceptically by jurors who question whether consent may well have been given.

A variety of attitudinal and demographic characteristics have been identified as being associated with rape myth acceptance. A persistent finding is that men are more likely to believe rape myths than are women (Flood and Pease 2009; Suarez and Gadalla 2010). Often associated with gender, a variety of attitudes towards women and the nature of heterosexual relationships have also been associated with rape myth acceptance. Factors that have been found to be associated with rape myth acceptance include: sex role stereotyping, adversarial sexual beliefs and acceptance of interpersonal violence (Burt 1980); hostile attitudes towards women; and a variety of other prejudices such as racism, classism and ageism (Suarez and Gadalla 2010). Flood and Pease (2009) also note the belief in traditional gender and sexual roles as being associated with beliefs supportive of violence against women. It therefore seems that support for rape myths may form part of a more general attitudinal orientation that consists of beliefs about women that are rooted in traditional gender/sex roles, prejudice and the acceptance of violence.

The Legal Framework, Consent and Rape Myths in Court

The majority of rapes (around 90%) are perpetrated by someone known to the victim (MOJ, HO, and ONS 2013). This means that the issue at hand in proving rape is not whether the accused actually had sex with the complainant (as this is not contested), but instead whether the complainant consented to sex ('consent') and/or whether the defendant reasonably believed that the complainant had consented to sex ('reasonable belief in consent') (Sexual Offences Act 2003, s. 1 [SOA]). Thus, the defence attempts to persuade the jury that the complainant had consented to sex and that the defendant believed she consented, and that such belief was reasonable in the circumstances. It is on the questions of consent and reasonable belief in consent that rape myths become particularly influential (Adler 1987; Lees 1996; Temkin et al. 2018). In this context, the majority of the evidence is likely to be oral testimony from the defendant and complainant. Rape myths are then used to make the defendant's claimed belief in consent seem reasonable (e.g. myths such as she flirted, she must have consented to sex, she invited him into her house after a date), and also, on a claim that the complainant did in fact consent, to undermine her credibility (e.g. myths such as women say 'no' when they mean 'yes'; she delayed reporting the rape and is therefore lying).

On the question of whether the complainant consented, the concept of consent is defined as follows: 'a person consents if he agrees by choice, and has the freedom and capacity to make that choice' (SOA, s. 74). A number of factors may affect the question of whether a legally valid consent was given. For example, if the complainant was so intoxicated that she lacked the capacity to consent, then the defendant will be liable for rape, unless he mistakenly believed she was consenting and this was based on reasonable grounds. The question of reasonableness of a belief in consent 'is to be determined having regard to all the circumstances', which includes any steps that the defendant has taken to ensure that the complainant did consent (SOA, s. 1(2)). Whilst the Act provides a framework for this judgement, it does not specify how this should be, or indeed actually is, operationalised by juries.

Research has shown that consent to sex (or refusal thereof) between individuals is conveyed using both verbal and non-verbal signals (e.g. Beres 2010; Beres et al. 2004), and that both men and women use and understand very subtle cues (Kitzinger and Frith 1999; O'Byrne et al. 2006, 2008). Conversely, the 'miscommunication model' (Tannen 1992) suggests that rape occurs because men cannot understand the 'ambiguous' signals given by women. Whilst the idea of rape being due to miscommunication seems to hold an intuitive appeal to the public (Ellison and Munro 2009c; O'Byrne et al. 2008), the evidence does not support this overly simplistic account of rape. A more convincing argument, made by authors such as Kitzinger and Frith (1999) and O'Byrne et al. (2006, 2008), is that the gendered stereotypes reflected in rape myths are used to excuse and minimise sexually aggressive behaviour by men and also to shift the blame to women and undermine the credibility of rape complainants.

There has long been evidence that rape myths are used during rape trials (Adler 1987; Lees 1996). These studies showed reliance on historical ideas such as that claims of rape are easy to make and hard to refute, or that promiscuous women are more likely to have consented and to lie about rape. Whilst it would be hoped that such ideas had fallen from use, the recent study by Temkin et al. (2018) showed both of these ideas, and a wide range of others, still being routinely used to undermine the credibility of complainants. Observational studies evidence the range and frequency of rape myth usage, showing that complainants frequently face distressing and humiliating questioning at the hands of the defence, and that myths are used to undermine the complainant's credibility and suggest it was her behaviour that precipitated events (Lees 1996).

More recent observational research has investigated the way in which the courts in England and Wales respond to rape, including the use of, and efforts to challenge rape myths (Smith and Skinner 2017). They conclude that rape myths are still routinely used in rape trials and form markers against which the 'normality' of the complainant's behaviour, and hence veracity of her account, is judged. Rape myths were also found to be part of a culture of 'rationality' identified in rape trials (Smith and Skinner 2012). Behaviour considered to be rational (e.g. appropriate emotionality, immediate reporting) was seen to be the ideal, and any deviation from this was therefore used to cast doubt on the truthfulness of the complainant. Rape myths were also employed to suggest that the complainant was undeserving and to undermine their credibility. Although there were some attempts by the prosecution, and to a lesser extent by the judges, to challenge such reliance on rape myths, the findings from both of these reports suggest that rape myths remain a yardstick against which cases and complainants may be judged. Thus, if a complainant does not behave in accordance with stereotyped myths about expectations of 'virtuous' and 'restrained' female sexuality and behaviour, then any deviation from these stereotypes will be emphasised by the defence to suggest that this was not 'rape' (Smith and Skinner 2012, 2017).

Temkin et al. (2018) also identified the reliance on rape myths as a starting point in the judgement of rape cases. This observational study identified that rape myths were used frequently, with a wide range of myths emerging in the trials. The myths were used in three identifiable ways. Firstly, if the case did not fit with the 'real rape' stereotype, then the defence would attempt to use this to argue that the incident could not have been rape. Secondly, rape myths were used to undermine the credibility of the complainant. The final distinct type of use was when there were myth-congruent features of the case, in which case these would be emphasised and these elements used to reduce the culpability of the defendant and shift the blame to the complainant. Challenges to the use of rape myths were inconsistent, with some judges choosing to employ the 'illustrations' in the Crown Court Bench Book (Judicial Studies Board [JSB] 2010),[1] whilst others did not. It was noted that even when this guidance was given, it was not always done effectively.

Taken together, the evidence clearly indicates that rape myths have a long and persistent history of being used during trials. Both Smith and Skinner (2012, 2017) and Temkin et al. (2018) found some evidence of attempts by prosecutors and judges to counter the impact of the myths. However, this was inconsistent and there is little evidence as to the effectiveness of such efforts. Whilst in no way a generalisable finding, Temkin et al. (2018) discuss one notable case, in which the defendant was convicted, during which both the judge and prosecution counsel made robust challenges. Further research is needed to assess the effectiveness of such challenges, but in the meantime such interventions should be encouraged to attempt to reduce the impact of rape myths. The following sections will consider in greater depth the influence these myths have on the practice of legal professionals in the courtroom, jury decision-making and victims' experience of court.

Legal Professionals' Attitudes and Practice

In the context of an adversarial trial, the attitudes of the lawyers, judges and jurors can be influential in determining the outcome. In an adversarial trial, lawyers have a great deal of control over what evidence is presented and the way in which it is done (Carson and Pakes 2003; Saks and Thompson 2003). Their attitudes and beliefs will therefore be likely to influence the decisions that they make in this regard. Furthermore, it would be expected that a lawyer who believes rape myths would be more likely to use them in making their case, and also be less likely to challenge them if they are used by the opposing side. Similarly, judges in adversarial trials oversee the conduct of the case and have a role in deciding what evidence can be presented to a jury (Saks and Thompson 2003), offering a further opportunity for rape myths to be influential.

In a series of interviews with barristers who practised in rape trials, Temkin (2000) identified a range of rape myth supportive attitudes from both defence and prosecution barristers. Some prosecution barristers clearly showed attitudes that were derogatory to rape complainants, based on the complainant's appearance, the way they behaved and features of their lifestyle. These placed the blame on the complainant and characterised her as unworthy, which these barristers argued made their job of prosecution in such cases more difficult. If barristers themselves believe rape myths, it is unlikely that they will recognise them as problematic or that prosecution barristers will seek to counter them when used by the defence.

Temkin and Krahé (2008) conducted interviews with a sample of judges and barristers, who were appropriately trained and qualified to work on rape cases, in England and Wales. The participants considered that there had been improvements in the Criminal Justice System (CJS) response to rape, but that there were still difficulties to overcome. Defence barristers were seen to rely on rape myths during cross-examination and in some cases to malign and harass the complainant. Also noted was the frequent prosecution failure to make relevant points or to challenge the behaviour of defence counsel (Temkin and Krahé 2008). Temkin and Krahé (2008) also carried out quantitative studies with both undergraduate and postgraduate law students in England, investigating their attitudes to rape and the extent to which these were associated with their judgements related to rape vignettes. As predicted, those who were supportive of victim precipitation rape myths were more likely to perceive the complainant as to blame and to exonerate the defendant, particularly when the case involved an acquaintance or ex-partner. Krahé et al. (2008) report a very similar pattern of findings based on studies with trainee lawyers in Germany. Again, rape myth acceptance and case details that deviated from the features of the 'real rape' stereotype were predictors of victim blame and defendant exoneration.

It might be assumed that legal training should mean that lawyers are more aware of the problematic nature of rape myths. However, research suggests that lawyers at different stages of training, and when qualified, may well believe these myths and are influenced by them when making judgements about a case. Such findings are of serious concern, as this may mean that prosecution lawyers and judges do not notice when the defence relies upon myths, or if they do, they may not see this as a source of argument that needs to be challenged. Such findings may help to explain the somewhat patchy interventions by the judges and prosecution identified by Temkin et al. (2018) and Smith and Skinner (2017).

The Impact of Rape Myths on Juror Decision-Making

Whilst there will be variability in the extent to which jury members accept rape myths, it is likely that in any group of 12 individuals there will be some agreement with at least some of the myths. By drawing on these myths as part of the defence case, jurors are being invited to fall back on stereotyped ideas of what rape is (or how it is commonly perceived) and use this in reaching the verdict on the case at hand (Temkin et al. 2018).

A recent systematic review of empirical research found that eight out of the nine studies included showed either full (six studies) or partial (two studies) support for the impact of rape myths on judgements in rape cases (Dinos et al. 2015). Significant differences were identified between studies conducted in the USA and those from Europe and the UK. The European/UK studies reported significant associations, with larger effect sizes, between rape myths and juror decisions than did those based in the USA. The studies included in the review all followed a similar methodology, involving participants completing a measure of rape myth acceptance, reading some case information and making a judgement about the case (verdict, victim blame or defendant blame). As such, these studies are based on the views of mock jurors, usually making individual rather than group decisions.[3] Nonetheless, the findings provide strong support for the hypothesis that rape myths affect people's decision-making in rape cases.

Jurors have a difficult job to do, as there is a double layer of interpretation involved when assessing a rape case. Firstly, the complainant and defendant give their interpretations of what happened, and then, the jurors have to interpret those accounts. To further complicate this, there is then the level of group discussion and decision-making that occurs in the jury. This means that there are multiple opportunities for rape myths to be introduced, and for them to influence juries' decisions.

In a qualitative study explicitly designed to explore how people interpret a 'reasonable belief in consent', Gray (2015) identified themes related to the giving or refusal of consent, the interpretation of consent, vulnerability and consent as a process. Participants largely rejected rape myth-based ideas relating to a woman's behaviour. They also saw that the majority of men are 'good guys', who would not assume that consent was given, based upon a woman behaving in a way consistent with a rape myth. Most rape myths were seen as a means by which 'bad guys' would seek to justify and normalise their behaviour, but not as a valid excuse. The notable exception to this pattern of responses was in situations where a woman could be perceived to have placed herself at risk. Women who invite a man back to her home, who accept a lift from a stranger or who get drunk were seen to have allowed themselves to become vulnerable and hence were attributed at least some blame for being raped. This is consistent with findings that victims who voluntarily drank alcohol or took recreational drugs were attributed some responsibility for their eventual rape (Finch and Munro 2005a, b).

Numerous studies have demonstrated the influence of rape myths, situational characteristics and observer characteristics on victim blaming, defendant exoneration and verdict (e.g. Frese et al. 2004; Gray 2006; Grubb and Harrower 2008; Hammond et al. 2011; Peterson and Muehlenhard 2004). Where situational characteristics are found to be influential on juror perceptions, these frequently relate to rape mythology, such as the role of alcohol/substance consumption (Finch and Munro 2005a; Grubb and Turner 2012; Lynch et al. 2013). Alcohol can be an influential factor in increased blame attribution to the victim and reduced responsibility of the defendant. Alcohol use can also be seen as a signal of a false rape allegation (consent given when drunk and later regretted), and also, if both parties are equally intoxicated, as making the event 'not really' rape (Gunby et al. 2012). Finch and Munro (2005b) also argue that the social acceptability of alcohol consumption affects the perception of rape and the responsibility of the complainant and defendant. In their mock jury study, whether either the victim had voluntarily consumed alcohol, or the defendant had surreptitiously administered it, participants were likely to see the complainant as at least somewhat responsible and be unwilling to characterise the event as rape. In contrast, where the defendant administered a drug such as Rohypnol, the event was much more clearly perceived to be rape. Thus, the consumption of alcohol in particular, whether voluntary or not, is particularly likely to lead jurors to conclude that an event is not rape.

Previous experience of sexual victimisation amongst those judging rape cases has also been suggested as a likely factor that would influence people's judgements. Surprisingly, Mason et al. (2004) found there was no difference in the judgements of victims and non-victims about whether a scenario was perceived to be an acquaintance rape or not, nor in the level of victim blaming. Regardless of victimisation status, rape myth acceptance was found to be associated with greater attribution of blame to the complainant. It is also noted that rape myths have been found to influence whether victims themselves actually recognise their experience as rape, particularly if there are stereotypical features of the event, such as 'not fighting back' (Peterson and Muehlenhard 2004; Weiss 2009). In this way, as well as influencing the judgements of potential jurors, rape myths can have a damaging effect on the decision-making of victims.

In a series of papers based upon an unusually complex and realistic mock trial study, Ellison and Munro (2009a, b, c) examine the impact of rape myths pertaining to victim resistance during rape, delayed reporting and a calm emotional demeanour in the aftermath of rape and whilst giving testimony. The idea that a 'true' victim of rape will always resist their assault, particularly putting up a physical struggle, was a robust belief (Ellison and Munro 2009a). This was particularly evident amongst the female participants who were inclined to claim that they were sure that they would physically resist rape. This expectation of resistance was less strong if the assailant was a stranger, but was still evident. Lack of injuries was often seen as an indicator that it was not rape, and even where bruising and scratches were present, participants frequently expected greater injury. Similarly, a delay in reporting the rape to the police was frequently seen as an indicator that the complainant had not actually been raped. A calm emotional demeanour when testifying in court was also counter to participants' expectations. However, it was evident that an emotional complainant was not universally accepted as evidence of veracity either, with some jurors suggesting that the emotion was being faked. These stereotypes about rape were readily brought into discussions, and whilst at times there were dissenting voices, the myths were significant influences in the decisions reached. In conclusion, Ellison and Munro (2009a) argue that the suggestion that jurors can be relied upon to judge a case without being influenced by their pre-existing attitudes and beliefs is erroneous.

Having established the presence and influence of rape myths in mock jury discussions, Ellison and Munro (2009b) also consider the influence of either an expert witness or judicial directions to educate jurors and counter the influence of rape myths. Overall, the guidance regarding calm emotional demeanour and delayed reporting was identified as having some success, with juries receiving this information being less likely to see these features as problematic for the prosecution case. However, the beliefs about victim resistance seemed to be harder to dislodge, with no difference identified in the nature of the discussions between members of those juries receiving education and those who did not. In relation to the source of the educational guidance, little difference was identified between the expert, who gave evidence in the earlier part of the mock trial (but after the complainant) and the judge who gave directions at the end.

Ellison and Munro (2009c) discuss how sexual scripts are drawn upon during the jury discussions to establish whether or not the complainant had consented to sex. Drawing on the expectations of 'normal' (i.e. consensual) sex, participants considered that if non-verbal behaviours associated with consensual sex were present, then the defendant was probably reasonable to expect that sex was likely. Many of these behaviours, such as inviting someone home, kissing, accepting a lift or drinking alcohol together, reflect rape myths, showing their influence in this context. Furthermore, some of the discussions reflected the view that the victim's resistance was not sufficient to counter the expectations of the defendant that had been raised by her earlier behaviour. However, participants also saw an explicit conversation to check consent as unrealistic and not the way normal sex unfolds. Thus, an evident contradiction occurs wherein jurors do not expect explicit checking of consent, but see the non-verbal signals as ambiguous.

In a context where it is not possible to study the working of real juries (Contempt of Court Act 1981, s. 8), mock jury and vignette-based studies are the closest facsimiles of real decision processes that are possible. Drawing on a variety of methodologies, there is good evidence that rape myths do influence the verdicts reached in rape cases, at least in trial simulation studies. Whilst there is some variability in the findings regarding specific myths, and also the cultural context, there is sufficient evidence to maintain concern that rape myths are likely to have a biasing influence on juror judgements, increasing the likelihood of acquittals. In addition to this impact on verdicts, rape myths are also problematic because of the way in which they contribute to the complainant's lived experience of court.

Complainants' Experiences of Court

Despite various efforts to improve victims' experiences of rape trials (discussed below), observational research over a substantial period has shown that rape myths are routinely brought into the courtroom, commonly by the defence counsel as a means of seeking to discredit the complainant and undermine her testimony (e.g. Lees 1996; Temkin et al. 2018). During the course of trial observations, researchers may observe signs of complainant's distress or discomfort, but such studies do not provide direct evidence of the way in which such practice is experienced by complainants. Unsurprisingly perhaps, research that has asked complainants about this has generally found that the experience is not good. Indeed, a number of women told Lees (1996) that they could not take part in her research because the experience of court was too traumatic for them to face reliving it. Those who did participate reported humiliating, demeaning, irrelevant questions and reported feeling as though they were the one being tried, rather than the defendant (Lees 1996).

Similar negative experiences of the court process for rape victims are reported by Wheatcroft et al. (2009), based upon interviews with rape complainants, police officers and rape support workers. Echoing the findings of other studies, this research highlighted the traumatising and humiliating nature of the cross-examination of complainants by the defence barristers, with one of the complainant participants describing it as a second rape. The behaviours of both judges and defence barristers were highlighted as being problematic for complainants, subjecting them to inappropriate comments and displaying victim-blaming attitudes.

Efforts to Challenge Rape Myths in the Courtroom

The problematic effects of rape myths have been recognised outside of the academic community, and we now turn to the various attempts to ameliorate their influence that have been introduced in England and Wales. Many politicians, activists, academics and members of the general public have sought to challenge the use of rape myths in the courtroom. For example, Jill Saward who died in early 2017 was the first rape victim in England and Wales to waive her right to anonymity. In the last few years of her life, she had set up Juries Understanding Rape is Essential Standard (JURIES) to campaign on mandatory briefings on myths and stereotypes about sexual violence for juries in rape, sexual assault and abuse trials. In this section of the chapter, we will outline the efforts that have been made in England and Wales to reduce the use of rape myths in trials and to counter their impact when they have been used. We will also consider what is known about the effectiveness of such measures.

What Has Been Done?

A key area of concern for policymakers, regarding the use of rape myths, has been the defence's reliance on sexual history evidence. Such evidence was an established part of rape trials (Temkin 2002) and was identified as being problematic for the implementation of justice in the Heilbron Report (1975) leading to the eventual introduction of section 41 of the YJCEA 1999. This provision restricts the occasions on which sexual history evidence can be used in court, requiring written application to the judge before the trial and substantially limiting cases where it can be allowed. However, in their study of the operation of section 41, Kelly et al. (2006) found that sexual history evidence occurred in two-thirds of the trials that they observed, but that the required application to the judge was only made in less than one-third of the cases. Furthermore, when sexual history evidence was introduced without the section 41 application, judges either did not notice or failed to take any action against the defence (Kelly et al. 2006). It thus seems that even legislative attempts to restrict the use of this very specific myth have a limited effect, indicating the pervasive reliance on such attitudes in court.

There are two key players in the courtroom when it comes to challenging rape myths, the judge and the prosecution barrister. In recent years, the CPS and the JSB have introduced guidance and recommendations about how judges and barristers should challenge rape myths.

Crown Prosecution Service

Specialist training for rape prosecutors was introduced in 2007 (CPS 2012). The training aims to reduce the use of rape myths by highlighting the realities of rape (Smith and Skinner 2017). CPS policy for the prosecution of rape also clearly states that prosecutors 'will robustly challenge such attitudes in the courtroom' (CPS 2012, p. 15). The Joint CPS and Police Action Plan on Rape (2014) further emphasises that the focus for investigators and prosecutors should be on the behaviour of the defendant rather than of the complainant. In 2012, the Director of

Public Prosecutions (DPP) set a challenge to those who work in the CJS 'How do we ensure that myths and stereotypes do not play any part in a jury's deliberations whether consciously or subconsciously?' (Saunders 2012). Shortly after the DPP laid down the gauntlet, Burrowes (2013), a clinical psychologist working in the area, produced a guide for prosecutors about rape myths and how to challenge them in the courtroom. This was endorsed by DPP Alison Saunders and has been fairly well received by researchers in the area (e.g. Smith and Skinner 2017). This document is freely available online but it is not possible to know how widely it has been read and whether its recommendations have been adopted by prosecutors.

Judicial Studies Board

The Crown Court Bench Book, published by the JSB (2010), sets out specimen directions for use by judges in the Crown Court. For example, judges in England and Wales are able to give directions to the jury regarding the danger of relying on stereotyped beliefs about rape, although they are not obliged to do so. In 2011, a *Companion to the Bench Book* was issued which took the form of checklists of matters which could and (depending on the issues in the case) might need to be dealt with when directing the jury on particular legal and evidential subjects (Tonking and Wait 2011). To address some apparent misunderstanding and confusion amongst judges regarding the previous guidance, in 2016 the Judicial College published a *Compendium* that it claims combines all of the strengths of the previously issued guidance into one document (Maddison et al. 2016). Chapter 20 of the Compendium focuses on sexual offences and clearly outlines the dangers of assumptions and stereotypes, essentially rape myths, and the steps judges can take to counteract them. The Compendium advises that directions regarding rape myths may be given at the outset of the trial or in their summing up. Judges are advised to discuss their direction with counsel and to make considerable efforts to ensure the direction 'reflects the facts of the case and retains a balanced approach' (Maddison et al. 2016: 20–22). The Compendium clearly states that there is a real danger that juries will be asked to make unwarranted assumptions by barristers and it is the judge's responsibility to warn the jury to guard against this. Specific examples of myths, particularly those that relate to the issues of consent and/or belief in consent, that the judge might need to warn against are listed. Alongside the guidance issued for judges, training has also been introduced for judges with a focus on the realities of rape and the aim of challenging rape myths (Smith and Skinner 2017).

Evaluating the Efforts of the CPS and Judicial Studies Board

There is extremely limited evidence available about the use and effectiveness of the available interventions to guard against rape myths in the courtroom. Some of the most comprehensive evaluative evidence available comes from an independent review of the investigation and prosecution of rape in London conducted by Dame Elish Angiolini in 2015. Angiolini (2015) observed that rape myths were on occasion influential in CPS judgements regarding the likelihood of obtaining a conviction, and that there was little evidence of the prosecution discussing strategies to combat these myths. She also found that the specialist training for rape prosecutors has not been adequately implemented. Although this was an independent review which lends it findings weight, it was not a systematic empirical evaluation of the work of the CPS and the JSB.

There have been other critiques of the training offered for prosecution barristers and judges, including that training can perpetuate stereotypes if interpretations of the course material are not checked (Stern 2010). Smith and Skinner (2017) provide an example from Smith (2009) of a barrister who thought his training had taught him to doubt any victim/survivor who was emotionally distressed. Rumney (2011), whilst largely praising the available training, because it is provided by experts and gives practical advice about legal decisions, also acknowledges that some legal professionals will attend training without challenging their perceptions. Indeed, in research undertaken in 2010, Smith and Skinner (2012) found that prosecution barristers still appeared ineffective at challenging rape myths. Furthermore, in a later paper, Smith and Skinner (2017) conclude that judges are being allowed to attend training and go on to try rape cases without any checks in place to demonstrate they have really engaged with the material. This leads back to the crucial problem for those working in this area: because systematic empirical evaluations of the training for judges and barristers do not exist, we cannot say with certainty how effective such training is.

In terms of the guidance available to judges and the consequences of increasing the number of judicial directions, there has been some debate about the effectiveness of these measures, but no comprehensive evaluations. Some have argued that guidance is more effective when given at the start of a trial (Leippe et al. 2004), and others have reported that barristers are sceptical of increasing the number of judicial directions (Carline and Gunby 2011). This scepticism seems to stem from a concern that the increase in judicial directions adds unnecessary complications to a trial and may lead jurors towards conviction. However, Ellison and Munro (2009b) argue that there are benefits to judicial directions and claim they are effective in lowering rape myth acceptance amongst jurors.

The introduction of Police and Crime Commissioners (PCC) has provided opportunities for regional initiatives in relation to all aspects of the CJS and one PCC has targeted rape trials. Northumbria's PCC, Vera Baird, has introduced a court observers' panel comprised of trained volunteers who are observing rape and some sexual abuse trials at Newcastle Crown Court (http://www.northumbria-pcc.gov.uk/court-observers-panel/). This scheme, running since January 2015, is the only one in the country. These observations aim to increase understanding within the court and build the confidence of victims to report rape and sexual abuse. No reports from the scheme have been made public at this time, and there is no evaluation evidence available in relation to the effectiveness of the panel's recommendations. However, the scheme's potential has been identified by other researchers in the field (e.g. Smith and Skinner 2017), and in a recent Guardian article (Denes 2017), which highlighted the scheme and provided insights into the kind of recommendations being made (the panel's reports are shared with a senior judge). In relation to rape myths, the panel praises judges who universally give 'myth busting' directives to the jury at the outset of a trial (Denes 2017).

Where Do We Go from Here?

As highlighted in the previous section, legal professionals receive training to counter stereotypes. Smith and Skinner (2015) recommend that good practice guidelines and practical training regarding stereotypes, rape myths and 'hypothetical rational scenarios' should be developed for prosecution barristers, and that specialist sexual violence courts should be developed to create centres of good practice.

There has been some discussion about the use of expert witnesses in rape trials. Keogh (2007) called for expert witnesses to outline the realities behind sexual violence, although Ellison and Munro (2009b) subsequently debated whether this would be more convincing than judicial directions. Smith and Skinner (2017) draw on Australian work which found mock jurors were equally convinced by judicial comments as by clinical psychologists (Goodman-Delahunty et al. 2011), to make the case that the focus should be on getting judicial directions correct rather than being distracted by the possibility of introducing expert witnesses. Although evidence does not currently exist as to whether judicial directions are most effective at the outset or closing stages of a rape trial, it could be argued that to be most effective they should be issued on both occasions. The judge giving the jury directives about rape myths at the beginning of the trial will prime the jury to be on the lookout for their use, and providing the warnings again at the end of the trial should allow them to be wary of relying upon them in their deliberations. However the messages are conveyed, there is a strong consensus that educational guidance and 'myth busting' directives for juries are necessary in rape cases. As Ellison and Munro (2009b) suggest, drawing on Lewis's (2006) work, educational guidance may have greatest impact when general expert testimony and judicial instructions are used together.

Another area for reform is around cross-examination, which, as outlined earlier in the chapter, is often experienced as re-traumatising by victim/survivors and is a key stage when rape myths are relied on by barristers. Henderson (2015) has made the case that reforms of cross-examination should be extended beyond vulnerable witnesses. She argues that:

> At a minimum, judges and advocates need to be more vigilant to prevent witnesses becoming confused and compliant. A complex vocabulary or complex syntax (for example, double negatives and multi-part questions) should be avoided and witnesses should be encouraged to seek clarification. (p. 93)

As has been demonstrated, there has been a raft of measures introduced but the problem remains that we have almost no monitoring or evaluation as to whether or how they work, and, given the limited data available, it is also not possible to draw conclusions about what works best.

Conclusions

This chapter has reviewed a wide range of literature related to the use and impact of rape myths in court. At the current time, evidence indicates that rape myths remain in common usage in trials, and that they can impact on verdicts. Long-established practice and the attitudes of members of the legal professions may well be influential in the persistence of rape myths (Smith and Skinner 2017; Temkin et al. 2018). Guidelines and policy developments have been introduced in an effort to encourage prosecutors and judges to act to counter rape myths when they are introduced. The evidence so far suggests that the implementation of these measures is somewhat inconsistent, but to date there is little evaluation of their efficacy.

At this juncture, it would seem that an urgent priority should be the systematic empirical evaluation of the implementation and effectiveness of efforts to challenge rape myths in the courtroom. The work being carried out in Northumbria by the Police and Crime Commissioner is a promising development but a rigorous, national programme of research is necessary to determine whether guidance is being followed, and, if so, whether it is having an effect. Furthermore, research is needed to develop an understanding of the way in which jurors utilise rape myths in their decision-making.

Continued work in this area, from academics, policymakers, practitioners, activists and the public, remains an important priority. The majority of rape victims still do not report their experience to the police, and the attrition rate remains high once victims do decide to report. Rape myths impact on decisions made by various actors throughout the process, including the victim's decision to report, the police response, the CPS decision of whether the case has a reasonable prospect of conviction and the practices of lawyers, judges and the decisions of the jury in court. Until such time as these beliefs are no longer commonplace amongst the public, the most promising means of reducing their impact on juries seem to be through education such as that encouraged through current guidance. This therefore emphasises the need for these forms of juror (and indeed lawyer and judicial) training to be evaluated and subjected to continuing development to improve justice in rape prosecutions.

Ultimately, if we are to effectively challenge rape myths in the courtroom, they must also be challenged and ideally eradicated in society. This is a hugely challenging task as rape myths are so deeply ingrained in our culture. However, if we are truly committed to reducing trauma and improving responses for victim/survivors of rape at every stage of the CJS, then we must try harder.

Notes

1. The Crown Court Bench Book (JSB 2010) has now been superseded by the Crown Court Compendium published by the Judicial College (Maddison et al. 2016).
2. In England and Wales, many barristers are self-employed and therefore will frequently take prosecution and defence work, according to what is available.
3. Mock jurors are often used as a methodological choice for reasons of experimental control/complexity of research design, etc.

References

Adler, Z. (1987). *Rape on trial*. London, UK: Routledge.

Angiolini, E. (2015). *Report of the independent review into the investigation and prosecution of rape in London*. Available at: http://www.cps.gov.uk/publications/equality/vaw/dame_elish_angiolini_rape_review_2015.pdf (Accessed 6 July 2017).

Beres, M. (2010). Sexual miscommunication? Untangling assumptions about sexual communication between casual sex partners. *Culture, Health and Sexuality, 12*(1), 1–14.

Beres, M. A., Herold, E., & Maitland, S. B. (2004). Sexual consent behaviors in same-sex relationships. *Archives of Sexual Behavior, 33*, 475–486.

Bohner, G., Eyssel, F., Pina, A., Siebler, F., & Viki, G. T. (2009). Rape myth acceptance: Cognitive, affective and behavioural effects of beliefs that blame the victim and exonerate the perpetrator. In M. Horvath & J. Brown (Eds.), *Rape: Challenging contemporary thinking* (pp. 17–45). Cullompton, UK: Willan.

Burrowes, N. (2013). *Responding to the challenge of rape myths in court: A guide for prosecutors*. Available at: http://nb-research.com/wp-content/uploads/2013/04/Responding-to-the-challenge-of-rape-myths-in-court_Nina-Burrowes.pdf (Accessed 6 July 2017).

Burt, M. R. (1980). Cultural myths and supports for rape. *Journal of Personality and Social Psychology, 38*(2), 217–230.

Carline, A., & Gunby, C. (2011). How an ordinary jury makes sense of it is a mystery: Barristers' perspectives on rape, consent and the sexual offences act 2003. *Liverpool Law Review, 32*(3), 237–250.

Carson, D., & Pakes, F. (2003). Advocacy: Getting the answers you want. In D. Carson & R. Bull (Eds.), *Handbook of psychology in legal contexts* (2nd ed., pp. 347–366). Chichester: Wiley.

Crown Prosecution Service. (2016). *CPS prosecuting and convicting more cases of rape, domestic abuse, sexual offences and child abuse than ever before*. Available at: http://www.cps.gov.uk/news/latest_news/vawg_report_2016/ (Accessed 6 July 2017).

Crown Prosecution Service and Association of Chief Police Officers. (2014). *Joint CPS and police action plan on rape*. Available at: https://www.cps.gov.uk/publications/equality/vaw/rape_action_plan_april_2015.pdf (Accessed 6 July 2017).

Denes, M. (2017, February 11). "It's always high drama. It's somebody's life at stake": Inside British rape trials. *The Guardian*. Available at: https://

www.theguardian.com/society/2017/feb/11/always-high-drama-stake-trials (Accessed 6 July 2017).

Dinos, S., Burrowes, N., Hammond, K., & Cunliffe, C. (2015). A systematic review of juries' assessment of rape victims: Do rape myths impact on juror decision-making? *International Journal of Law, Crime and Justice, 43*(1), 36–49.

Ellison, L., & Munro, V. E. (2009a). Reacting to rape: Exploring mock jurors' assessments of complainant credibility. *British Journal of Criminology, 49*(2), 202–219.

Ellison, L., & Munro, V. E. (2009b). Turning mirrors into windows? Assessing the impact of (mock) juror education in rape trials. *British Journal of Criminology, 49*(3), 363–383.

Ellison, L., & Munro, V. E. (2009c). Of 'normal sex' and 'real rape': Exploring the use of socio-sexual scripts in (mock) jury deliberation. *Social and Legal Studies, 18*(3), 291–312.

Estrich, S. (1987). *Real rape: How the legal system victimizes women who say no.* Boston: Harvard University Press.

Finch, E., & Munro, V. E. (2005a). Juror stereotypes and blame attribution in rape cases involving intoxicants: The findings of a pilot study. *British Journal of Criminology, 45*(1), 25–38.

Finch, E., & Munro, V. E. (2005b). The demon drink and the demonized woman: Socio-sexual stereotypes and responsibility attribution in rape trials involving intoxicants. *Social and Legal Studies, 16*(4), 591–614.

Flood, M., & Pease, B. (2009). Factors influencing attitudes to violence against women. *Trauma, Violence, and Abuse, 10*(2), 125–142.

Frese, B., Moya, M., & Megías, J. L. (2004). Social perceptions of rape: How rape myth acceptance modulates the influence of situational factors. *Journal of Interpersonal Violence, 19*(2), 143–161.

Frith, H. (2009). Sexual scripts, sexual refusals and rape. In M. Horvath & J. Brown (Eds.), *Rape: Challenging contemporary thinking* (pp. 99–124). Cullompton, UK: Willan.

Gerger, H., Kley, H., Bohner, G., & Siebler, F. (2007). The Acceptance of Modern Myths About Sexual Aggression (AMMSA) scale: Development and validation in German and English. *Aggressive Behavior, 33*(5), 422–440.

Goodman-Delahunty, J., Cossins, A., & O'Brien, K. (2011). A comparison of expert evidence and judicial directions to counter misconceptions in child sexual abuse trials. *Australian and New Zealand Journal of Criminology, 44*(2), 196–217.

Gray, J. M. (2006). Rape myth beliefs and prejudiced decision guidance: Effects on decisions of guilt in a case of date rape. *Legal and Criminological Psychology, 11*(1), 75–80.

Gray, J. M. (2015). What constitutes a "reasonable belief" in consent to sex? A thematic analysis. *Journal of Sexual Aggression, 21*(3), 337–353.

Grubb, A., & Harrower, J. (2008). Attribution of blame in cases of rape: An analysis of participant gender, type of rape and perceived similarity to the victim. *Aggression and Violent Behavior, 13*(5), 396–405.

Grubb, A., & Turner, E. (2012). Attribution of blame in rape cases: A review of the impact of rape myth acceptance, gender role conformity and substance use on victim blaming. *Aggression and Violent Behavior, 17*(5), 443–452.

Gunby, C., Carline, A., & Beynon, C. (2012). Regretting it after? Focus group perspectives on alcohol consumption, nonconsensual sex and false allegations of rape. *Social and Legal Studies, 22*(1), 87–106.

Hammond, E. M., Berry, M. A., & Rodriguez, D. N. (2011). The influence of rape myth acceptance, sexual attitudes, and belief in a just world on attributions of responsibility in a date rape scenario. *Legal and Criminological Psychology, 16*(2), 242–252.

Henderson, E. (2015). Best evidence or best interests? What does the case law say about the function of criminal cross-examination? *The International Journal of Evidence and Proof, 20*(3), 183–199.

Her Majesty's Inspectorate of Constabulary and Her Majesty's Crown Prosecution Service Inspectorate. (2012). *Forging the links, rape investigation and prosecution.* Available at: https://www.justiceinspectorates.gov.uk/hmic/media/forging-the-links-rape-investigation-and-prosecution-20120228.pdf (Accessed 6 July 2017).

Judicial Studies Board. (2010). *Crown Court Bench Book: Directing the jury.* Available at: https://keithhotten.files.wordpress.com/2014/05/benchbook_criminal_2010.pdf (Accessed 6 July 2017).

Kelly, L., Temkin, J., & Griffiths, S. (2006). *Section 41: An evaluation of new legislation limiting sexual history evidence in rape trials* (Home Office Online Report 20/06). Available at: http://citeseerx.ist.psu.edu/viewdoc/download?doi=10.1.1.628.3925&rep=rep1&type=pdf (Accessed 6 July 2017).

Keogh, A. (2007). Rape trauma syndrome: Time to open the floodgates? *Journal of Forensic and Legal Medicine, 14*(4), 221–224.

Kitzinger, C., & Frith, H. (1999). Just say no? The use of conversation analysis in developing a feminist perspective on sexual refusal. *Discourse and Society, 10*(3), 293–316.

Krahé, B., Temkin, J., Bieneck, S., & Berger, A. (2008). Prospective lawyers' rape stereotypes and schematic decision-making about rape cases. *Psychology, Crime & Law, 14*(5), 461–479.

Lees, S. (1996). *Carnal knowledge: Rape on trial.* London, UK: Hamish Hamilton.

Leippe, M., Eisenstadt, D., Rauch, S., & Seib, H. (2004). Timing of eyewitness expert testimony, jurors' need for cognition, and case strength as determinants of trial verdicts. *Journal of Applied Psychology, 89*(3), 524–541.

Lewis, P. (2006). Expert evidence of delay in complaint in childhood sexual abuse prosecutions. *International Journal of Evidence & Proof, 10*(3), 157–179.

Lynch, K. R., Wasarhaley, N. E., Golding, J. M., & Simcic, T. (2013). Who bought the drinks? Juror perceptions of intoxication in a rape trial. *Journal of Interpersonal Violence, 28*(16), 3205–3222.

Maddison, D., Ormerod, D., Tonking, S., & Wait, J. (2016). *The Crown Court Compendium: Part 1: Jury and trial management and summing up.* Available at: https://www.judiciary.gov.uk/wp-content/uploads/2016/06/crown-court-compendium-pt1-jury-and-trial-management-and-summing-up-feb2017.pdf (Accessed 6 July 2017).

Mason, G. E., Riger, S., & Foley, L. A. (2004). The impact of past sexual experiences on attributions of responsibility for rape. *Journal of Interpersonal Violence, 19*(10), 1157–1171.

Ministry of Justice, Home Office, and the Office for National Statistics. (2013). *An overview of sexual offending in England and Wales* (Statistics Bulletin). Available at: https://www.gov.uk/government/uploads/system/uploads/attachment_data/file/214970/sexual-offending-overview-jan-2013.pdf (Accessed 6 July 2017).

O'Byrne, R., Rapley, M., & Hansen, S. (2006). 'You couldn't say "no", could you?': Young men's understandings of sexual refusal. *Feminism and Psychology, 16*(2), 133–154.

O'Byrne, R., Hansen, S., & Rapley, M. (2008). "If a girl doesn't say 'no'…": Young men, rape and claims of "insufficient knowledge". *Journal of Community and Applied Social Psychology, 18*(3), 168–193.

Payne, D. L., Lonsway, K. A., & Fitzgerald, L. F. (1999). Rape myth acceptance: Exploration of its structure and its measurement using the Illinois rape myth acceptance scale. *Journal of Research in Personality, 33*(1), 27–68.

Peterson, Z. D., & Muehlenhard, C. L. (2004). Was it rape? The function of women's rape myth acceptance and definitions of sex in labeling their own experiences. *Sex Roles, 51*(3/4), 129–144.

Rumney, P. (2011). Judicial training and rape. *Journal of Criminal Law, 75*(6), 473–481.

Saks, M. J., & Thompson, W. C. (2003). Assessing evidence: Proving facts (2nd ed.). In D. Carson & R. Bull (Eds.), *Handbook of psychology in legal contexts* (pp. 329–345). Chichester: Wiley.

Saunders, A. (2012, January 30). Speech on the prosecution of rape and serious sexual offences. *Crown Prosecution Service.* Available at: http://www.cps.gov.uk/news/articles/speech_on_the_prosecution_of_rape_and_serious_sexual_offences_by_alison_saunders_chief_crown_prosecutor_for_london/ (Accessed 6 July 2017).

Smith, O. (2009). *An investigation into the effects of court culture on barristers' opinions of responses to rape* (BSc dissertation, University of Bath, Bath, UK).

Smith, O., & Skinner, T. (2012). Observing court responses to victims of rape and sexual assault. *Feminist Criminology, 7*(4), 298–326.

Smith, O., & Skinner, T. (2015). *Court responses to rape and sexual assault in the UK.* Available at: http://www.bath.ac.uk/ipr/our-publications/policy-briefs/court-response-to-rape.html (Accessed 6 July 2017).

Smith, O., & Skinner, T. (2017). How rape myths are used and challenged in rape and sexual assault trials. *Social and Legal Studies, 26*(4), 441–466.

Stern, V. (2010). *The Stern review: A report by Baroness Stern CBE of an independent review into how rape complaints are handled by public authorities in England and Wales.* London: Home Office. Available at: http://webarchive.nationalarchives.gov.uk/20110608162919/, http://www.equalities.gov.uk/pdf/Stern_Review_acc_FINAL.pdf (Accessed 6 July 2017).

Stewart, M., Dobbin, S. A., & Gatowski, S. I. (1996). "Real rapes" and "real victims": The shared reliance on common cultural definitions of rape. *Feminist Legal Studies, 4*, 159–177.

Suarez, E., & Gadalla, T. M. (2010). Stop blaming the victim: A meta-analysis on rape myths. *Journal of Interpersonal Violence, 25*(11), 2010–2035.

Tannen, D. (1992). *You just don't understand: Women and men in conversation.* London: Virago.

Temkin, J. (2000). Prosecuting and defending rape: Perspectives from the bar. *Journal of Law and Society, 27*, 219–248.

Temkin, J. (2002). *Rape and the legal process* (2nd ed.). Oxford: Oxford University Press.

Temkin, J., & Krahé, B. (2008). *Sexual assault and the justice gap: A question of attitude.* Oxford: Hart.

Temkin, J., Gray, J. M., & Barrett, J. (2018). Different functions of rape myth use in court: Findings from a trial observation study. *Feminist Criminology, 13*(2), 205–226.

Tonking, S., & Wait, J. (2011). *Crown Court Bench Book Companion*. Available at: https://www.judiciary.gov.uk/wp-content/uploads/JCO/Documents/eLetters/Bench+Book+Companion_revised+complete+march+2012.pdf (Accessed 6 July 2017).

Weiss, K. G. (2009). "Boys will be boys" and other gendered accounts: An exploration of victims' excuses and justifications for unwanted sexual contact and coercion. *Violence Against Women, 15*(7), 810–834.

Wheatcroft, J. M., Wagstaff, G. F., & Moran, A. (2009). Revictimizing the victim? How rape victims experience the UK legal system. *Victims and Offenders: An International Journal of Evidence-Based Research, Policy and Practice, 4*(3), 265–284.

3

False Allegations of Sexual Violence: The Reality

Charlotte Triggs OBE

At the outset it is important that we acknowledge the very damaging impact that a false allegation of rape or sexual assault – be it either malicious or misguided – can have on the person falsely accused. Reputations can be ruined and lives can be devastated as a result. (Crown Prosecution Service [CPS] 2013a, p. 3)

Introduction

'Women lie about rape!'; 'Most rape allegations are false!'; 'Rape is just regret sex!'

For those with knowledge and experience of sexual violence, comments like these come as no surprise. They reflect the commonly expressed opinions of many in society, including some professionals. If the word 'rape' is replaced with 'theft', 'assault' or 'homicide', such expressions become unfamiliar.

C. Triggs OBE (✉)
London, UK

E. Milne et al. (eds.), *Women and the Criminal Justice System*,
https://doi.org/10.1007/978-3-319-76774-1_3

This chapter aims to explore what is meant by false allegations, how they are defined and by whom, and how societal assumptions about their nature and frequency impact on the perceptions of the men and women responsible for handling rape across England and Wales, whether as an officer with one of the 43 police forces or as a CPS prosecutor. It will address the wider context within which society understands sexual violence and ask why those alleging they have been raped risk being judged negatively by their peers and labelled as liars. In particular, this chapter will also look at how the criminal justice system tackles false allegations and how it treats women who are thought to have made a false rape allegation.

Before exploring the subject of false allegations, it is important to understand how rape is defined in law. Section 1 of the Sexual Offences Act 2003 (hereafter SOA) states that rape occurs when a person, A, intentionally penetrates another person, B's, vagina, anus or mouth with his penis. B does not consent and A does not reasonably believe that B consents. There is no more serious sexual offence than rape and it attracts a maximum penalty of life imprisonment, on a par with offences including murder and robbery.

The absence of the complainant's consent is fundamental to what constitutes 'rape'. Questions of consent arise in two ways—did the complainant consent to the act of penetration, and, as a separate issue, did the defendant reasonably believe she/he was consenting at the time. The basic definition is provided in section 74 of the SOA which states that consent can only be given by a person who 'agrees by choice and has the freedom and capacity to make that choice'. This definition is then supplemented by a set of circumstances where consent is presumed to be absent in sections 75 and 76.

The meaning of consent gives rise to complex issues which fall outside the scope of this chapter, but a few brief points will be noted to demonstrate the scope of rape in the criminal law. As is evident from the definitions contained in sections 1 and 74 of the SOA, the legal definition of rape does not require that the defendant used force, as it is understood in everyday usage; neither does it require that the complainant resisted, either physically or verbally (*R v Malone* 1998). According to the definition of consent in section 74, where sex was agreed to on the basis of certain deceptions or threats, this may mean that there was no consent because the complainant did not 'agree by choice'. This has the potential for wide interpretation, but to note one recent example, it has been held that a jury may conclude that there was no consent where the defendant deliberately lied as to whether they were wearing a condom in circumstances where it was clear that consent would only be given where a condom was used (*Assange v Swedish Judicial Authority* 2011). A deception as to agreeing to withdraw prior to ejaculation may in certain circumstances also mean there was no consent (*R(F) v Director of Public Prosecutions* 2013). Further, there will also be no consent where the complainant lost their capacity to consent due to intoxication through alcohol or drugs. This gives rise to complexities because the stage at which an individual may become incapable will vary between one person and another. However, the courts have recognised that capacity to consent 'may evaporate well before a complainant becomes unconscious' (*R v Bree* 2007).

The above provides only a very brief introduction to the concept of consent in the context of sexual offences. The key point to highlight is that the legal definition of absence of consent, and therefore 'rape', is much broader than how rape is widely understood. The role of rape myths will be discussed below, but at this stage it is worth noting that there is a mismatch between the legal definition of rape, and how rape is understood according to popular perceptions, something which can feed into the construction of what constitutes a 'false rape allegation'.

Rape can be difficult to prosecute for a number of reasons. Often occurring in private, it is likely that the only witnesses are the complainant and the perpetrator. Their accounts may be contradictory, the complainant says she/he did not consent and the alleged perpetrator says he reasonably believed that they did consent. Both requirements (no consent and no reasonable belief in consent) may be difficult to prove. The investigating police officer will pursue all lines of enquiry to establish the context in which the offence occurred. This may include obtaining statements from witnesses who saw the complainant and suspect before and after the incident as well as interrogating telephone records and social media. However, the credibility of both the complainant and the defendant is usually paramount. At trial, the defence will be intent on discrediting the complainant's credibility.

Satisfying a jury so that they are sure[1] the defendant raped the complainant is not easy. Jurors, like the rest of society, are likely to have their own belief systems, which may influence their perception of sexual violence and what they consider to constitute the crime of rape. It will be for the trial advocates and judge to explain the legal definitions of 'consent' and 'rape' enabling jurors to make informed decisions based on the evidence. However, it is not only jurors whose decisions may be affected by 'rape myths'. Indeed, criminal justice professionals, including police officers and CPS prosecutors, are not immune from such influences and beliefs, issues which may affect their assessment of the complainant's account and of his/her credibility. If a case is to progress successfully to prosecution, investigators and prosecutors will generally need to assess the complainant as being a credible witness and to decide that the particular circumstances match the various elements that constitute the offence of 'rape' (e.g. see research by Hohl and Stanko 2015).

In this regard, sexual violence including rape is often misunderstood. Indeed, public perception has been shown as inaccurate and beset by what are commonly described as myths and stereotypes discussed in detail in Chapter 2 of this book (Gray and Horvath, this volume). One example of a 'rape myth' is the perception that 'real' rape is committed by a masked stranger in a dark alley. However, evidence shows that perpetrators are most likely to be known to their victims and that rape by a stranger is less common than rape by family members, partners, former partners or friends. Indeed, according to a 2013 Overview of Sexual Offending, '[a]round 90 per cent of complainants of the most serious sexual offences in the previous year knew the perpetrator', (Ministry of Justice et al. 2013, p. 6). Furthermore, society may expect a person who has been raped to act in a specific way, to struggle and fight off their attacker and to report the crime immediately. They may presume that the victim will suffer extensive injuries, especially to their genital area. Such cultural perceptions of what constitutes a 'real' rape may affect professional assessments of whether a rape took place and, as will be discussed later in this chapter, may lead police officers and prosecutors to decide that a reported incident of rape is 'false'.

Newspaper Reporting of False Allegations and Rape Prosecutions

How 'rape' is perceived may be influenced by the way it is represented in various media. For example, a search of UK online newspapers will generate a significant number of stories involving women convicted of criminal offences as a result of lying about sex. To illustrate this point, this chapter will refer to just three such reports.

In the *MailOnline*, the headline '*Woman jailed for falsely accusing two soldiers of trying to rape her because she was ashamed about drunken cocaine-fuelled threesome*' was used to describe a 20-year-old woman who, it was reported, panicked when her boyfriend heard rumours about her sexual activity with two servicemen. Ashamed to admit she had 'cheated on him' the woman made up an allegation of rape. The boyfriend 'made her go to the police to report the "attack", and [she] even gave a "tearful" account of the apparent crime to officers and "illicitly gained their empathy"'. According to the report, the young woman was jailed for two and a half years (Duell 2015).

An account of another case from the *MailOnline*, this time from a Scottish court, appeared under the headline '*Woman who falsely claimed she had been raped so she could resit her A-levels is jailed for 2 years*'. The article explained that the police had recovered the 20-year-old's journal, which documented 'her increasingly alarming thoughts and fantasies, including the names and offences of rapists and sexual offenders from around Scotland'. In fact, the man she named as her attacker was in prison at the relevant time and could not have been guilty of committing the alleged offence. The woman was prosecuted and convicted. It appears the case was taken very seriously as reflected by the term of imprisonment.

Referring to the investigation of the young woman's case, a woman police officer was quoted as saying, 'I had concerns about her hiding her face and running out of the room'. 'I had the impression it was very well planned. I didn't see any real distress or anything like that'. According to the newspaper, the Sheriff was left baffled by her activities, telling her: 'In many years in these courts I have come across the whole range of hateful, hideous and downright bizarre things that people do but I doubt that I have encountered a course of conduct so strange, so needless and so hard to fathom as yours' (Baker 2015).

The third case, from southern England, told of '*Two women jailed after having threesome with man and accusing him of sexual assault*' (Fifield 2015). The same story reported in another online paper (Johnson 2015) described the defendants as 'two wicked women who concocted a pack of lies'. Aged 29 and 30 years, they were jailed for 18 months and eight months, respectively, for lying 'to cops following romp'.

These are just three examples, but they give some indication of the circumstances which can give rise to a criminal charge on the basis of having made a false rape allegation, and of the way these cases are reported in the media. These newspaper reports, however, do not provide a full or objective account of these cases, and, indeed, are of a type that tends to sensationalise these incidents and reinforce gender stereotypes. Aspects that these three reports have in common are the use of a sensational headline accompanied by a photograph of the offender(s). In the first and third reports, the more salacious and titillating elements of the stories are emphasised. Both refer to a 'threesome' and use words such as 'romp' with its saucy connotations and implications with regard to the sexual character of the offender, namely that she was promiscuous. 'Cheating' adds weight to the stereotype of the woman who is deceitful and whom men should not trust. Such women are described as 'wicked' in the third report. The ease with which reports such as these can be found may suggest to their readers that the prosecution of women for telling lies about rape is common. The same readers may get the impression that women do this either deliberately to get innocent men into trouble or to save their own skin, when there is a risk their partner will find out they cheated on him. These reports tend to reflect and reinforce a stereotypical view, that women 'cry rape'.

Conversely, many successful rape prosecutions, resulting in the conviction and imprisonment of a defendant, may escape any media attention due to restrictions on reporting of rape prosecutions which mean most cases cannot be reported in the way described above. Section 1 of the Sexual Offences (Amendment) Act 1992 provides lifelong anonymity to victims of sexual offences and prevents the publication of any photographs or information that could lead to their identification. Where naming the offender would lead to the victim's identification, publication of their name will not be permitted in order to avoid indirect identification of the victim. As already noted, the majority of victims know their perpetrator with many being their spouse, partner, father or brother (Ministry of Justice et al. 2013). If the perpetrator cannot be named or a photograph included there will be few, if any, interesting details available for publication. This gives no opportunity for titillating headlines.

The reports of false allegations included in this section indicate some of the complexities of these cases in terms of the range of factual circumstances involved, and what sort of conduct involving 'false allegations' will be subjected to criminalisation, something that is touched on again later in this chapter. Further, these reports highlight that media reporting of this issue may draw on and reinforce common stereotypes and myths about rape and especially about those who falsely accused others of rape. For those with little or no knowledge of sexual violence who rely on newspapers for information, such reports may add weight to the myths and stereotypes affecting this area of human activity. Certainly, it seems possible that reports about false allegations, such as those referred to above, give support to the stereotype that women lie about rape. Likewise, although evidence shows that most rapists know their victims, the requirement for newspapers to avoid breaching victims' anonymity and concentrate on stories involving victims and perpetrators who are unrelated may leave readers to conclude that the more widely reported stranger rape is the norm. The issue of myths and stereotypes, which has already been touched upon, will be discussed again in the following section where the meaning of a false rape allegation and the impact of rape myths on how the police and prosecutors handle rape and false rape allegations are explored.

False Allegations and Misunderstandings Surrounding Rape

The term 'false allegation' has no legal or even generally accepted definition. Although it is regularly used, its meaning will vary depending on the perception of the person using the term. In other words, a 'false allegation' means different things to different people. The prevalence of false rape allegations is a hotly contested topic about which there are opposing views. In her 2010 report into how rape is handled by public authorities, Baroness Vivien Stern commented, 'The question of false allegations comes up time and again in any meeting or discussion about rape, with some arguing that the number is large and others insisting that the prevalence is grossly exaggerated' (Stern 2010, p. 41).

Recent research commissioned by the Ministry of Justice explored what was meant by 'false allegations' in 299 rape cases recorded by the police in 2008/2009. Although the files interrogated by the researchers had been reported to the police as allegations of rape, some police officers and prosecutors concluded that some allegations were false. In terms of how these professionals understood the meaning of a false allegation, the researchers found there was no agreed definition but rather that a 'variety of definitions of false allegations of rape were found to be in operation amongst police and prosecutors. These ranged from a broadly drawn definition relating to intoxicated complainants (and poor recollection of details), delays in reporting, witness retractions, lack of physical injury and lack of medical evidence, and a narrower definition based on situations where the complaint was considered malicious' (Burton et al. 2012, p. 19).

Relying on the so-called broadly drawn definition would lead to classifying 12% of rape cases in the sample as false (Burton et al. 2012, p. 21). However, do the issues described actually indicate that an allegation is false? In other words, are delayed reporting, retracting an allegation or lack of physical injury evidence that the complainant fabricated the charge? If not, then it would seem that misunderstanding of sexual violence and its impact on victims may lead to genuine allegations being classified as 'false'. This is problematic, not only because it means that cases of rape are not being prosecuted, but also because the genuine complainant may face the risk of criminal prosecution for making a false allegation.

The assumption that genuine victims of sexual violence will promptly report to the police and that any delay in reporting is an indication that they are lying is not supported by evidence gathered by the British Crime Survey (now Crime Survey England and Wales). According to its 2013 report, 'An Overview of Sexual Offending in England and Wales', 'Around a quarter (28 per cent) of females had not told anyone about the incident. One in seven had told the police about the incident (15 per cent), and all of these respondents had also told somebody else. Fifty-seven per cent of females told someone about the incident, but did not tell the police. For those who did tell someone about their experience, the main group that victims confided in were friends, relatives or neighbours (65 per cent)' (Ministry of Justice et al. 2013, pp. 16–17).

There are many reasons why a victim of sexual violence will delay, if not permanently avoid, reporting to the police. Focus groups taking part in the 2015 Independent Review into the Investigation and Prosecution of Rape in London (hereafter the Angiolini Review) cited guilt, shame and wanting to protect their privacy, for example. Others described how being in a relationship with a perpetrator meant they faced complex barriers to reporting (Angiolini 2015, pp. 51–52). Later in this chapter, we consider what happened when one victim of domestic abuse, having overcome the barriers to report rape, decided to retract.

The expectation that a person who has been raped will always have injuries, including defensive injuries resulting from having put up a struggle, as well as to their genital area, is yet another myth. In fact, lack of genital or other injury by no means proves that the sexual activity was consensual. Freezing rather than fighting is a common response to trauma, including sexual violence, and can effectively reduce injury that might have been incurred in the course of any struggle or resistance (Lodrick 2007, pp. 5–6). Research that compared the incidence of genital injury in consensual and non-consensual sexual activity revealed that most complainants of rape (77%) do not sustain any genital injury, although women are more likely to sustain a genital injury from an assault than during consensual intercourse (5.9%) (McLean et al. 2011).

Misunderstandings surrounding rape, such as those referred to above, have long been recognised. A 2005 Home Office research study explained that rather than describing these as myths,

> [w]e prefer to discuss powerful stereotypes that function to limit the definition of what counts as "real rape", in terms of the contexts and relationships within which sex without consent takes place. As a number of researchers and legal scholars have pointed out... despite extensive legal reform, "real rapes" continue to be understood as those committed by strangers, involving weapons and documented injury. The failure of criminal justice systems to address these stereotypes means that the processes involved in responding to reported rapes – from early investigation through to courtroom advocacy – can serve to reinforce, rather than challenge, narrow understandings of the crime of rape, who it happens to and who perpetrates it. (Kelly et al. 2005, p. 2)

As previously stated, in addition to a 'broadly drawn' definition of false allegations identified by the authors of the Ministry of Justice research referred to above, a narrower definition limited to complaints that were perceived as deliberately malicious was also applied (Burton et al. 2012, pp. 19–21). Using this definition, just three per cent of allegations of rape examined by the researchers would classify as false, compared to the 12% when using the 'broadly drawn' definition (Burton et al. 2012, p. 21). This is a noteworthy difference which supports Baroness Stern's observation (noted above) of starkly divided opinion about the number of false allegations.

In 2015, the Angiolini Review found a wide range of opinions about the incidence of false allegations handled by the Metropolitan Police Service (MPS). Amongst those attending focus groups of MPS officers, some expressed the opinion that a large number of rape allegations were false. In common with the Ministry of Justice research mentioned above (Burton et al. 2012), there was no consensus on what makes an allegation false, or on the proportion of reported rapes which might be false. One officer, exceptionally, estimated that it might be as high as 30% of the cases he dealt with (Angiolini 2015, p. 41). Examples of false allegations provided to the Review included reporting rape 'to cover up a one-night stand' or an affair. A term used by several officers was 'regret sex' (Angiolini 2015, pp. 40–41). This explanation together with the concept of 'young girls' lying their way out of trouble was consistent with the Ministry of Justice's 'broadly drawn' definition.

Although not every officer who spoke to the Angiolini Review agreed that false allegations were common, the review reported that,

> It was a matter of serious concern that there was a ready assumption that so many allegations are false and about what the explanation for this might be. Reasons why officers might be inclined to label a report as false could include the type of issues linked to allegations of rape. Some complainants are extremely challenging to deal with and there were a number of examples of aggressive, drunken complainants often with underlying mental health issues. Police officers may simply not be equipped in terms of expertise, let alone time, to unravel the heavy emotional and other baggage and decipher the reality of the complainant's experience. Human nature dictates that in such circumstances officers may be more empathetic to those whom they perceive as more obviously 'deserving complainants', those who are co-operative and whose circumstances potentially point towards, rather than away from, a successful prosecution. (Angiolini 2015, p. 41)

An explanation suggested by some Detective Inspectors for the tendency to label allegations as false was 'burn-out' and 'compassion fatigue'. They believed that unacceptable workloads may have left some officers incapable of recognising any but the most 'deserving' of complainants (Angiolini 2015, p. 42). The Angiolini Review sought the views of psychologists employed by the Havens, London's specialist Sexual Assault Referral Centres (SARCs), to explain why so many officers were convinced that false allegations were rife. The psychologists suggested that the lack of occupational health support available to police officers working in sexual offences teams left them susceptible to 'vicarious trauma'. The review heard that vicarious trauma 'can de-sensitise officers, leading to fatigue, lack of ability to cope and, significantly, lack of ability to empathise' with complainants (Angiolini 2015, p. 42).

The absence of a specific definition of what constitutes a false allegation leaves the whole question open to individual interpretation. This is troubling, especially when some police officers, the very professionals responsible for objective and thorough investigation of rape cases, apparently classify as false cases that may well be genuine and capable of effective prosecution. Misconstruing victims' behaviour through reliance on myths and stereotypes raises serious questions about police training and supervision. Not only may they drop genuine cases due to a mistaken belief that the allegation is false, they may also consider prosecuting truthful complainants for making a false allegation. These are issues to be addressed in the next section.

Prosecuting False Allegations

As identified previously, distinguishing the false allegation from the genuine is not always straightforward. As highlighted in the previous section, by succumbing to myths the police may mistakenly consider an allegation to be false, based on a misunderstanding of the realities of how victims behave and the impact of trauma. When this happens, cases may not be referred to the CPS for a review and potential charging decision. Even where the case is sent to the CPS for a charging decision, the prosecutor making that decision may mistakenly succumb to myths and conclude the allegation is false. However, it would be wrong to interpret all CPS decisions not to prosecute as meaning the allegation was regarded as false. When deciding whether to bring charges, prosecutors must apply the two-stage test set out in the Code for Crown Prosecutors. This means reviewing all the evidence supplied by the police and being satisfied that there is sufficient evidence to provide a realistic prospect of conviction *and* that a prosecution is in the public interest (CPS 2013b). A prosecutor's decision that there is insufficient evidence to prosecute should not be mistaken for meaning the allegation was false. As stated in the Code, 'A case which does not pass the evidential stage must not proceed, no matter how serious or sensitive it may be' (CPS 2013b, para. 4.4).

If, following an investigation, the police conclude that a false allegation has been made, they may refer the case to the CPS for a charging
decision in respect of the woman who made the allegation. The absence
in England and Wales of a definition or specific criminal offence cov-
ering the making of a false allegation complicates the task of the CPS
prosecutor. When reviewing evidence involving false allegations, prosecutors routinely choose between charges of Perverting the Course of
Justice and Wasting Police Time. Perverting the Course of Justice is a
common law offence (not defined in statute), triable only on indictment (in the Crown Court with a judge and jury) and with a maximum sentence of life imprisonment. The offence is committed where
a person does an act which has a tendency to pervert, and which is
intended to pervert, the course of public justice (*R v Vreones*). Wasting
Police Time is defined in section 5(2) of the Criminal Law Act 1967.
The offence is committed 'where a person causes any wasteful employment of the police by knowingly making to any person a false report
tending to show that an offence has been committed, or to give rise to
apprehension for the safety of any persons or property, or tending to
show that he has information material to any police inquiry'. It is a less
serious offence than Perverting the Course of Justice, being triable only
summarily (in the Magistrates' Court) and, on conviction, the maximum sentence of imprisonment is six months or a fine or both. In common with other summary offences, there is a six-month time limit for
commencing criminal proceedings.

Wasting Police Time is one of the few cases requiring the consent of
the Director of Public Prosecutions (DPP) to prosecute (Criminal Law
Act 1967, s. 5(3)). Neither Perverting the Course of Justice nor Wasting
Police Time is restricted to behaviour involving false allegations of rape
or other sexual offences and both may be used to prosecute a wide
range of offending. Official Ministry of Justice crime statistics do not
distinguish between prosecutions for making false allegations of sexual
offending and any other prosecution of these offences and, therefore,
there are no official crime figures on prosecutions for making a false
allegation.

Some of the complex issues surrounding false allegations, including
the criminal justice response and the pressures experienced by

complainants, are clearly demonstrated by the case of *R v A* (2010). This case involved an allegation of rape made in November 2009 by 'Sarah' (not her real name), the mother of four young children in a 999 call. The police responded by arranging for her to go to a women's refuge. The next day she was video interviewed and, based on Sarah's evidence, her husband was arrested and charged with six offences including vaginal, oral and anal rape. In court, he was remanded in custody before being given conditional bail at a subsequent hearing. A breach of his bail conditions resulted in a further remand in custody before he was once more released on bail. Some weeks later, Sarah told the police that she wanted to withdraw her complaint against her husband although she maintained that her allegations were true. The CPS decided, against Sarah's wishes, that the prosecution should continue because of the seriousness of the offending. On 18 January 2010, the husband entered pleas of not guilty and a trial was fixed for May.

On 7 February, Sarah asked the detective in charge of the investigation what would happen, 'if I say I made it all up, I've lied about the rape?' (*R v A* 2010, para. 11). On 11 February, she told the police she had lied and her husband had never raped her. Following this, she was arrested and cautioned and later provided a written witness statement confirming the allegations of rape were false. Despite police scepticism and their testing of the complainant's retraction, Sarah maintained her allegation of rape was a lie. Finally, the prosecution was left with no choice but to end the case against the husband by offering no evidence. Not guilty verdicts were recorded.

On 16 April, Sarah was interviewed by the police under caution. She continued to insist the original allegation had been false and was charged with perverting the course of justice on the basis that she had made false allegations against her husband, resulting in him being charged and spending time in custody awaiting trial. However, following a court hearing, she contacted the police to say that the original allegation of rape was true and it was her retraction which had been false. She was then charged by the CPS with a second offence of attempting to pervert the course of justice. This was an alternative to the existing charge and was on the basis that she had falsely withdrawn a true allegation. Sarah pleaded guilty to the new charge, admitting that her original allegations of rape were true and she had lied when she told the police that they were not. She was sentenced in the Crown Court to eight months imprisonment. She appealed against the severity of the sentence and within days the sentence was reduced by the Court of Appeal to a community order.

Sarah's explanation for withdrawing her support for her husband's prosecution is summarised in the Court of Appeal judgment delivered by the Lord Chief Justice, Lord Judge. In it, he acknowledged the pressure to which she had been subject:

> She said that she had received a visit from her husband's sister who told her to say that she had lied and that if she did, she would receive a suspended sentence because the children were living with her. She felt under pressure. During the time when her husband had been on bail and had been seeing the children, she had also felt under pressure. She had been given to understand that if her husband had been convicted the sentence on him would be something in the order of ten years' imprisonment.
>
> The appellant explained her position to the author of the pre-sentence report. She said that, following the arrest of her husband and his remand in custody, she had felt an immense sense of guilt. She believed that simply by the instigation of proceedings to divorce her husband would be sufficient for her own purposes, and so she decided to withdraw her complaint. When her husband was released on bail he contacted her. She said that she was in an emotional and very confused state at the time. She told the author of the report that she had suffered from years of domestic abuse and was very fearful of her husband but, wanting to give her children a family Christmas at which their father was present, she continued to communicate with him. This created an immense pressure on her. Her husband sought to persuade her to retract her original statement and so, due to fear of repercussions from him, she had agreed. (*R v A* 2010, paras. 16–17)

The Lord Chief Justice went on to identify the extreme vulnerability experienced by victims of domestic abuse who have been subjected to 'dominance, power and control' by the very man 'in whom she is entitled to repose her trust' (*R v A* 2010, para. 21). Warning against any future prosecutions of similar cases the Lord Chief Justice expressed the firm view that, 'This is an exceptional case. We hope that it will be very exceptional for cases of this kind to be prosecuted to conviction in the Crown Court' (*R v A* 2010, para. 23).

The response of those at the CPS with ultimate responsibility for steering this case through the criminal justice system demonstrates their regret at Sarah's prosecution. At the hearing of her appeal against sentence, the DPP's then Principal Legal Adviser Alison Levitt QC did not oppose Sarah's appeal. Responding publicly to the case, Keir Starmer QC, then DPP and head of the CPS, launched a package of measures designed to increase public confidence in the CPS handling of rape allegations. Later, in an article for *The Guardian*, (Starmer 2010) he set out his commitment to justice being done in rape cases. He acknowledged that, 'there have been cases recently where our conduct has been scrutinised and where, as director of public prosecutions, I do not consider justice was done or was seen to be done'. He then went on to refer directly to Sarah's case, saying, 'a woman was prosecuted for perverting the course of justice after making a rape allegation, retracting it and then withdrawing that retraction'. He accepted that the CPS had been criticised and that there had been 'legitimate questions' about the handling of the case.

The DPP's package of measures designed to improve public confidence in how the CPS handled rape included new legal guidance for CPS prosecutors in cases involving allegedly false rape and domestic violence allegations. Published in July 2011, the guidance was informed by a public consultation process including a round-table discussion at which interested parties and stakeholder groups contributed their views on the factors that prosecutors should consider when dealing with this type of case (CPS 2011). The current guidance, which has been revised since its original publication, states that in the context of making a false rape or domestic violence allegation prosecutions for perverting the course of justice and wasting police,

> will be extremely rare and by their very nature they will be complex and require sensitive handling. On the one hand, victims of rape and / or domestic abuse making truthful allegations require the support of the criminal justice system. They should not be deterred from reporting their

allegations. Nor should they be criminalised for merely retracting an allegation because true allegations can be retracted for a broad range of reasons. (CPS 2017, para. 3)

To avoid the potential risk of a genuine victim being mistakenly prosecuted, the guidance states that 'if the evidence is such that the original allegation might reasonably be true then there is not a realistic prospect of conviction and no charge should be brought' (CPS 2017, para. 13). In addition, prosecutors must consider any vulnerability to which the person making the false allegation was subject, including mental health issues, learning difficulties, their youth and any substance misuse. They must also explore the background to the allegation, especially any history of domestic or sexual abuse, and avoid succumbing to the myths and stereotypes that commonly apply to rape (CPS 2017, paras. 6–7).

The guidance, while recognising the need to protect the innocent from false allegations of rape, also directed that genuine victims retracting truthful allegations (often as a result of pressure or violence) should not be prosecuted (CPS 2017, paras. 19–21). Any such prosecution might have the adverse effect of deterring other victims from coming forward. Furthermore, charging two alternative counts of perverting the course of justice, as in Sarah's case, is specifically to be avoided (CPS 2017, para. 24). To avoid any mistaken or ill-informed decision to prosecute the CPS guidance sets out 'handling arrangements' designed to ensure that only specialist prosecutors make charging decisions in this type of case, and that they are subject to ratification at a senior level (CPS 2017, para. 4).

As part of the package of measures to improve the handling of rape, the DPP introduced the requirement for CPS prosecutors to refer to him all cases submitted by the police to the CPS that involved an allegedly false allegation of rape, domestic violence or both. The purpose of the referral was for the DPP personally to oversee the charging decisions in these cases. This requirement was effective from January 2011 for a period of 17 months, during which 121 cases involving an allegedly false allegation of rape and 11 involving both rape and domestic violence were considered by the DPP. Out of these cases, the DPP authorised 35 prosecutions for making false allegations of rape and a further 3 for making false allegations of both rape and domestic violence. By way of comparison, there were during the same period 5651 prosecutions for rape. Clearly, on this evidence, the number of prosecutions for false allegations (0.67%) is minimal compared with prosecutions for rape (CPS 2013a, pp. 5–6, 10–11).

Following the 17-month period during which the DPP took personal responsibility for charging this category of case, the CPS published a report analysing the results of the exercise. Nearly half the suspects referred to the CPS by the police for alleged false allegations were aged 21 or younger and eleven were aged under sixteen (CPS 2013a, p. 11). In 38 per cent of all cases, the initial report to the police was made not by the suspect themselves but by a third party. Of those suspects aged under 18, more than half had not contacted the police themselves.

As the report explained, 'It was a feature of these cases that the suspect later reported that the whole thing had spiralled out of control and he or she had felt unable to stop the investigation' (CPS 2013a, p. 14). Also of note was the finding that, '18% of suspects had a mental health problem that had been identified by a medical assessor' (CPS 2013a, p. 17). Furthermore, 33% had consumed alcohol and/or drugs at the time of the incident or of making the report (CPS 2013a, p. 19). Many of the cases analysed did not involve deliberate malice.

Examples of specific cases included a 14-year-old who had engaged in sexual activity with a 17-year-old. She told her father she had been raped because she did not want him to think badly of her. The father then reported the offence to the police. It was not clear that the 14-year-old fully understood the seriousness of her actions (CPS 2013a, pp. 15–16). In another case, a 40-year-old woman told her son she had been raped. The case was reported to the police by a third party. When the alleged perpetrator was arrested, he said the sex was consensual. In fact, the woman had a significant learning disability and was unlikely to have sufficient mental capacity to understand the consequences of making a false statement (CPS 2013a, pp. 17–19). In other cases, younger suspects 'showed a clear failure to think about (or even awareness of) the seriousness of making an allegation of rape' (CPS 2013a, p. 26).

What the 2013 CPS review clearly demonstrates is the complexities involved in cases where a false allegation has allegedly been made.

This means that when deciding whether to prosecute a person for making a false allegation of a sexual offence, prosecutors must carry out an almost forensic scrutiny of the evidence and circumstances. This will include not only the suspect's actions but also their situation, including any vulnerabilities by which they are affected, their intention and the background to the alleged offence. A key finding of the CPS Review was that, 'in dealing with these cases, the prosecution must be able to prove to the criminal standard that the initial complaint was in fact false' (CPS 2013a, p. 27). Prosecutors must therefore be able to justify, based on the evidence and not their assumptions or beliefs, that there is no possibility of the allegation being true. Also of note in the CPS review is the specific acknowledgement and confrontation of the risk of investigators and prosecutors succumbing to rape myths and stereotypes. In order to avoid decisions based on such perceptions, prosecutors are specifically instructed to, 'challenge investigators if such assumptions have been incorporated into reports' (CPS 2013a, p. 30).

In terms of how the CPS prosecutes false allegations of rape, *R v A* was highly significant. A case in which, according to the then DPP, justice 'was not seen to be done' led directly to the introduction of detailed guidance for crown prosecutors to apply when deciding whether or not to prosecute false allegations of rape. Issues highlighted by the Court of Appeal in its judgment were included in the advice to prosecutors. They included the need to scrutinise the background, especially in a domestic relationship, and to be aware of the extreme vulnerability that can exist where an individual is a victim of long-term domestic abuse (CPS 2017, paras. 8, 20, 21). Importantly, the guidelines also direct prosecutors not to be influenced by myths and stereotypes in their assessment of whether an allegation of rape is false, and to take account of any vulnerabilities of the suspect, including their mental health, age and maturity (CPS 2017, paras. 6, 7.)

The introduction by the CPS of its *Guidance on Charging Perverting the Course of Justice and Wasting Police Time in Cases Involving Allegedly False Allegations of Rape and/or Domestic Abuse* was designed to improve public confidence in how the CPS handles rape. This followed the case of *R v A* which risked causing reputational damage to, and reducing confidence in, the CPS. By holding a public consultation to inform the content of the guidance, the DPP demonstrated a willingness to listen to the views of others, and especially to those organisations that support victims. Since its publication, the guidance has been kept updated and the handling arrangements and requirement for ratification of decisions have remained in force. It is hoped and expected that the guidance will provide an effective deterrent to the future occurrence of a case similar to *R v A*.

While the work of the CPS in this area is welcomed, its contribution to the criminal justice system is necessarily limited by its reliance on the police for case referrals. Crucially, it is the police who provide the first point of contact for complainants and act as gatekeepers to the criminal justice system, determining which cases will be referred to the CPS for a charging decision. Research into attrition in rape cases has repeatedly shown that many cases never make it as far as the CPS (e.g. see Kelly et al. 2005; Hohl and Stanko 2015). This reinforces the need to ensure that police decisions are demonstrably based on the same level of detailed scrutiny as CPS decisions when dealing with this complex and sensitive area.

As mentioned at the beginning of this chapter, there are 43 police forces across England and Wales, compared with one CPS. This gives the CPS an advantage when it comes to disseminating guidance and monitoring how it is applied, one that individual police forces lack, given the decentralized way in which they are organised. When providing the initial response to complainants and determining how crimes are officially recorded and investigated, police officers need informed understanding of sexual assault and its impact and to demonstrate that they have not succumbed to the adverse influence of myths and stereotypes.

Conclusion

Unlike other offences, rape is the subject of a range of entrenched myths and stereotypes which can impact on the effectiveness of the criminal justice system, from the early stages of a police investigation to the weighing of the evidence by a jury. Factors such as a complainant's failure to fight back, lack of injuries and late reporting, all of which are entirely explicable in rape cases, are routinely misinterpreted and used to discredit the complainant's account. Such myths and stereotypes are highly influential.

'False allegations' have no accepted meaning or legal definition and the expression's use is entirely dependent on an individual's personal interpretation; nor is there a specific criminal offence for which any person guilty of making a false allegation can be prosecuted. Perverting the Course of Justice and Wasting Police Time are the offences of choice and are at opposing ends of the spectrum in terms of seriousness and sentence. Their use for offences arising from false allegation is not separated from their use for any other type of offending and does not feature as part of the official published crime statistics. There have been cases where justice was not seen to be done. Sarah, who was convicted and imprisoned for falsely retracting a true allegation of rape, is one example. Were her case to be reviewed now, Sarah could expect to be shown compassion and understanding as a victim of domestic violence who, as a result of family pressure and extreme vulnerability, retracted a genuine allegation of rape. Her case was highly influential in the introduction and crafting of new CPS guidance. This requires prosecutors to give careful and detailed consideration when reviewing cases involving allegedly false rape reports.

In contrast to the impression given by some newspaper reporting, cases involving false allegations tend to be complex. Police officers and prosecutors must be robust in following the relevant guidance and be open to signs of vulnerability, especially mental health issues or learning difficulties, exhibited by alleged perpetrators of false rape reports. They should also take account of the age and maturity of the person making the allegation and whether they are aware of the seriousness and potential consequences of their actions.

The myth that women cry rape is strongly held amongst many in society, including some professionals, and the publicity that prosecutions for false allegations attracts may contribute to society's belief that false allegations are prolific. However, contrary to these myths, and the publicity generated by cases of false rape allegations in the media, CPS research reveals that the number of false allegation prosecutions is tiny when compared to the number of rape prosecutions.

So, what is the truth behind statements such as, 'Women lie about rape!', 'Most rape allegations are false!', 'Rape is just regret sex!'? As we have seen, the issue of false allegations is a complex one and these statements by no means reflect the reality of rape or shed light on the actual incidence of false allegations. However, until common myths and stereotypes loosen their grip on the comprehension of rape by our wider society, misunderstanding of this most sensitive of subjects is likely to continue together with heated dispute.

Finally, what can be done to bring balance and understanding to this problem? While CPS acknowledgment of mistakes led to clarification of the issues and clear guidance for practitioners, the argument in the public arena continues to rage, based on ill-informed myths and stereotypes. The need for those who understand sexual violence to ensure greater public education, as well as continuing training and supervision for professionals handling rape and false allegations, remains paramount.

Note

1. The prosecution must prove 'beyond reasonable doubt' that the defendant is guilty (*Woolmington v DPP* 1935), which is explained to juries as meaning they must be 'sure' of the defendant's guilt (*R v Summers* 1952).

References

Angiolini, E. (2015, April 30). *Report of the independent review into the investigation and prosecution of rape in London.* Available at: https://www.cps.gov.uk/Publications/equality/vaw/dame_elish_angiolini_rape_review_2015.pdf (Accessed 14 November 2017).
Baker, K. (2015, December 24). Woman who falsely claimed she had been raped so she could resit her A-levels is jailed for 2 years. *MailOnline.* Available at: http://www.dailymail.co.uk/news/article-3372802/Woman-falsely-claimed-raped-jailed-two-years.html (Accessed 17 November 2017).

Burton, M., McLeod, R., de Guzmán, V., Evans, R., Lambert, H., & Cass, G. (2012). *Understanding the progression of cases through the criminal justice system: Evidence drawn from a selection of casefiles* (Ministry of Justice Research Series 11/12). Available at: https://www.gov.uk/government/uploads/system/uploads/attachment_data/file/217471/understanding-progression-serious-cases.pdf (Accessed 14 November 2017).

Crown Prosecution Service. (2011, July). *A consultation on CPS interim guidance on perverting the course of justice—Charging in cases involving rape and/or domestic violence allegations.* Available at: http://webarchive.nationalarchives.gov.uk/20110710225820/http://www.cps.gov.uk/consultations/summary_of_responses_on_perverting_course_of_justice.pdf (Accessed 14 November 2017).

Crown Prosecution Service (Levitt, A., and CPS Equality and Diversity Unit). (2013a). *Charging perverting the course of justice and wasting police time in cases involving allegedly false rape and domestic violence allegations—Joint report to the Director of Public Prosecutions.*

Crown Prosecution Service. (2013b). *The code for crown prosecutors.* Available at: https://www.cps.gov.uk/publications/docs/code_2013_accessible_english.pdf (Accessed 14 November 2017).

Crown Prosecution Service. (2017). *Guidance for charging perverting the course of justice and wasting police time in cases involving allegedly false allegations of rape and/or domestic abuse.* Available at: http://www.cps.gov.uk/legal/p_to_r/perverting_the_course_of_justice_-_rape_and_dv_allegations/ (Accessed 14 November 2017).

Duell, M. (2015, March 26). Woman jailed for falsely accusing two soldiers of trying to rape her because she was ashamed about drunken cocaine-fuelled threesome. *MailOnline.* Available at: http://www.dailymail.co.uk/news/article-3013207/Woman-jailed-falsely-accusing-two-soldiers-trying-rape-ashamed-drunken-cocaine-fuelled-threesome.html (Accessed 13 November 2017).

Fifield, N. (2015, July 25). Two women jailed after having threesome with man and accusing him of sexual assault. *The Mirror.* Available at: http://www.mirror.co.uk/news/uk-news/two-women-jailed-after-having-6138718 (Accessed 17 November 2017).

Hohl, K., & Stanko, E. (2015). Complaints of rape in the criminal justice system: Fresh evidence on the attrition problem in England and Wales. *European Journal of Criminology, 12*(3), 324–341.

Johnson, J. (2015, June 30). Friends are sentenced for inventing sex attack lies against man. *Southern Daily Echo*. Available at: http://www.dailyecho.co.uk/news/13360705._Wicked__woman_jailed_for_false_sex_allegations/ (Accessed 17 November 2017).

Kelly, L., Lovett, J., & Regan, L. (2005, February). *A gap or a chasm? Attrition in reported rape cases* (Home Office Research Study 293). Available at: http://webarchive.nationalarchives.gov.uk/20110218141141/http://rds.homeoffice.gov.uk/rds/pdfs05/hors293.pdf (Accessed 14 November 2017).

Lodrick, Z. (2007). Psychological trauma—What every trauma worker should know. *The British Journal of Psychotherapy Integration, 4*(2). Available at: http://www.zoelodrick.co.uk/training/article-1 (Accessed 13 November 2017).

McLean, I., Roberts, S., White, C., & Paul, S. (2011). Female genital injuries resulting from consensual and non-consensual vaginal intercourse. *Forensic Science International, 204*(1–3), 27–33.

Ministry of Justice, Home Office & Office of National Statistics. (2013, January 10). *An overview of sexual offending in England and Wales*. Available at: https://www.gov.uk/government/uploads/system/uploads/attachment_data/file/214970/sexual-offending-overview-jan-2013.pdf (Accessed 14 November 2017).

Starmer, K. (2010, December 16). Rape: Justice will be done. *The Guardian*. Available at: https://www.theguardian.com/commentisfree/2010/dec/16/justice-for-victims-of-rape (Accessed 14 November 2017).

Stern, V. (2010). *A report by Baroness Vivien Stern CBE of an independent review into how rape complaints are handled by the public authorities in England and Wales* (Government Equalities Office & Home Office). Available at: http://webarchive.nationalarchives.gov.uk/20110608162919/http://www.equalities.gov.uk/pdf/Stern_Review_acc_FINAL.pdf (Accessed 13 November 2017).

Assange v Swedish Judicial Authority [2011] EWHC 2849.

R v A [2010] EWCA Crim 2913.

R v Bree [2007] EWCA 256.

R v Malone [1998] 2 Cr App R 447.

R v Summers (Alfred) [1952] 1 All E.R. 1059.

R v Vreones [1891] 1 Q.B. 360.

R(F) v Director of Public Prosecutions [2013] EWHC 945.

Woolmington v D.P.P [1935] A.C. 462.

4

Domestic Abuse: Predicting, Assessing and Responding to Risk in the Criminal Justice System and Beyond

Aviah Sarah Day, Angela Jenner and Ruth Weir

Introduction

This chapter brings together early findings from three Ph.D. projects on domestic abuse, each taking a different approach. The first explores the issues of underreporting and the predictors of risk; the second focuses on the police response to domestic abuse, highlighting gaps in service

A. S. Day (✉)
University of Essex,
London, UK
e-mail: sday@essex.ac.uk

A. Jenner
London Metropolitan University,
Essex, UK
e-mail: ajenne@essex.ac.uk

R. Weir
Department of Sociology, University of Essex,
Colchester, Essex, UK
e-mail: rweir@essex.ac.uk

© The Author(s) 2018
E. Milne et al. (eds.), *Women and the Criminal Justice System*,
https://doi.org/10.1007/978-3-319-76774-1_4

67

provision to victims; and the final project looks at specialist courts and the work of independent domestic violence. This chapter cannot do justice to all three of the projects here; however, it is worth noting that, together, they form a body of research with the potential to make a significant contribution to the field. Indeed, the motivation for each of the projects is to add to current efforts to improve responses to domestic abuse within the criminal justice system and beyond. This chapter will focus on the ways in which practitioners might predict, assess and respond to risk in relation to domestic abuse.

Defining Domestic Abuse

A review of the literature on domestic abuse will reveal that there is no single, universally accepted, definition of domestic abuse—neither is there widespread agreement on terminology (domestic abuse, domestic violence, intimate partner violence, violence against women). The same may be said for the numerous organisations and agencies involved in the response to domestic abuse (e.g. police, social services, health services, charities); each provides their own terminology and/or definition in line with their role and responsibilities (Hughes and Jenner, forthcoming). For the purposes of this chapter the definition of domestic violence and abuse offered by the Home Office will be applied:

> any incident or pattern of incidents of controlling, coercive, threatening behaviour, violence or abuse between those aged 16 or over who are, or have been, intimate partners or family members regardless of gender or sexuality. The abuse can encompass, but is not limited to: psychological; physical; sexual; financial; emotional. (Home Office 2013)

This definition, as currently applied within the UK criminal justice system, is gender neutral and incorporates a wide range of behaviours, not all of which might be taken to be 'violent', hence the more inclusive term domestic abuse. The ever-expanding 'official' definition reflects society's current understanding of the issue—based on research findings and it now also includes young people aged 16 or over and extends to family members, not just those in intimate relationships. Feminist-informed definitions are more likely to adopt the term domestic violence and express the gendered nature of the problem, highlighting patterns of controlling and coercive behaviour. However, this does not necessarily fit well with a criminal justice approach, which tends to be more concerned with specific 'incidents' and the application of the law. It is not possible within this chapter to cover all the complexities of the debate on acceptable definitions and/or terminology and how this might impact on our response to the problem. However, it is important to note that, for many reasons, definitions and terminology, as well as resources and services, are likely to differ at the international, national and local levels. Whilst we might applaud the overall progress in terms of recognising a wider range of abusive behaviours affecting a more diverse range of victims, we should also note that any lack of agreement regarding the issue is also likely to have an impact on how various practitioners and victims themselves understand and respond to risk in relation to domestic abuse.

Understanding and Responding to Domestic Abuse

Regardless of any criticism, the ongoing debates regarding definitions of domestic abuse and the recent definition as provided by the Home Office reflect an increased awareness and improved levels of understanding concerning the impact and extent of the problem. It is now widely accepted that anyone may experience domestic abuse, regardless of class, ethnicity, age or gender. Whilst the extent of the problem is difficult to measure for a variety of reasons—underreporting (many victims do not disclose the abuse to anybody), non-recording (criminal justice agencies may not record all forms of abuse due to the focus on criminal 'incidents'), definitional discrepancies (not all tools designed to measure prevalence use the same definition) and a range of other methodological issues (e.g. difference in reporting between face-to-face interviews and self-completion methods)—we know that the problem is widespread. According to Crime Survey England and Wales 2016, largely considered to be the best data on domestic abuse in the UK (Walby et al. 2015), 'an estimated 2 million adults aged 16 and 59 had experienced domestic abuse in the last year' (Flatley 2016). Despite some disagreement, studies consistently show that women are much more likely to be victims than men and the focus of this chapter reflects this. Women were the victims in 67% of incidents of domestic abuse according to 2015/2016 Crime Survey in England and Wales (CSEW) (Flatley 2016). The impact of domestic abuse on women and on society in general is immeasurable. In financial terms, Walby (2009) reported the overall cost of domestic abuse to society at £15.7 billion a year.

The human cost is of greater concern—in 2012, 77 women were killed by their partners or ex-partners (Her Majesty's Inspectorate of the Constabulary [HMIC] 2014).

Women have also been central to placing key issues in relation to our response to domestic abuse firmly on the agenda in developing policy and practice. Whilst throughout history domestic abuse has been largely regarded as a 'personal problem' offering little if any protection or legal support to victims, over the last 40 years, Britain has witnessed a revolution in how society views and responds. This is due largely to feminist and non-governmental organisation (NGO) campaigns that have sought to highlight the serious impact of domestic abuse on victims and families (Harwin 2006). The women's movement against male violence was enhanced by Pizzey's early academic and activist work in developing community-based refuges in the 1970s and attention eventually fell on the criminal justice system's lack of response to women in danger. Feminist academics and activists have campaigned for domestic abuse to be treated by the state with the same severity as other violent crimes (Radford and Stanko 1995). The drive to change the law as well as apply existing legal options to the private sphere has constituted a seismic change in the criminalisation of violence against women (Walklate 2008). As noted above, the definition of domestic abuse has expanded significantly in recent years. Alongside this, there have been many policy and practice developments to address the problem that now involves a range of agencies. Women at risk of harm today may have a number of housing, civil and criminal justice options available to them (Holder 1999) offering some protection from the perpetrator. Despite the recognition of domestic abuse as a 'public' issue, which entitles victims to support and protection as well as a criminal justice response, there remain many issues to be addressed.

As suggested above, domestic abuse is still one of the most underreported crimes. The 2015/2016 CSEW estimated that only 21% of abuse is reported to the police (Flatley 2016). This leaves a substantial hidden problem, which hinders the development of appropriate support to victims. It is also imprudent to presume that what victims need from services will be the same for all. It cannot be assumed that the victims who do not report their abuse to the police are the same in profile as those who do. More research is needed around the nature of these unreported incidents, including the severity, the demographic composition and the cost to services. In particular, a more comprehensive understanding of difference is required to account for gender (Newburn and Stanko 2002), sexuality (Farley 1996), ethnicity (Thiara and Gill 2009) and geographical distribution (CWASU 2012).

Figure 4.1 illustrates that risk factors contributing to domestic abuse operate across multiple levels. At the lowest level, they include the attitudes, behaviours, health and social history of the individual. This level

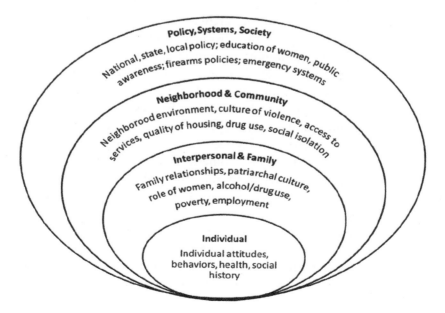

Fig. 4.1 Conceptual model relating individual, social and ecological factors to domestic abuse; Bayer et al. (2015)

is nested within the second layer which includes the influence that family and interpersonal relationships have on the individual, as well as factors such as the existence of patriarchal culture, alcohol and drug use, poverty and employment. The next level, the neighbourhood and community in which individuals live, can influence the level of abuse, with variables such as the neighbourhood environment, culture of violence, access to services, quality of housing, drug use and social isolation potentially contributing (Beyer et al. 2015). By understanding the first three levels and the potential variation in predictors of abuse between agencies, the fourth level of policy, systems and society can be challenged and shaped.

To date, most research has focused on individual factors of abuse, a recent systematic review found only a small number of studies at the neighbourhood level, 23 studies were from the USA and Canada and the remaining 14 were from Africa, Asia and South America. No research was identified from Europe, although one study from Spain has been carried since the systemic review was published (Beyer et al. 2015; Gracia et al. 2014). The research from the Essex studies will be discussed in more detail in the following section. Once complete, it is hoped these will make an important contribution to understandings of domestic abuse risk and the development of services for victims. Having the ability to predict the individuals and areas that are most at risk of victimisation by using predictive models can help estimate the true scale of the problem and enable policy makers to find new ways to encourage victims to report their abuse and to receive a more targeted service.

Encouraging victims to report domestic abuse is clearly important. In 2014, HMIC (2014) reported that the police receive an emergency call for help in relation to domestic abuse every 30 seconds and that domestic abuse related crime is 8% of total crime. For those victims who do make what is often a difficult decision to report to the police, it is vital that they receive an appropriate response. On average, two women a week are murdered by their partner or ex-partner in the UK (Office for National Statistics 2015)—a number of these women will have had some contact with the police prior to their death. Not surprisingly then, domestic abuse is a priority for most police forces across England and Wales. However, HMIC (2014) also reported that:

'This stated intent is not translating into operational reality in most forces' (p. 6). Whilst there is no way of knowing if police intervention might have prevented any domestic homicides, the police are often criticised for a general lack of understanding of the risk to victims (Hanmer et al. 1989/2013: 194).

Predicting and policing domestic abuse risk are complex issues. As well as developing statistical and/or geographical models to learn more about risk factors and updating policies and practices to reflect such learning, it is imperative that we also have a more in-depth understanding of how police officers understand risk in relation to domestic abuse. We also need to know more about how officers' understandings of the problem might affect risk assessment and risk management processes on a day-to-day basis at the operational level. Some of the Essex research, discussed later, takes a qualitative approach to reviewing police responses to risk, with a focus on looking at police responses from the perspective of victims. As a collaborative project between the University of Essex and Essex Police, this project has allowed for a great deal of learning and knowledge sharing, including unique access to police data and observations of operational processes and practice. As well as direct involvement in training packages, recommendations have also been made (through written and verbal reports) as to how the police response to domestic abuse in Essex might be improved.

We know that the response to domestic abuse does not always begin and/or end with the police. Ensuring victims receive the help and support they need to take their case through the courts and also to live safely beyond the criminal justice process is paramount, and it is now widely acknowledged that this can only be achieved through coordinated action and the delivery of a range of services via multi-agency partnerships. Effective multi-agency partnerships are key to delivering an appropriate response to domestic abuse both within and beyond the criminal justice system. For example, independent domestic violence advisors (IDVAs) are key to the criminal justice response and the delivery of a range of support services to victims. All IDVAs receive specialist nationally accredited training that allows for a more in-depth understanding of domestic abuse risk factors; they work independently alongside police and criminal justice agencies to ensure that the focus remains on victims; and they are likely to pay more careful attention to victims' appraisals of their situation (Robinson and Howarth 2012). The women's sector has consistently highlighted the importance of listening to and empowering victims—indeed, it is also considered that victims are fairly successful at assessing their own risk (Bowen 2011). Whilst studies suggest that engagement with an IDVA might deliver improvements in safety, the extent to which partnerships such as this are considered effective will depend largely on local and organisational arrangements. As such, it is essential to conduct professional evaluations of all initiatives which aim to reduce the risk of harm to DV victims.

The police are in a unique position, being the only helping agency open 24 hours a day and having the power to physically intervene in incidents of domestic violence where necessary. Therefore, understanding how the police assess and respond to risk is crucial. Whilst endeavours to improve on the first response by officers are essential, it is also widely acknowledged that ongoing support of survivors is necessary in preventing further incidents of violence. Effective multi-agency partnerships are now widely acknowledged to be key in the management of ongoing risk to survivors of domestic violence. For example, Independent Domestic Violence Advocates (IDVAs) were introduced by the government in 2005 to support survivors through the criminal justice system, whilst offering a range of practical support in assessing and lowering risk. Whilst IDVAs are now available in almost every locality nationally, the origins of domestic violence advocacy can be found in localised, collaborative initiatives between feminist organisations and the criminal justice system. Aside from IDVAs, collaboration between the women's sector and the criminal justice system has given rise to a number of innovative criminal justice programmes, which will be the focus of the last section of this chapter.

This section will focus on the work of Standing Together Against Domestic Violence (hitherto Standing Together), a feminist organisation that has pioneered local partnerships. Standing Together's criminal justice projects were inspired by similar endeavours in Duluth, Minnesota (the Duluth Programme), which provided a blueprint for women's organisations work with the criminal justice system to address domestic violence. The authors of the programme proposed that each stage of the criminal justice system and its policies could be reshaped to ensure survivor safety and perpetrator accountability. The research discussed later in the chapter involves an evaluation of Standing Together's initiatives: the Specialist Domestic Violence Courts (SDVCs) based in West London and the Impact Project based in Hammersmith Police Station. In developing such initiatives, Standing Together has sought to transform the reputation of the criminal justice system and utilise it to protect survivors and hold perpetrators to account. Since Standing Together launched the second SDVC nationally 2013, there are now 137 in England and Wales.

In the somewhat brief discussion of responses to domestic abuse thus far, we can appreciate that there have been a range of developments that might be considered improvements. However, there is still a way to go in the improvement to services and development of effective strategies, within and beyond the criminal justice system, that work to reduce the risk of harm to victims. The following three sections discuss current research projects highlighting a range of key issues in predicting, assessing and responding to domestic abuse risk. Each of the projects aims to add to the knowledge base of 'what works' in responding to domestic abuse.

Predicting Domestic Abuse in Essex

Essex is a large police force area (comprising Essex County and Southend and Thurrock Unitary authorities) with a population of 1.725 million and a mixture of rural, urban and coastal areas. In terms of income, the area is diverse, with the most deprived area in England and Wales being in Tendring district and some of the most affluent areas in the country in Uttlesford. In 2014, Essex was one of four areas to pilot the Department for Communities and Local Government (DCLG) Whole Place Community Budget (WPCB). The aim of the WPCB was to trial a new way of working which involved integrating public service delivery—working across agencies, rather than on specific organisation-led programmes or projects. The pilots aimed to identify services that were fragmented and high cost, shifting the focus from organisational responsibility to a pooled response. The pilots were driven by an economic motivation to maximise provision whilst cutting duplication and waste with a focus on early intervention and action (Local Government Association [LGA] 2015). In Essex, reducing domestic abuse was identified as one of the work streams.

The starting point in this work stream was to research what was already known about the extent of domestic abuse in Essex. It quickly became apparent that there was little information concerning the true scale of the problem. Service delivery was largely based upon police statistics, with figures augmented to account for those who had not reported their abuse to the police, based on multiplying the figure that reported to the police by the CSEW percentage non-reporters. Assumptions were made that those who reported their abuse to the police were the same in characteristics to those who had not. Between November 2011 and December 2014, there were 88,136 incidents of domestic abuse reported in Essex. Within this time, there were 46,871 victims, with 34% of victims reporting more than one incident.

It was from this initial research that two policy questions emerged. Firstly, where should Essex County Council focus their resources and services to have the most impact in reducing domestic abuse? This question sought to identify whether a blanket policy across the whole geographic area should be used, or whether a more targeted response would be more effective in reducing the problem. Secondly, can Essex County Council rely on Essex Police recorded crime data to predict the service requirements of those who do not report their abuse to the police? This questioned the assumption that those who report their abuse to the police share the same characteristics and have the same needs as those who do not.

These policy questions focus on individual- and neighbourhood-level predictors of abuse, but with little previous research at the neighbourhood level, it was not known how valuable they could be in identifying risk. And this leads on to a third research question—are individual or neighbourhood variables better at predicting domestic abuse?

In order to consider these questions, a range of methods were used to reflect the different levels. At the individual level and family level, more traditional statistical models, including logistic regression, were used to see whether factors such as gender, age, ethnicity and responses to the DASH (Domestic Abuse, Stalking and Honour-Based Violence risk assessment tool) can predict domestic abuse and reporting patterns (the DASH is discussed in more detail on page 15). One of the difficulties in finding predictors of police-reported domestic abuse at the individual level is that these are only the known cases. There is no baseline for comparison with those who do not report their abuse to the police. Therefore, a proxy measure of repeat victimisation was used. The rationale for this is that it is likely that victims of more serious incidents or abuse that is escalating are more likely to have been to the police more than once. Of course, the caveat to this could be that a victim has a bad experience with the police and will not report to them again.

At the neighbourhood level, models were produced using a Geographic Information System (GIS) to predict the rate of domestic abuse in each census Lower Super Output Area (LSOA), each representing a population of approximately 1500 people.

A GIS not only offers the ability to map the location of crime but also allows researchers to predict where crime is most likely to be concentrated in the future. This type of modelling has been applied to other crime types but not domestic abuse. The most promising geographic predictive models have used multiple variables to predict future crime rates (Chainey and Ratcliffe 2005). These variables include structural and cultural factors that are available at the neighbourhood level. In this research a methodology called Geographically Weighted Regression was used (Fotheringham et al. 2002).

Individual, Family, and Interpersonal-Level Risk

Early research findings do not challenge the widely held view that domestic abuse is a gendered issue, with 72% of Essex Police victims being female, which is slightly higher than the 67% reported to the CSEW (Flatley 2016). When looking at the number of victims, rather than incidents, the proportion of female victims increases to 78%, with the majority aged between 15 and 49, and the peak age for both male and female victims being 20–24.

Victims classified as white European experienced 89% of abuse for both males and females, followed by those recorded as African/Caribbean and those of unknown ethnicity. Analysis of victim's ethnicity has been made difficult as the classification used by the police does not align with the census ethnicity classification, making it challenging to identify ethnicities where domestic abuse is more prolific.

For instance, the North London Domestic Violence Survey found understanding of domestic abuse among black African and black Caribbean respondents to be polar opposites, with black African's having the lowest level of recognition among any ethnicity and black Caribbean the highest (Mooney 1999). The IC codes used by the police combine the two ethnicities creating an ecological fallacy and no real understanding of the individual ethnicities.

Examining the relationship between victim and perpetrator offers some quite different victim typologies to that found when focusing on the whole incident dataset. The gendered nature of abuse is very clear for partners and ex-partners, but less so for other relationships, such as those between children and their parents and those between siblings.

Referring to the conceptual model of Beyer et al. (2015) that frames this analysis there are still gaps in our understanding of individual-level factors, the police data do not have attitude data or individual's health or social history. It has, however, identified significant variables, particularly gender. As the conceptual models suggest, multiple factors across different levels contribute to domestic abuse. The next step was to look at contextual factors at the neighbourhood level.

Neighbourhood Level

Initial findings from neighbourhood-level analysis in Essex are that 81% of the domestic abuse rate can be explained using all of the following variables: the anti-social behaviour rate; income; health, barriers to housing and living environment deprivation scores; the proportion of Black, Asian and Minority Ethic (BAME) population; population density; and the proportion of young people in a neighbourhood. What is also interesting is that the relationship between each of the variables is not geographically consistent, with variables having more influence on the rate of domestic abuse in some areas and less in others, whilst some of the relationships between variables are negative in some areas and positive in others. For example, a higher proportion of young people predicted a higher domestic abuse rate in some areas and but a lower one in others. These findings have clear implications for targeted policy interventions.

The next step is to test this model with data from other agencies, including the NHS and Children and Family Court Advisory and Support Service (CAFCASS), to identify whether the predictors also apply to those who have not reported their abuse to the police. The early findings have found predictors at both the individual and neighbourhood levels and a further step that can now be taken is to see whether a multilevel model, which factors in both levels, is the best overall predictor of the risk of domestic abuse.

With an increased understanding of the predictors, appropriate mechanisms can be designed to try to encourage at-risk populations to report to the police and to overcome barriers that may deter victims from talking to others about their abuse. One of these barriers could be the experience that victims have when reporting to the police and the next section will explore the ways in which front-line police officers interpret and manage risk.

Improving Police Responses to Domestic Abuse

It is vital that victims receive appropriate levels of protection and support from the police if further incidents of domestic abuse are to be prevented and perpetrators held to account. We know that victims do not always receive an appropriate and/or effective response from the police, leaving scope for improvement. It is within this context that the research discussed in this section was planned. Its key purpose has been to review the policing of domestic abuse in Essex and consider some of the issues that affect police response. Full access to police files and processes was granted allowing for an in-depth qualitative analysis of policing activity in relation to domestic abuse. The work adds to current efforts to improve performance by aligning, more closely, 'what police do' with 'what victims need'. The project is by no means complete, and a great deal of work is yet to be done to meet the aims and objectives. However, at this stage, it is possible to discuss some of the key areas of consideration in relation to risk assessment and risk management.

Policing Domestic Violence—Risk

Undoubtedly, responding to calls for help in relation to domestic abuse presents considerable challenges to police services, especially in assessing and managing risk. Many organisations, including the police, now use a standardised model for identifying, assessing and managing risk in relation to domestic abuse. The DASH model (2009) was accredited by the Association of Chief Police Officers (ACPO) in 2009 and is now used by most police forces, as well as some partner organisations across the UK, thus, achieving a level of consistency in terms of sharing knowledge about risk within and between agencies. The DASH risk assessment tool consists of screening questions, which assist with identifying and assessing risk. The DASH, according to Richards (2016), has been built on good practice (including other evidence-based risk models such as SPECCS + Risk Identification), and the risk factors that are included are derived from extensive research on a range of domestic abuse incidents and multi-agency Domestic Homicide Reviews (DHRs—introduced by section 9 of the Domestic Violence, Crime and Victims Act 2004). Despite developments in terms of the definition and legislation regarding domestic abuse since 2009, the DASH risk assessment tool has remained largely unchanged and unchallenged since its introduction. The College of Policing admit that they have 'found no research or evaluation to support the adoption of any one particular risk assessment tool over another' (College of Policing 2016) and so the DASH model continues to be widely used and supported by practitioners in the field. At the time of writing, the DASH is currently under review, and some discussion of the expectations and achievements in terms of police risk assessments has already been published (see Ariza et al. 2016). It remains to be seen if this will result in any significant changes to the process of risk assessment for the police.

At this point, it would be helpful to consider Hoyle's (2008: 326) summary of the process of risk assessment and risk management for domestic violence:

> Risk assessment processes in domestic violence cases are focused on the medium and long-term, as much as on responding effectively at the scene. They are based on the need to secure victims' safety, better manage potentially lethal situations, and to gather and make sensible use of intelligence. They are aimed at preventing serious injury and death by putting into place a risk management plan. The main purpose of risk management and assessment is to improve the protection and interventions for families who are experiencing domestic violence and to target those interventions on those cases that need them most because they present the highest risk.

Thus, the purpose of police risk assessments is to offer a level of protection that is in line with the level of risk—with a particular emphasis on ensuring that resources are directed towards those that are deemed to be *high* risk. It may then be argued that the process of risk assessment may be something of a 'rationing device' (Radford and Gill 2006) rather than a means of putting effective strategies in place that might offer an appropriate level of protection to *all* victims, not just those who are judged to be high risk.

Offering an appropriate level of protection to all victims whilst responding to increasing domestic abuse incidents is a challenge for all police forces. It is important to acknowledge this, particularly in the current climate of cuts to police budgets and multi-agency domestic abuse services in general. The impact of this on victims is a cause for concern, as calls for help in relation to domestic abuse are increasing nationally. Despite domestic abuse still being significantly underreported, there has been a rise in police-recorded domestic abuse. There was a 23% increase in England and Wales in the 12 months to June 2016—in Essex there was an increase of 24% in police-recorded domestic abuse representing 12% of all recorded crime in Essex. At the same time, the Essex Police budget has been cut significantly and the workforce has been reduced by 17% since 2010 (HMIC 2017). This is likely to have a negative impact upon domestic abuse responses, as well as other areas of policing activity where there are risks to vulnerable victims. This research has found that officers in Essex are frustrated with what they perceive to be a lack of resources for responding to domestic abuse. In particular, officers are concerned about the time it may take them to respond to a domestic abuse incident whilst they are also being directed to their next job which might also involve vulnerable victims— one officer referred to this as being a 'slave to the radio' (comment from front-line officer 2016). It is perhaps not difficult to see how risk assessments and risk management may be planned with resources in mind, rather than the needs of victims being the primary driving force behind decision-making.

A lack of resources is far from being the only issue. In 2015, Essex Police were judged to be 'inadequate' in the HMIC PEEL effectiveness report in relation to vulnerability, 'because it was failing to properly support and safeguard vulnerable people'; however, following a revisit in 2016, it was deemed that there had been 'significant progress and *a complete change of mindset* and approach to vulnerability' (HMIC 2017: 41; emphasis added). Policing is particularly resistant to change (College of Policing 2015), so to declare a 'complete change of mindset' in such a short period of time is perhaps overstating the extent of the progress made. However, this research suggests that Essex Police have taken significant steps towards improving their performance in relation to recognising and responding to vulnerability generally. The extent to which this has a real impact upon day-to-day operational processes and the front-line response to domestic abuse is less clear. There is evidence of a lack of knowledge and understanding in some areas of domestic abuse policing. The HMIC also found 'instances of officers undertaking roles and investigations for which they were not qualified or trained and with little obvious support from more experienced colleagues' (HMIC 2017: 47). To encourage meaningful change from the bottom-up, front-line officers require a high level of knowledge and understanding in terms of confronting domestic abuse and, more specifically, the needs of a diverse range of victims. More in-depth training could be provided to develop confidence and professional judgement to keep front-line officers up to date with developments in terms of awareness, policy and practice.

Policing Domestic Abuse—Professional Practice

A reading of the domestic abuse policy of any of the 43 police forces in England and Wales will reveal a well-informed professional approach towards responding to domestic abuse. Indeed, they are all guided by and expected to have regard to Authorised Professional Practice (APP) on domestic abuse, developed and owned by the College of Policing (College of Policing 2016). The APP on domestic abuse includes a comprehensive section on '*Understanding risk and vulnerability in the context of domestic abuse*' which covers risk identification and assessment as well as risk factors and vulnerabilities that may be associated with domestic abuse. It also highlights particular issues affecting certain groups of victims as well as the different kinds of relationships within which the abuse may occur. Whilst the College of Policing acknowledge that there may 'be circumstances where it is perfectly legitimate to deviate from APP', they also state that there must be 'a clear rationale for doing so' (College of Policing 2016). This may be considered a reminder to all officers and staff that decision-making processes require accountability, particularly if they are to depart from APP. In public protection training and professional development sessions at Essex Police, officers were concerned that there should be a policy for any action they were being advised to take, with one officer (sergeant) stating 'the police are most scared of the police'. Others expressed frustration with going against the wishes of victims, as well as being restricted in terms of applying what they deemed to be their own professional judgement. Developments in policing, such as the introduction of APP frameworks, national risk models (e.g. DASH 2009) and recording protocols (National Crime Recording Standards introduced in 2002), do indeed have the potential to limit the opportunity for officers to exercise discretion in their response to domestic violence. But perhaps with good reason!

The factors that influence officers' decision-making in their responses to domestic violence are less clear. However, as argued by Ericson and Haggerty (1997): 'The conventional sociological wisdom is that the most influential rule-structure is the one provided by the occupational culture of fellow officers' (Ericson and Haggerty 1997: 31). Indeed, decades of research on police culture refers to the 'uninformed and sexist attitudes of officers' (Myhill and Johnson 2015: 4) and the negative impact this has on responses to domestic abuse (Hanmer et al. 1989/2013; Loftus 2009). It is known that domestic violence has long been viewed by officers as 'rubbish' work (Loftus 2009) or not something they should have to deal with as 'crime fighters'. In a domestic abuse training session, a front-line officer declared 'we are not social workers'. Unsurprisingly then, police discretion, particularly in relation to domestic abuse, is an issue that is still 'hotly contested' (Myhill and Johnson 2015: 2).

Well-designed, well-informed, evidence-based policies may go some way to counteracting the more negative aspects of police culture and reduce the likelihood of poor judgement. However, the complexities of intimate and familial relationships and the unique circumstances behind each call for help might not always fit with standard operating procedures (SOP) and/or APP frameworks. Furthermore, it is important to note that the DASH risk assessment model should not be based entirely on actuarial calculations (i.e. number of 'yes' responses to questions regarding risk factors). Ultimately, the final decision as to the risk grading, as well as the level of protection to be offered to victims, often lies with the attending officer/s. For those victims who are deemed to be high risk, secondary risk assessments are likely to be carried out by more experienced staff in dedicated domestic abuse units, but this activity varies across police forces, as does the level of expertise. As such, it is imperative that officers make an informed decision based on professional judgement. The extent to which professional judgement is applied will depend on the level of knowledge, skill and experience of each involved. Victims are unlikely to engage with officers if they feel there is a lack of understanding and empathy, thus, diminishing the officers' capacity to gain the information required to make an informed judgement about risk. Victims are 'experts by experience', and as suggested above, they are found to be particularly successful at judging their own risk (Bowen 2011). Front-line officers need to feel confident that they have the knowledge and skills to encourage victims to share their experiences. Through listening to the voices of victims, officers are likely to learn more about the risk involved in each incident of domestic abuse. Independent Domestic Violence Advisors may take a more effective approach by encouraging victims to speak about their experiences, engage with safeguarding procedures and support prosecution. There is also evidence to suggest that practitioners from outside support agencies consider a wider range of factors than the police in assessing risk for domestic abuse victims (Robinson and Howarth 2012), and the following section looks more closely at the collaboration between women's services and the criminal justice system and the effectiveness of this approach.

A Women's Sector and Criminal Justice System Alliance: A Strategy Against Domestic Abuse

In the late 1980s and early 1990s, parts of the feminist movement against domestic abuse drew attention to the criminal justice system as a potential remedy in risk management. It was felt by some that the inadequate police response (as discussed above) could be reformed, so that a safer justice system be utilised as part of a wider strategy to challenge male domination in the home. Those feminists who looked to criminal justice reform were particularly concerned about the ongoing risk to survivors who were unable or unwilling to flee to a refuge, who invariably remained in the community, where their perpetrator may have free and uninterrupted access to re-abuse them. If done properly, it was argued, the police and courts have the potential to lower risk to women. This would be done by physically removing perpetrators from the scene through arrest and then applying sanctions at court to prevent repeat incidents (Shepard and Pence 1999).

Feminist activists and researchers have successfully won acknowledgement in policy and law, highlighting the importance of an adequate response to domestic abuse. The most significant policy change came in 2005 when the government announced a roll-out of SDVCs and Independent Domestic Violence Advocates (IDVAs) through its National Domestic Violence Delivery Plan in England and Wales

(Home Office 2005). This marked a significant shift in policy and practice on a national scale. However, this was the culmination of many years of local feminist organisations collaborating with the police and courts, to establish system reform that aimed to increase support to survivors and hold perpetrators to account.

Standing Together Against Domestic Violence was the organisation under the focus of the research discussed in this section and opened one of the first SDVCs nationally in 2002 in West London and opened a second in Westminster in 2013. The first SDVC opened in 1999 in Leeds, and there are now 137 such courts in England and Wales.

From the beginning, the overarching goals of the Standing Together courts were to utilise a multi-agency framework to implement safety measures, as well as to increase the number of perpetrators being held to account through successful prosecutions. Whilst largely successful in both, it was felt that improvements could be made on the second goal through the enhancement of evidence gathering from the police before cases come to court. It was on this basis that The Impact Project was launched at Hammersmith Police Station in 2015. The aim of the initiative was to increase the number of successful convictions by locating domestic abuse specialists in the police station to review cases for evidence as well as offer on-site support to survivors through an IDVA. However, the focus of this section will be based on the SDVCs, as it is here where the most significant decisions are made regarding immediate and medium-term risk.

The research, conducted over three years, consisted of court observations, analysis of case studies and interviews with members of staff from all agencies involved. The data yielded then underwent an Intersectionality-Based Policy Analysis. This involved utilising the concept of intersectionality to locate survivors (with particular attention towards those marginalised through power structures, i.e. 'race', migration status or social class) and the likely impact of these criminal justice initiatives in their lives. An additional point of analysis involved identifying power structures between survivors, local domestic abuse services and national justice agencies, and the power relations between and across all three. As such initiatives are relatively new and even the most pioneering among them have taken years to settle into permanency, research that seeks to understand whether this strategy is one that may work for survivors from all communities is vital.

Specialist Domestic Violence Courts

Specialist courts were first established in the USA in the 1980s, but similar initiatives have since been introduced in Canada, Australia, South Africa and the UK. The strategy has been utilised most commonly where traditional adversarial approaches have been deemed ineffective in cases such as drugs offences and domestic abuse (Casey and Rottman 2003).

In the UK, the SDVC programme involves dedicating one courtroom, one day a week to be used for domestic abuse cases. These cases are siphoned off to focus resources. In the courts under examination by this research, domestic abuse cases are discussed every Wednesday. A specially trained, dedicated prosecutor whose sole focus is on domestic abuse cases presents to the magistrates. The magistrates or District Judges are selected from a pool of those who are trained to deal with such cases and the dynamics of domestic abuse. To the side of the court sits an IDVA, making a note of important updates that need to be fed back to the survivor and communicating safety needs to the court. She will also be made available to support any survivors who come to the court to give evidence in a trial, who are unsupported by a domestic abuse service. The probation officer also sits in the court and will have been trained in making recommendations in collaboration with the other stakeholders with a view to managing risk. Lastly, the coordinator is employed by Standing Together and oversees all proceedings, monitoring and addressing any ongoing problems, whilst facilitating information sharing between agencies. Standing Together has provided the training to all stakeholders in the SDVC. From observations of the court in process, it is clear that a great deal of information is shared between the partners and this information is used to make decisions based on *risk*, as illustrated by the case study below.

Case Study

Hammersmith SDVC

A defendant has been brought to court after a night in custody following an arrest for common assault. His defence solicitor makes an application for unconditional bail. The police have provided the prosecutor with an antecedents report and call-out history, which shows several police call-outs to the address and a previous case of common assault that was discontinued at trial. The IDVA passes information, via the coordinator informing that whilst the defendant was on bail for that offence, he breached bail on a number of occasions, but that went unreported. This information had come from a phone call with the survivor that morning. That is put in the magistrates bundle but is not reported verbally in open court, to protect the survivor. The magistrate asks the prosecutor if a risk assessment has been completed. The prosecutor looks through his bundle and confirms that the police completed a CAADA DASH (now Safe Lives) risk assessment at the scene and the resulting score.

In this setting, the courtroom was a complex but proactive multi-agency forum, in which each agency was expected to have come to court prepared and with the relevant information to hand. Each agency has specific access to intelligence, ranging from antecedents to the expressed concerns of the survivors. The SDVC has laid out procedural expectations for all to follow, meaning that the responsibility to investigate, enquire and gather information about risk lies with the professionals in the courtroom. The role of the court coordinator is to provide assurance of accountability, and where there is a failure to maintain procedures, the relevant agencies will be challenged in the out of court steering committee. This level of attention to detail and risk was identified as a theme in all the observed cases in the courts, including first appearances, trials and at sentencing.

The role of the IDVA is particularly crucial in bridging the gap between the complexity of the court and the inexperience of the survivor. Research has found that less educated women having their cases heard in traditional court settings often feel the process is so mystifying that they have no understanding of the options available to them or the consequences of any decisions made (Miller 2005). Through the IDVA the survivor is able to communicate her safety concerns, and the IDVA, being more familiar with the court process, is able to navigate it in a way that ensures the safety of the women. In cases observed for this research, the IDVA was seen making phone calls before and after the court session, ensuring that she was updated on all proceedings as soon as possible, and had the opportunity to feed in relevant information right up until the moment the court session opened. The survivor did not need to take any obvious part in proceedings, as she will not be named in open court and does not need to attend. Yet she remains central to proceedings covertly. Such a programme provides more safety options to survivors, especially those who might not otherwise be able to successfully navigate such an institution to focus on her interests.

Whilst the SDVC programme demonstrates real potential in placing more power in the hands of survivors to influence and understand court proceedings, investment in a criminal justice remedy was not without its flaws. As discussed above, a criminal justice strategy on domestic abuse often relies on increasing the arrest rate of perpetrators, usually involving mandatory or pro-arrest policies. However, an unexpected consequence of such policies has been a significant increase in the number of *women* arrested for domestic abuse (Hester 2009). Although women certainly do perpetrate violence in the home, the steep increase has generally been attributed to the phenomenon of 'mutual arrest' or 'cross fillings' that has been identified as a problem associated with new mandatory arrest policies (Buzawa and Buzawa 1990; Chesney-Lind 1997; Greenfield and Snell 1999). Here, the police may arrest both parties if they are unable to discern who the perpetrator is, or in some cases, the perpetrator is successfully able to manipulate the criminal justice system to arrest his victim (Chesney-Lind 1989; Miller 2005).

There were examples of such cases coming through the SDVC, with practitioners sometimes identifying a woman being prosecuted as more likely to be the victim than the perpetrator. One practitioner identified a case in which a female defendant, who was probably the survivor of the abuse, was brought before the court as a defendant. She felt that the bail conditions and an eventual conviction actually helped the survivor to end the abusive relationship. It has been argued that increasing criminal justice initiatives at the same time as shrinking welfare provision has seen a 'punitive turn' in the way social problems are dealt with. Where housing, benefits and community services were previously the main means of addressing this, increasingly it is the police and court that do so, with the additional imposition of sanctions and punishment—even of survivors of abuse (Bumiller 2008; Sweet 2016; Richie 2012).

Reliance on criminal justice sanctions being placed on perpetrators, as well as survivors, as a method of risk mediation has been referred to by some as 'carceral feminism' (Richie 2012; Sweet 2016). It may be that as welfare provision dwindles, concurrent investment in criminal justice initiatives is leaving some practitioners, perhaps understandably, to look pragmatically at what is left to prevent further incidents. However, understanding this from an intersectional perspective, we cannot assume that all survivors are equally likely to fall foul of initiatives devised to support them. For example, research has shown that women of colour that come into contact with the criminal justice system face significantly more punitive responses compared with white women at every stage, with women of colour more likely to be arrested and charged with more serious offences and to be prosecuted, convicted, and to serve time in prison (Chesney-Lind 1997; Greenfield and Snell 1999; Miller 2001; Allard 2002; Uhrig 2016).

Therefore, whilst the SDVC programme certainly has the potential to offer some survivors empowerment and safety through the criminal justice system, we must be cautious. The criminal justice system is certainly not experienced as a liberating institution by all survivors of domestic abuse. For some, contact with the police may increase their risk rather than lower it, especially if the justice system is unwittingly being utilised by perpetrators to further abuse women. Additional to this, if an increase in criminal justice initiatives is accompanied by the severing of all other routes to a life free from abuse, the gains made by the SDVC programme may be undermined by an overreliance on punitive remedies.

Conclusion

As stated above, we have come a long way in terms of working towards a more appropriate response to domestic abuse. Yet there is also still a long way to go to ensure that we are giving all victims the opportunity to speak about their experiences in a context where they are going to be offered the guidance and support they need, as well as a criminal justice response that addresses the harms they have endured. This can only be achieved through coordinated action by key services and continued efforts to consider 'what works' in terms of responding to domestic abuse. It is regrettable that many feminists, academics, activists, women's groups, campaigners and victims are still experiencing some of the same issues they were in the 1970s/1980s. Academic research, such as the collaborative projects highlighted here, can open up the opportunity for all those currently involved to learn more about 'what works' and has the potential to drive further improvements in domestic violence responses. The three projects highlighted here represent just a fraction of the research undertaken by women, for women, to improve the experience of women in the criminal justice system. It is through learning more about women's experiences within the criminal justice system and beyond that we are likely to improve the response to domestic abuse for *all* victims.

References

Allard, P. (2002). *Life sentences: Denying welfare benefits to women convicted of drug offenses*. Washington, DC: The Sentencing Project.

Ariza, J. J. M., Robinson, A., & Myhill, A. (2016). Cheaper, faster, better: Expectations and achievements in police risk assessment of domestic abuse. *Policing, 10*(4).

Beyer, K., et al. (2015). Neighborhood environment and intimate partner violence: A systematic review. *Trauma, Violence, & Abuse, 16*(1), 16–47.

Bowen, E. (2011). An overview of partner violence risk assessment and the potential of female victim risk appraisals. *Aggression and Violent Behaviour, 16*, 214–226.

Bumiller, K. (2008). *In an abusive state: How neoliberalism appropriated the feminist movement against sexual violence*. Duke University Press.

Buzawa, E. S., & Buzawa, C. (1990). *Domestic violence: The criminal justice response*. Thousand Oaks: Sage.

Casey, P. M., & Rottman, D. B. (2003). *Problem-solving courts: Models and trends*. Williamsburg, VA: National Center for State Courts.

Chainey, S., & Ratcliffe, J. (2005). *GIS and crime mapping*. London: Wiley.

Child and Woman Abuse Studies Unit. (2012). *Women's journeys in response to domestic violence*. Available at: http://www.cwasu.org/.

Chesney-Lind, M. (1989). Girls' crime and woman's place: Toward a feminist model of female delinquency. *Crime & Delinquency, 3*(10), 5–29.

Chesney-Lind, M. (1997). *The female offender*. Thousand Oaks, CA: Sage.

College of Policing. (2015). *Leadership Review*, [online]. Available at: http://www.college.police.uk/leadershipreview (Accessed 5 August 2015).

College of Policing. (2016). *Authorised professional practice: Understanding risk and vulnerability in the context of domestic abuse*. Available at: https://www.app.college.police.uk/legal-information/.

Ericson, R. V., & Haggerty, K. D. (1997). *Policing the risk society*. Oxford: Clarenden Press.

Farley, N. A. (1996). Survey of factors contributing to gay and lesbian domestic violence. *Journal of Gay and Lesbian Social Services, 4*(1).

Flatley, J. (2016). *Intimate personal violence and partner abuse*. London: Office for National Statistics.

Fotheringham, S. A., Brunsdon, C., & Charlton, M. (2002). *Geographically weighted regression: The analysis of spatially varying relationship*. Chichester: Wiley.

Gracia, E., López-Quílez, A., Marco, M., Lladosa, S., & Lila, M. (2014). Exploring neighborhood influences on small-area variations in intimate partner violence risk: A bayesian random-effects modeling approach. *International Journal of Environmental Research and Public Health, 11*(1), 866–882.

Greenfield, L. A., & Snell, T. L. (1999). *Women offenders*. Washington, DC. NCJ175688.

Hanmer, J., Radner, J., & Stanko, E. A. (1989/2013). *Women, policing and male violence: International perspectives. Routledge revivals*. Oxon: Routledge.

Harwin, N. (2006). Putting a stop to domestic violence in the United Kingdom: Challenges and opportunities. *Violence Against Women, 12*(6), 556–567.

Her Majesty's Inspectorate of Constabulary. (2014). *Everybody's business: Improving police response to domestic violence*. Available at: www.hmic.gov.uk.

Her Majesty's Inspectorate of Constabulary. (2015). *PEEL: Police effectiveness 2015 (vulnerability)—An inspection of Essex Police*. Available at: https://www.justiceinspectorates.gov.uk/hmic/wp-content/uploads/police-effectiveness-vulnerability-2015-essex.pdf.

Her Majesty's Inspectorate of Constabulary. (2017). *Essex Police (profile)*. Available at: http://www.justiceinspectorates.gov.uk/hmic/essex/.

Hester, M. (2009, June). Who does what to whom? Gender and domestic violence perpetrators. *Violence Against Women Research Group School for Policy Studies University of Bristol*, 1–19. https://doi.org/10.1177/1477370813479078.

Holder, R. (1999). Creating an unholy alliance: Inter-agency developments on domestic violence in Hammersmith and Fulham. In N. Harwin, G. Hague, & E. Malos (Eds.), *The multi-agency approach to domestic violence: New opportunities, old challenges?* London: Whiting and Birch Ltd.

Home Office. (2005). *Domestic violence: A national report*. London.

Home Office. (2013). New government domestic violence and abuse definition. *Circular 003/2013*.

Hoyle, C. (2008). Will she be safe? A critical analysis of risk assessment in domestic violence cases. *Children and Youth Services Review, 30*(3), 323–337.

Local Government Association. (2015). *Whole place*. Available at: http://www.local.gov.uk/community-budgets/-/journal_content/56/10180/3692233/ARTICLE.

Loftus, B. (2009). *Police culture in a changing world*. Oxford: Oxford University Press.

Miller, S. L. (2001). The paradox of women arrested for domestic violence: Criminal justice professionals and service providers respond. *Violence Against Women, 7*, 1339–1376.

Miller, S. L. (2005). *Victims as offenders: The paradox of women's violence in relationships*. New York: Rutgers University Press.

Mooney, J. (1999). *The North London domestic violence survey*. Centre for Criminology: Middlesex University.

Myhill, A., & Johnson, K. (2015). Police use of discretion in response to domestic violence. *Criminology and Criminal Justice, 16*(1), 3–20.

Newburn, T., & Stanko, E. A. (2002). When men are victims: The failure of victimology and victim services. In T. Newburn & E. A. Stanko (Eds.), *Just boys doing business? Men, masculinities and crime*. London, UK: Sage.

Office for National Statistics. (2015). *Crime statistics, focus on violent crime and sexual offences, 2013/14. Chapter 4: Violent crime and sexual offences—Intimate personal violence and serious sexual assault*. Available at: http://www.ons.gov.uk/ons/dcp171776_394500.pdf.

Radford, L., & Gill, A. (2006). Losing the plot? Researching community safety partnership work against domestic violence. *The Howard Journal, 45*(4), 369–387.

Radford, J., & Stanko, E. (1995). Violence against women and children. In M. Hester, L. Kelly, & J. Radford (Eds.), *Women, violence and male power* (pp. 65–68). Buckingham: Open University Press.

Richards, L. in partnership with CAADA. (2009). *Domestic Abuse, Stalking and Harrasment and Honour Based Violence (DASH 2009) risk identification and assessment and management model.* Available at: http://www.dashrisk-checklist.co.uk/wp-content/uploads/2016/09/DASH-2009.pdf.

Richards, L. (2016). *DASH risk model.* Available at: http://www.dashriskcheck-list.co.uk/.

Richie, B. E. (2012, May 22). *Arrested justice: Black women, violence, and America's prison nation.* New York: New York University Press.

Robinson, A. L., & Howarth, E. (2012). Judging risk: Key determinants in British domestic violence cases. *Journal of Interpersonal Violence, 27*(8), 1489–1518.

Shepard, M. F., & Pence, E. L. (1999). *Coordinating community responses to domestic violence: Lessons from Duluth and beyond.* Thousand Oaks, CA: Sage.

Sweet, E. L. (2016). Carceral feminism. *Dialogues in Human Geography, 6*(2), 202–205. https://doi.org/10.1177/2043820616655041.

Thiara, R., & Gill, A. (2009). *Violence against women in South Asian communities: Issues for policy and practice.* London: Jessica Kingsley.

Uhrig, N. (2016). *Black, Asian and minority ethnic disproportionality in the criminal justice system in England and Wales.* Ministry of Justice Analytical Services.

Walby, S. (2009). *The cost of domestic violence up-date 2009.* Lancaster University. Available at: www.lancs.ac.uk/fass/doc_library/sociology/Cost_of_domestic_violence_update.doc.

Walby, S., Towers, J., & Francis, B. (2015). Is violent crime increasing or decreasing? A new methodology to measure repeat attacks making visible the significance of gender and domestic relations. *The British Journal of Criminology, 56*(6), 1203–1234.

Walklate, S. (2008). What is to be done about violence against women? Gender, violence, cosmopolitanism and the law. *British Journal of Criminology, 48*(1), 39–54.

5

Criminalising Neonaticide: Reflections on Law and Practice in England and Wales

Karen Brennan and Emma Milne

Introduction

Ruth Percival, a 28-year-old woman, gave birth to her son on the toilet in her home in November 2014. The child was born with the umbilical cord wrapped around his neck and was reported by Ruth's father to have 'appeared "sallow and lifeless" and he thought was "obviously deceased"' (*The Telegraph* 2017). Ruth and her father were initially arrested on suspicion of murder and conspiracy to conceal the birth of a child. Over two years later, both charges were dropped, and Ruth and her father were arrested on suspicion of child neglect; later this charge would also be dropped. Despite a prolonged investigation and several

K. Brennan (✉)
School of Law, University of Essex, Colchester,
Essex, UK
e-mail: kbrennan@essex.ac.uk
E. Milne (✉)
Department of Criminology and Sociology, Middlesex University,
London, UK
e-mail: e.milne@mdx.ac.uk

© The Author(s) 2018
E. Milne et al. (eds.), *Women and the Criminal Justice System*,
https://doi.org/10.1007/978-3-319-76774-1_5

post-mortems, the cause of death of the baby boy remained 'unascertained'. A coroner's inquest, conducted almost two years after the death of the child, was halted when the coroner decided to adjourn the inquest and refer the case to the Director of Public Prosecutions; consequently, Ruth and her father faced a third criminal investigation over the death of the baby. The referral came after three medical professionals presented evidence at the inquest that the baby had been born alive, suggesting that he could have survived if the correct medical attention had been given. Dr. Ruth Gottstein, a consultant neonatologist, told the court 'If resuscitation had been initiated, I think the baby would survived' (Parveen 2016). Further suspicion was aroused following evidence that Ruth had placed the baby in the outside bin (Ruth and her father denied this); that paramedics had not been called immediately following the birth; and that the child's body was left alone in the house whilst Ruth and her father attended a previously arranged doctor's appointment after cleaning the blood from the bathroom floor. The investigations into the birth and death of Ruth's child ended after 28 months, when the Crown Prosecution Service (CPS) decided that there was 'insufficient evidence to provide a realistic prospect of conviction for a criminal prosecution' (*The Telegraph* 2017).

This case illustrates some of the typical features of the phenomenon of 'neonaticide', newborn child killing: a single woman experiencing an unwanted pregnancy and giving birth alone, resulting in the death of her baby. Such cases are unusual in Western modern society and are emotionally distressing for the public and professionals. The Percival case also highlights a number of issues with regard to criminalising women whose babies die at birth. First, it highlights the efforts of the police and CPS to investigate this particular case with the aim of initiating prosecution, despite the limited evidence available to them. Second, it demonstrates that there are limits to the reach of the criminal law in cases involving the deaths of neonates following 'secret' births. Finally, the case raises questions about the purpose and appropriateness of criminalisation in cases of maternal neonaticide.

The purpose of this chapter is to examine these issues, and to this end, we do the following: first, we provide an outline of the literature on the circumstances and incidence of neonaticide; second, we discuss some of the problems that arise in connection with convicting women of criminal offences, particularly homicide crimes, when their babies die following a 'secret birth'; third, we briefly outline what we know about criminal justice practice in these cases, and, finally, we offer some reflections for future research and practice.

What Is Neonaticide?

The term 'neonaticide' was first used by Resnick (1969, 1970) to describe the killing of an infant within the first twenty-four hours of life. Resnick and others argue that it is a distinct form of child homicide. It is usually committed by the mother in the context of an unwanted pregnancy (d'Orbán 1979; Friedman and Friedman 2010; Meyer and Oberman 2001; Porter and Gavin 2010). The term neonaticide is widely used within medical, legal, psychiatric, psychological and criminological literature, and many attempts have been made to understand its causes and consider prevention.

It is difficult to determine the rate of neonaticide. Scholars have commented on the inaccuracy of official statistics; Wilczynski (1997) argues there is a large 'dark figure' of child killing (victim aged under 16 years), estimating that true incidents of child homicide are 3–7 times higher than official statistics report. In the UK, no official record of how many children are killed within the first day of life is kept. The Home Office records the number of homicides that occur each year in the Homicide Index. However, as we discuss below, proving a homicide has occurred can be very difficult in cases of neonaticide. In some cases, the death of a foetus/newborn child may be recorded under the criminal offence of concealment of birth (COB). Section 60 of the Offences Against the Person Act 1861 (OAPA) makes it an offence to conceal the dead body of a baby in order to conceal the fact the infant had been born; it is irrelevant for the purposes of conviction how and when death was caused. Therefore, cases of suspected COB may also be cases of neonaticide. Due to the close connection between COB and newborn homicide (Milne forthcoming), it is possible that some deaths will be recorded in both the Homicide Index and the police recorded statistics for concealment, producing a duplicate count. Despite the shortcomings, the data presented in Table 5.1 offer the most comprehensive picture of known neonaticide cases, and taken together, the average is 7 deaths per year. Drawing upon Wilczynski's (1997) conclusion that actual figures are, at least, three times higher than official statistics, the possible number of neonaticides to occur each year is 21.[1]

Neonaticide is almost exclusively committed by women. Much of the literature constructs a stereotype of the neonaticidal woman: she is young, often a teenager, single, lives with her parents, comes from a low socio-economic background and has few economic, social or emotional resources to deal with a pregnancy (See Alder and Baker 1997; Craig 2004; d'Orbán 1979; Resnick 1969; Porter and Gavin 2010). Such women have also been described as 'passive', not taking active steps to address their pregnancy (Spinelli 2003; Beyer et al. 2008; Amon et al. 2012). However, not all women fit the stereotype. For example, perpetrators older than teenagers have been identified in numerous studies.

Table 5.1 Estimated number occurrence of neonaticide 2002/2003 to 2015/2016

Year	Offences currently recorded as homicide, victims one day old or less[a]	Police recorded crime: Concealing an infant death close to birth[b]	Total
2002/2003	3	7	10
2003/2004	2	6	8
2004/2005	0	6	6
2005/2006	0	8	8
2006/2007	3	4	7
2007/2008	1	8	9
2008/2009	5	8	13
2009/2010	0	6	6
2010/2011	1	9	10
2011/2012	1	5	6
2012/2013	1	2	3
2013/2014	2	2	4
2014/2015	1	5	5
2015/2016	2	5	5
Annual mean	2	6	7

[a]Data as at 14 November 2016; figures are subject to revision as cases are dealt with by the police and the courts, or as further information becomes available. Data obtained from Homicide Index, Home Office
[b]Data obtained from Office for National Statistics (2016)

A review of coroner's reports and death certificates in Finland and Austria conducted by Amon et al. (2012) concluded that perpetrators' average age was 28. There is also dispute in the literature about perpetrators' socio-economic background. For example, Beyer et al. (2008), in their review of law enforcement case files in the USA, concluded that the majority of the offenders were middle class, with only 5 out of 37 women identified as working class. Similarly, a review of cases in the USA using newspaper reports, conducted by Meyer and Oberman (2001), found suspected women came from diverse socio-economic backgrounds and across ethnic groups. Many studies reported that perpetrators are not always single, childless or living with their parents. Amon et al. (2012) noted that 16 of 28 perpetrators were married or living with a partner and all sixteen reported having sexual relationships during the pregnancy. Beyer et al. (2008) found that 15 of 40 perpetrators had experienced previous pregnancies.

One similarity between cases of neonaticide is that women keep their pregnancy secret from the wider world and specifically from the individuals around them whose response to their pregnancy they fear, such as parents, other relatives and partners. In this regard, neonaticide often follows a concealed or denied pregnancy, a fact which creates difficulties for detection and any subsequent prosecution. Debate exists within the literature as to the extent to which a woman can be unaware that she is pregnant. For example, several scholars argue that women in this situation must have some awareness of their pregnancies, but then deny knowledge of this to themselves or others (Spinelli 2003; Brezinka et al. 1994; Miller 2003). Others have argued that there is a distinction between a woman who knows she is pregnant and thus conceals her pregnancy from others, and those who have only an unconscious awareness of their pregnancy and so are in denial about its existence (Wessel et al. 2002; Vellut et al. 2012). Other scholars have also documented the co-occurrence of denial and concealment, arguing women can experience both at different times during their pregnancy (Amon et al. 2012; Meyer and Oberman 2001; Brezinka et al. 1994). From the literature, it is difficult to conclude the extent to which a woman may be aware of her pregnancy prior to the onset of labour and subsequent delivery.

The connection between concealed/denied birth and neonaticide has led a number of scholars to conclude that concealed or denied pregnancy is a risk factor for neonaticide (Beier et al. 2006; Beyer et al. 2008; Craig 2004; Friedman and Friedman 2010; Porter and Gavin 2010). However, as Spinelli (2010) argues, neonaticide is not the usual outcome for a concealed/denied pregnancy. Data pertaining to the number of concealed/denied pregnancies each year would support this conclusion. Whilst we have no accurate figures of the number of concealed/denied pregnancies each year, researchers have estimated that they occur from one in every 2455 births (study from Germany, Wessel et al. 2002) to 1 in 1000 (study in France, Pierronne et al. 2002; cited in Gonçalves et al. 2014). Using a study from Wales that concludes concealed pregnancies occur one in 2500 deliveries (Nirmal et al. 2006), we can estimate that approximately 280 concealed/denied pregnancies occurred in England and Wales in 2015, based on 700,999 babies being delivered, live and stillborn (Office for National Statistics 2016). As outlined earlier in the chapter, we do not know the exact instances of neonaticide that occur, although approximately seven cases are recorded each year. Regardless of our lack of certainty in these figures, it is very unlikely that the rate of neonaticide is close to 280. Consequently, it is reasonable to conclude that whilst neonaticide often occurs after a concealed/denied pregnancy, a concealed/denied pregnancy is not always a predictor of risk.

Criminalising 'Neonaticide'

Whilst the literature may term deaths of babies in the period immediately surrounding birth as 'neonaticides', the criminal law's approach is somewhat different. To start with, there is no specific crime of 'neonaticide'. A range of offences which include standard homicide offences (murder and manslaughter) and specific statutory crimes tailored to the fact that death occurred in the context of pregnancy and childbirth (such as infanticide, child destruction, COB) may be used to criminalise women whose infants die around birth. Second, the fact that a baby dies at or around the time of a concealed and unassisted birth does not necessarily mean that the mother has committed any crime. This is the case even if death is ostensibly due to (morally) blameworthy conduct on her part, such as an act of violence or neglect to ensure for safe delivery of her baby. Whether a crime has been committed will depend on whether the legal requirements for a specific offence have been met on the evidence available. The criminalisation of women for the deaths of their babies at birth gives rise to myriad complexities. Many of the difficulties stem from the law's distinction between the foetus and a legal person, and the different levels of protection offered to each. Some of the issues that arise in connection with criminalising women for the deaths of their babies at birth will now be briefly explored.

The Born Alive Rule

In everyday language, the terms 'child', 'baby', and 'infant' may be aptly used to capture the identity and status of those who die around the time of birth. Legally, however, the situation is complicated by the demarcation between the foetus and legal persons that is created by the born alive rule. Where neonaticide is suspected the law on homicide requires proof that the victim had achieved legal personhood, that they were a 'reasonable being in rerum natura' (Coke 1681, pp. 50–51). This means that a conviction for murder, manslaughter or infanticide is only possible if, at the time death occurred, the victim was 'born alive'.

To be born alive, the body of the infant must be fully expelled from the birth canal, so that no part of the infant remains inside the mother, and there must be an independent existence (Davies 1937, pp. 206–208; Ormerod and Laird 2015, p. 559). Historically, there was a lack of clarity as to what constituted an independent existence, there being 'no authorised definition of live birth in the theory of law' (Atkinson 1904, p. 134). Questions relating to whether and when the child had breathed, whether the child had an independent circulation and whether the umbilical cord had been cut were considered important (Atkinson 1904). The current accepted test, stemming from nineteenth-century case law, for an independent existence, is evidence of an independent circulation (*R. v. Enoch and Pulley*). The umbilical cord does not need to be severed (*R. v. Crutchley*; *R. v. Reeves*; *R. v. Trilloe*). Breathing is a factor to consider, but it is not decisive (*R. v. Poulton*; *R. v. Brain*; *R. v. Sellis*). Whilst the test is now clear, proving that an independent circulation was established may still give rise to difficulties (Ormerod and Laird 2015, p. 559).

Where death occurs before a neonate has achieved legal personhood, no homicide offence has been committed. In such cases, depending on the factual circumstances involved, the prosecution may be able to rely on some other offence which does not require the victim to have achieved legal personhood, such as COB, procuring a miscarriage (OAPA 1861 s. 58) or child destruction (Infant Life (Preservation) Act 1929, s. 1). However, although each of these offences allows for conviction for an offence in the absence of a live birth, they have their own unique requirements which may on the evidence preclude successful prosecution.

The relationship between the born alive rule and the other requirements for establishing liability for any of the existing homicide offences might mean that even if a neonate dies after it has achieved legal personhood, there may be other reasons, connected with the legal distinction between foetuses and legal persons, which preclude a homicide conviction. For example, whilst acts done pre-birth which result in the death of the neonate after a 'live birth' will satisfy the *actus reus* (conduct) requirement for murder, problems may arise in establishing the *mens rea* (mental fault) for that offence in such circumstances due to the legal distinction between the foetus and a 'human being' (Temkin 1986; Simester et al. 2016, pp. 375–376; *Attorney General's Reference* (*No. 3 of 1994*)). This can give rise to complex issues that are beyond the scope of this chapter.

Criminalising Neglect

Cases of 'neonaticide' discussed in the literature show that the death of an infant at the time of birth is not always due to a positive and deliberate act of violence (Beier et al. 2006). Neonates may die for a variety of reasons, including failure to ensure safe delivery by seeking medical assistance; failure during an unassisted birth to perform certain tasks to ensure the survival of the newborn, such as cutting and tying the umbilical cord; mishandling of the neonate during or after birth (e.g. accidental strangulation or suffocation when trying to expel the baby from the birth canal); and leaving the child to die after birth. There are two issues that arise in cases where death was not due to a deliberate act of violence but to conduct which may be termed 'neglect'. The first issue relates to restrictions on imposing criminal liability for an 'omission' rather than a positive 'act'. The second is connected with the level of criminal, as opposed to moral, fault involved, and whether the woman can be held liable for a homicide offence where death was due to maternal neglect.

First, many of the above examples of neglect involve 'omissions' rather than 'acts'. Overall, the criminal law is slow to criminalise individuals for their omissions. There are some limited circumstances where the law imposes a 'duty to act' and where failure to act may result in criminal liability being imposed for a crime such as homicide. One of the well-recognised duties is that which a parent owes to their child (Simester et al. 2016, pp. 75–76). The issue of whether a woman has a duty to act with regard to her unborn child, however, is complicated by the born alive rule. Whilst there are no recent authorities explicitly on this point, it would seem that the parental duty to act only arises after the child has been born alive. The older case law establishes that a decision to give birth alone, and therefore fail to prepare for birth, is not sufficient to allow for a homicide conviction; neglect before birth does not suffice, and there must be evidence of neglect after the child is born (*R. v. Knights; R. v. Izod*).

In terms of more recent authorities, we must look to the civil law. In the civil law, rather than criminal, a woman does not owe her foetus a 'duty of care' and therefore cannot be sued by her child for harm she causes to it through her negligent behaviour whilst the child was a foetus. The only exception involves injury caused as a result of a road traffic accident. However, in such instances a child would claim compensation through its mother's motor insurance.[2] In the medical law context, women who have mental capacity can refuse treatment (e.g. a caesarean section), even where this carries a risk of death for the foetus/child (*St George's Healthcare NHS Trust v. S*; Cave 2004, pp. 62–74). The Court of Appeal recently indicated—in a case to do with whether women who cause serious harm to their foetus (and child) by drinking excessively during pregnancy can be liable for a criminal offence under our existing law—that the approach to the issue of maternal duty of care towards the foetus in the above civil contexts would similarly apply in the criminal law (*Criminal Injuries Compensation Authority v. First-tier Tribunal*).

Whilst the concept of a 'duty of care' in criminal law is not the same as a 'duty to act' (Ormerod and Laird 2015, pp. 638–641), the indication from the above is that women have no duty to act to protect their foetus from harm or death and so cannot be liable for homicide where death was caused by a pre-'live birth' omission. In other words, it seems that a woman has no duty to act with regard to her foetus. Consequently, she cannot be liable for homicide for an omission made prior to or during birth which led to the death of the baby, even if death occurred after a live birth. The issue of criminalising women for the deaths of their newborn infants as a consequence of their failure to act appropriately with regard to ensuring the survival and health of the foetus/unborn child highlights moral and legal questions which point to a tension between maternal autonomy and maternal responsibility. As the law stands, it seems that autonomy is given greater primacy, even where this poses a risk to the health or life of the foetus/child born alive.

Second, the question of liability for homicide in the event of the baby dying as a result of neglect after birth is complicated by the requirements for mental fault. To be liable for murder, it is necessary to show an intention to kill or an intention to cause really serious harm (*R. v. Moloney*). Cases involving 'neglect' would not meet this threshold, though it should be highlighted that a murder conviction can be sustained on the basis of an omission, for example a failure to care for the baby (providing this occurred after a live birth), if this was done for the purpose of causing death or seriously harming the baby. In the absence of violence, however, it will surely be difficult to prove such intent, particularly given the woman's likely physical and mental condition following an unassisted labour. The more appropriate offence to charge in cases involving neglect of the baby after birth, where there is no evidence of an intention to kill or seriously harm, is gross negligence manslaughter.[3] However, there may also be problems in securing a conviction for that offence because the test for 'gross negligence' requires the jury to consider whether the accused '*deserves*' to be convicted (*R. v. Adomako*, p. 187). This allows for moral rather than legal judgments about the seriousness of her conduct in the circumstances involved. As a result, the law lacks certainty—what one jury may consider criminal, another may not (Simester et al. 2016, pp. 419–420). Certainly, it is feasible that in a case involving the typical neonaticide facts outlined above, a jury would conclude that the mother does not deserve conviction for manslaughter.

Impact of Mental State on Mental Fault Requirements

The literature on neonaticide highlights that women and girls whose neonates die in the context of an unassisted birth may experience particular effects on their mental state. For example, in some cases, they may lose consciousness as a result of the physical trauma of an unassisted birth; in others, they may claim that they did not know what they were doing at the time, or that they experienced a sense of dissociation. In particular, research has shown that women who kill neonates can experience active fear and cognitive denial of pregnancy. Meyer and Oberman (2001) argue that this leads women to delay any decision about the pregnancy until it is too late; consequently, the birth of the child comes as a shock to the woman who kills from fear and panic in this situation. Furthermore, it is known for women not to remember the birth, and some women with a more profound denial will not recall the pregnancy. Spinelli (2003) draws similar conclusions after conducting psychiatric interviews with seventeen American women who were accused of killing their newborn children. Spinelli categorised the women as having unassisted births associated with dissociative psychosis in 10 cases, dissociative hallucinations in 14 and intermittent amnesia delivery in 14 cases. Each woman described 'watching' herself during the birth. Twelve experienced dissociative hallucinations ranging from an internal commentary to critical and argumentative voices; 14 experienced brief amnesia; nine described associated psychotic symptoms at the sight of the infant. When the women awoke from the dissociative hallucination, it was to find a dead newborn child whose presence they could not explain.

The fact that the accused was unconscious, in a dissociative state, or had some other mental disorder, may affect her criminal liability in a number of ways. It may, for example, give rise to a defence, such as automatism, insanity (*M'Naghten's Case* (1843) 10 C and F 200; 8 ER 718) or, on a murder charge only, the partial defence of diminished responsibility (Homicide Act 1957).[4] In particular, the offence/defence of infanticide may be used. Infanticide operates as an alternative to murder or manslaughter in cases where a woman, by a 'wilful act or omission', kills her baby (aged under 12 months) whilst the 'balance of her mind was disturbed by reason of her not having fully recovered from the effect of giving birth to the child or by reason of the effect of lactation consequent the birth of the child' (Infanticide Act 1938, ss. 1 and 2). Although the statute extends to victims aged under 12 months, when it was originally enacted in 1922, it was primarily focused on facilitating lenient treatment of women who killed their babies at birth due a reluctance to convict her of murder and condemn her to death (Davies 1937, 1938; Brennan 2013a).

Although infanticide allows for a more lenient approach, feminists have criticised this law on the ground that it medicalises the offender, explaining her crime as the product of a biologically produced mental disturbance and failing to acknowledge any social, economic, and political causes (Morris and Wilczynski 1993). However, research into the history of this law shows that the mental disturbance rationale was based on a lay understanding of infanticide which could take account of the social and other causes of infanticide (Ward 1999; Kramar 2005; Kramar and Watson 2006; Brennan 2013b). In terms of how the law has been applied in practice, research has shown that it allows for 'covert recognition' of social causes (Morris and Wilczynski 1993) and that it operates as a 'legal device' to facilitate lenient treatment of at least some girls and women who kill their babies at birth (Mackay 1993, p. 29).

Other jurisdictions that have adopted the same law have had a similar experience (Brennan forthcoming-b).

In summary, 'infanticide' may be a particularly apt charge or conviction option in cases of 'neonaticide', and to some extent, it is tailor-made for these cases. Although the requirements for murder or manslaughter must also be proven, it would seem that the specific medical rationale of the infanticide law is not difficult to meet, and so those who kill their babies at birth may be convicted of infanticide even where there is little evidence of a specific mental disorder. An infanticide conviction generally results in exceptionally lenient sentences (in the context of homicide); offenders are rarely imprisoned (Walker 1968). However, there may be wider social implications of a prosecution, such as being prevented from raising any subsequent children, even if the neonaticide occurred when the woman was a teenager and her future pregnancy occurred many years later in very different circumstances.

Criminal Justice Practice in Cases of Neonaticide

There is very little research available on how cases of 'neonaticide' are currently dealt with by the criminal authorities in England and Wales. The Ruth Percival case mentioned in the introduction indicates that the CPS seriously considers initiating prosecutions in these cases, and is willing to explore a range of criminal offence options in this regard. However, before prosecuting for a specific offence, there must be 'sufficient evidence [of the requirements for that offence] to provide a realistic prospect of conviction' (CPS 2013, para. 4.4). As the Percival case highlights, there may be difficulties in cases of suspected neonaticide in meeting the requirement for evidential sufficiency. This is supported by the above analysis of some of the complexities involved in seeking to establish the requirements for criminal offences, particularly for homicide, in typical cases of suspected neonaticide. These cases pose unique challenges which may preclude criminalisation of a woman whose baby dies following a secret birth due to there being insufficient evidence to support a criminal charge. Further, even where there is sufficient evidence to charge with an offence, the CPS is not obliged to prosecute because the second part of the test for prosecution must be met, namely that prosecution is in the 'public interest' (CPS 2013, paras. 4.7–4.12). This gives the CPS discretion to not prosecute. A recent case in Preston where a woman was convicted of murdering her newborn baby after a concealed birth (Milne 2017a) indicates, however, that successful prosecutions do take place, and further, that prosecutors will not necessarily shy away from seeking the law's ultimate sanction, notwithstanding the existence of more lenient options, such as infanticide. The Percival and Preston cases are just two recent examples, but what we do not have is an overall picture of how the criminal justice system disposes of suspected neonaticide.

Empirical work by Mackay (1993, 2006) which focuses specifically on the use of the infanticide law gives an indication of how some suspected neonaticides are dealt with, indicating a tendency towards a lenient response. In a 1980s study, he observed that 'cases which may lead to an infanticide or related charge tend to be of the type where prosecutorial discretion is likely to the exercised in the female defendant's favour' (1993, p. 29): no prosecution was taken in 11 of the 21 newborn victim cases in his sample, in most cases because it was considered to not be in the public interest to prosecute. A subsequent study of infanticide convictions involving 15 newborn victims during the period 1990–2003 evidences a tendency to charge with murder but to dispose of the case as 'infanticide' (Mackay 2006). The accused in the newborn sample had all pleaded guilty to infanticide, but in nine of these cases the original charge had been murder, with infanticide being later added to the indictment. None of the 15 was given a custodial sentence. The approach taken by the CPS in the second study may suggest lenient treatment of women suspected of killing their babies at birth. However, the sample only focuses on those convicted of infanticide and so provides no indication of how others who were suspected of killing their babies at birth during the same period, but who were not disposed of under the infanticide law, were treated. Limited available research into the outcome of all cases of neonaticide prevents a firm conclusion from being drawn. Furthermore, the discretion available to the CPS when deciding whether to prosecute and what kind of charge to bring means that it is not possible to generalise in these cases. For some women, leniency appears to drive prosecutorial decisions, but this suggestion cannot be applied across all cases.

The Neonaticidal Woman and the Criminal Justice System—Some Reflections

Our analysis of the legal dynamics of cases of neonaticide leads us to four reflections. The first relates to the language that surrounds newborn child killing and specifically the use of the term 'neonaticide' in both academic literature and wider social use. As illustrated above, the term neonaticide is employed within the literature to describe the death of a child/foetus in various circumstances, ranging from the child born alive and then violently killed by its mother, to the foetus that dies before or during labour, whatever the cause of death. Scholarly analyses of neonaticide have included deaths that may not have been acts of homicide, due to for example a lack of evidence of the legal requirements for imposing liability (e.g. live birth). As such, the appropriateness of the term 'neonaticide' as a catch-all term to cover all cases where the death of the foetus/baby occurs at birth needs to be considered. As a general term to describe a typology of killing it can be useful. However, within a legal context, 'neonaticide', as a concept, does not encapsulate the complexities that surround these deaths. We would caution against the application of this term to describe the deaths of infants/foetuses.

Our second reflection relates to the complexities involved in prosecuting cases of suspected neonaticide, the issue of consistency in criminal justice practice and the need for further research. As highlighted by the case of Ruth Percival, due to the typical circumstances involved in cases of suspected neonaticide, prosecutors may face difficulty in passing the first requirement for prosecution—evidential sufficiency—despite the range of offences at their disposal. There is also an issue of consistency in approach given the variety of options open to prosecutors in terms of the offences they can consider; the fact that they have discretion to not prosecute on public interest grounds; and have the option to accept a guilty plea for another offence (e.g. an infanticide plea on a murder charge).

Whilst we do not seek to challenge prosecutorial discretion per se, we do wish to highlight the risk for inconsistency between cases with similar factual backgrounds. In the USA, for example, Oberman's (1996) research has shown that cases of suspected neonaticide can result in widely disparate criminal outcomes, ranging from first-degree murder charges (and prison sentences of over 30 years) to charges for misdemeanours with very lenient sentencing. Whilst the American and English approaches are not directly comparable, for example the latter has a specific infanticide law and a tendency towards more lenient outcomes (Maier-Katkin and Ogle 1997), Oberman's (1996) research does highlight the risk of inconsistency in approach.

What is needed is further research to consider the application of the law across cases to assess a number of issues, including consideration of the following: the charges brought in cases involving suspected neonaticides; the outcome of prosecutions; the role and impact of guilty pleas; the extent to which the CPS exercises discretion to not prosecute; the extent to which all of the foregoing are affected by the factual background, such as whether differences in decisions and outcomes can be explained by differences in the evidence and the circumstances. In this regard, questions about the role of non-legal factors in the processing of these cases should also be addressed. For example, do judgments about suspected neonaticide offenders as women and mothers play a role in how they are dealt with by the criminal justice system (Morris and Wilczynski 1993; Allen 1987; Brennan forthcoming-a)? Another interesting issue to consider is the role of social norms in the criminal justice response to these cases (Brennan forthcoming-b). Due to the sensitive nature of this area of law and the discretion of the police and CPS, we suggest that such research would need to be conducted with the support of criminal justice bodies.

Our third reflection directly speaks to the aims of this book—the implications of criminal justice involvement with women, in this instance with regard to cases of suspected neonaticide. Considering the nature of these cases, specifically the vulnerability of the offender, we believe it is important to consider whether the involvement of criminal justice in such cases is the most appropriate response. There is a significant body of evidence supporting the claim that women involved in cases of suspected neonaticide are vulnerable. As outlined in this chapter, they are often young and single. Furthermore, research has demonstrated that women's responses to their pregnancies—concealment/denial of the pregnancy, solo birth and death of the infant—can be attributed to the fear of the reaction of others to her pregnancy (Alder and Baker 1997; Meyer and Oberman 2001; Spinelli 2003). For example, Beyer et al. (2008) conclude from their review of law enforcement files in the USA that women are often motivated by fear, associated with the shame and guilt of being pregnant and concern about the reaction of parents, partners and others if the pregnancy is discovered. Oberman (2003) advocates that maternal filicide is deeply embedded in and responsive to the societies in which it occurs, citing contemporary American policies towards single parents.

Considering the context and the nature of cases of neonaticide, the suitability and purpose of criminalising these women needs to be considered. For instance, it can hardly be said that convicting women of a homicide offence, or any other crime available to prosecutors in this area, will act as a means of preventing similar instances by other women. To suggest that the law will act as a deterrent seems to imply that women may become pregnant for the purpose of killing the foetus/newborn. Certainly, it ignores the context of this crime, in particular the fact that it may follow a denied pregnancy where birth comes as a shock and where the woman may act out of fear and desperation; in other words, that her mental and emotional state is such that she is incapable of being deterred.

It is undoubtedly symbolically important for the law to say that the killing of an infant who has achieved legal personhood will be treated as seriously as other homicides. To suggest otherwise would not only raise moral questions about the sanctity of human life, but also human rights concerns about the right to life of infants, for example under article 2 of the European Convention on Human Rights. It seems morally abhorrent to suggest that those who kill the most vulnerable in our society should not be subject to criminal sanction. A full examination of the ethical, legal and philosophical questions that arise is beyond the scope of this article. At this point, the most that can be said is that the vulnerability of women who kill their babies at birth suggests that caution is needed regarding whether and when they should be criminalised. In this regard, prosecutorial discretion to not prosecute under the public interest test may be particularly important in terms of ensuring that vulnerable girls and women are not criminalised, but this carries disadvantages, particularly with regard to consistency in approach. Minimal criminalisation involving an appropriate lenient conviction with a non-custodial sentence, such as can be provided under the infanticide law, may also provide a suitable balance between protecting vulnerable girls/women from further trauma through harsh criminal sanction, whilst at the same time at least symbolically vindicating the life of the baby (Brennan forthcoming-a).

This leads to our final reflection—if the law is unlikely to assist in the protection of newborn children and to assist vulnerable pregnant women from seeking help prior to going into labour, then what will? A number of scholars have concluded their studies into concealed/denied pregnancy and its connection with neonaticide by advocating that increased surveillance of all women of childbearing age is an appropriate preventative measure, including conducting regular pregnancy tests (Jenkins et al. 2011; Kaplan and Grotowski 1996). Whilst such measures may capture a proportion of the women who fail to appreciate that they are pregnant until the later stages, such a proposal cannot hope to stop all cases of neonaticide. Furthermore, such testing would be obstructive and invasive for all women, prioritising the welfare of a child that is not yet conceived over the ability of women to control and regulate their own bodies (Brazier 1999). Instead, the provision of support for vulnerable women would be a more appropriate and likely more successful programme for prevention. This could take the form of community support for women living with the threat of abusive relationships and those living in poverty. For young women, comprehensive, state regulated and mandated sexual health education which promotes the use of contraception, and support if a pregnancy occurs, would also be a reasonable measure for prevention.

Notes

1. Analysis presented here is based on the research conducted by Milne (2017b).
2. A duty of care, in other words liability for injury caused by negligence, is imposed in the case of road traffic accidents due to the existence of compulsory third-party motor insurance (Congenital Disabilities (Civil Liability) Act 1976, ss. 1(1) and 2; Cave 2004, p. 55).
3. Infanticide could be used as an alternative charge or conviction providing both the requirements for gross negligence manslaughter and the additional infanticide requirements had been proven, including the fact that the woman had a disturbance in the balance of the mind caused by the effect of childbirth (Infanticide Act 1938, ss. 1(1) and 1(2)).
4. Discussion of these defences is outside the scope of this chapter.

References

Case Law

Adomako [1995] 1 AC 171.
Attorney General's Reference (No. 3 of 1994) [1997] 3 All ER 936.
Brain (1834) 6 C. and P. 349.
Criminal Injuries Compensation Authority v. First-tier Tribunal (Social Entitlement Chamber) (British Pregnancy Advisory Service and others intervening) [2014] EWCA Civ 1554.
Crutchley (1839) 7 C. and P. 814.
Enoch and Pulley (1833) 5 C. and P. 539.
Izod (1904) 20 Cox 690.
Knights (1860) 2 F and F 46.
M'Naghten's Case (1843) 10 C and F 200; 8 ER 718.
Moloney [1985] AC 905.
Poulton (1832) 5 C. and P. 329.
Reeves (1839) 9 C. and P. 25.
Sellis (1837) 7 C. and P. 850.
St George's Healthcare NHS Trust v. S [1998] 3 All ER 673.
Trilloe (1842) C. and M. 650; 2 Mood. 260.

Alder, C. M., & Baker, J. (1997). Maternal filicide: More than one story to be told. *Women and Criminal Justice, 9*(2), 15–39.

Allen, H. (1987). *Justice unbalanced: Gender, psychiatry, and judicial decisions.* Milton Keynes: Open University Press.

Amon, S., Putkonen, H., Weizmann-Henelius, G., Almiron, M., Formann, A., Voracek, M., et al. (2012). Potential predictors in neonaticide: The impact of the circumstances of pregnancy. *Archives of Women's Mental Health, 15*(3), 167–174.

Atkinson, S. B. (1904). Life, birth and live-birth. *Law Quarterly Review, 20*(2), 134–159.

Beier, K. M., Wille, R., & Wessel, J. (2006). Denial of pregnancy as a reproductive dysfunction: A proposal for international classification systems. *Journal of Psychosomatic Research, 61*(5), 723–730.

Beyer, K., McAuliffe Mack, S., & Shelton, J. L. (2008). Investigative analysis of neonaticide: An exploratory study. *Criminal Justice and Behavior, 35*(4), 522–535.

Brazier, M. (1999). Liberty, responsibility, maternity. *Current Legal Problems, 52*(1), 359–391.

Brennan, K. (2013a). "A fine mixture of pity and justice:" The criminal justice response to infanticide in Ireland 1922–1949. *Law and History Review, 31*(4), 793–841.

Brennan, K. (2013b). "Traditions of English liberal thought": A history of the enactment of an infanticide law in Ireland. *Irish Jurist, 50*, 100–137.

Brennan, K. (forthcoming-a). Murdering mothers and gentle judges: paternalism, patriarchy and infanticide. *Yale Journal of Law and Feminism.*

Brennan, K. (forthcoming-b). Social norms and the law in responding to infanticide. *Legal Studies.*

Brezinka, C., Brezinka, C., Biebl, W., & Kinzl, J. (1994). Denial of pregnancy: Obstetrical aspects. *Journal of Psychosomatic Obstetrics & Gynecology, 15*(1), 1–8.

Cave, E. (2004). *The mother of all crimes: Human rights, criminalization and the child born alive.* Aldershot: Ashgate.

Coke, E. (1681). *The fourth part of the institutes of the laws of England: Concerning the jurisdiction of courts* (6th ed.). London: Printed by W. Rawlins, for Thomas Basset at the George near St. Dunstans Church in Fleet-street.

Craig, M. (2004). Perinatal risk factors for neonaticide and infant homicide: Can we identify those at risk? *Journal of the Royal Society of Medicine, 97*(2), 57–61.

Crown Prosecution Service. (2013). *The code for crown prosecutors.* Available at: https://www.cps.gov.uk/publications/docs/code_2013_accessible_english.pdf.

Davies, D. S. (1937). Child killing in English law, Part I. *The Modern Law Review, 1*(3), 202–223.

Davies, D. S. (1938). Child killing in English law, Part II. *The Modern Law Review, 1*(4), 269–287.

d'Orbán, P. T. (1979). Women who kill their children. *The British Journal of Psychiatry, 134*(6), 560–571.

Friedman, S. H., & Friedman, J. B. (2010). Parents who kill their children. *Pediatrics in Review, 31*(2), 10–16.

Gonçalves, T., Macedo, M., & Conz, J. (2014). Non-psychotic denial of pregnancy: A psychoanalytical comprehension. *Interamerican Journal of Psychology, 48*(1), 23–29.

Jenkins, A., Millar, S., & Robins, J. (2011). Denial of pregnancy: A literature review and discussion of ethical and legal issues. *Journal of the Royal Society of Medicine, 104*(7), 286–291.

Kaplan, R., & Grotowski, T. (1996). Denied pregnancy. *Australian and New Zealand Journal of Psychiatry, 30*(6), 861–863.

Kramar, K. J. (2005). *Unwilling mothers, unwanted babies: Infanticide in Canada.* Vancouver: UBC Press.

Kramar, K. J., & Watson, W. D. (2006). The insanities of reproduction: Medico-legal knowledge and the development of infanticide law. *Social & Legal Studies, 15*(2), 237–255.

Mackay, R. D. (1993). The consequences of killing very young children. *Criminal Law Review,* (January), 21–30.

Mackay, R. D. (2006). Appendix D: Infanticide and related diminished responsibility manslaughters: An empirical study. *Murder, Manslaughter and Infanticide: Project 6 of the Ninth Programme of Law Reform: Homicide.* Available at: http://lawcommission.justice.gov.uk/docs/lc304_Murder_Manslaughter_and_Infanticide_Report.pdf.

Maier-Katkin, D., & Ogle, R. S. (1997). Policy and disparity: The punishment of infanticide in Britain and America. *International Journal of Comparative and Applied Criminal Justice, 21*(2), 305–316.

Meyer, C. L., & Oberman, M. (2001). *Mothers who kill their children: Understanding the acts of moms from Susan Smith to the "Prom Mom"*. New York: New York University Press.

Miller, L. J. (2003). Denial of pregnancy. In M. G. Spinelli (Ed.), *Infanticide: Psychosocial and legal perspectives on mothers who kill* (pp. 81–104). Washington, DC: American Psychiatric.

Milne, E. (2017a). Murder or infanticide? Understanding the causes behind the most shocking of crimes. *The Conversation* (30 June). Available at: https://theconversation.com/murder-or-infanticide-understanding-the-causes-behind-the-most-shocking-of-crimes-79808 (Accessed 17 July 2017).

Milne, E. (2017b). *Suspicious perinatal death and the law: Criminalising mothers who do not conform*. (PhD, University of Essex, UK). Available at: http://repository.essex.ac.uk/20474/.

Milne, E. (forthcoming). Concealment of birth: Time to repeal a 200-year-old convenient stop-gap?.

Morris, A., & Wilczynski, A. (1993). Rocking the cradle: Mothers who kill their children. In H. Birch (Ed.), *Moving targets: Women, murder, and representation* (pp. 198–217). London: Virago.

Nirmal, D., Thijs, I., Bethel, J., & Bhal, P. S. (2006). The incidence and outcome of concealed pregnancies among hospital deliveries: An 11-year population-based study in South Glamorgan. *Journal of Obstetrics and Gynaecology, 26*(2), 118–121.

Oberman, M. (1996). Mothers who kill: Coming to terms with modern American infanticide. *American Criminal Law Review, 34*(1), 1–110.

Oberman, M. (2003). Mothers who kill: Cross-cultural patterns in and perspectives on contemporary maternal filicide. *International Journal of Law and Psychiatry, 26*(5), 493–514.

Office for National Statistics. (2016). *Births in England and Wales: 2015* (13 July). Available at: http://www.ons.gov.uk/peoplepopulationandcommunity/birthsdeathsandmarriages/livebirths/bulletins/birthsummarytablesenglandandwales/2015-the-number-of-stillbirths-decreased-in-2015 (Accessed 30 August 2016).

Ormerod, D., & Laird, K. (2015). *Smith and Hogan's Criminal Law* (14th ed.). Oxford: Oxford University Press.

Parveen, N. (2016). Prosecutors to re-examine vicarage death of newborn baby. *The Guardian* (5 October edn). Available at: https://www.theguardian.com/uk-news/2016/oct/05/prosecutors-to-re-examine-vicarage-death-of-newborn-baby (Accessed 15 May 2017).

Porter, T., & Gavin, H. (2010). Infanticide and neonaticide: A review of 40 years of research literature on incidence and causes. *Trauma, Violence, & Abuse, 11*(3), 99–112.

Resnick, P. J. (1969). Child murder by parents: A psychiatric review of filicide. *American Journal of Psychiatry, 126*(3), 325–334.

Resnick, P. J. (1970). Murder of the newborn: A psychiatric review of neonaticide. *American journal of psychiatry, 126*(10), 1414–1420.

Simester, A. P., Spencer, J. R., Stark, F., Sullivan, G. R., & Virgo, G. J. (2016). *Simester and Sullivan's criminal law: Theory and doctrine* (6th ed.). Oxford and London: Hart.

Spinelli, M. G. (2003). Neonaticide: A systematic investigation of 17 cases. In M. G. Spinelli (Ed.), *Infanticide: Psychosocial and legal perspectives on mothers who kill* (pp. 105–118). Washington, DC: American Psychiatric.

Spinelli, M. G. (2010). Denial of pregnancy: A psychodynamic paradigm. *Journal of American Academy of Psychoanalysis, 38*(1), 117–131.

Temkin, J. (1986). Pre-natal injury, homicide and the draft criminal code. *Cambridge Law Review, 45*(3), 414–429.

The Telegraph. (2017). '"Insufficient evidence" to charge anyone over baby's death at vicarage'. *The Telegraph* (20 March edn). Available at: http://www.telegraph.co.uk/news/2017/03/20/insufficient-evidence-charge-anyone-babys-death-vicarage/ (Accessed 15 May 2017).

Vellut, N., Cook, J. M., & Tursz, A. (2012). Analysis of the relationship between neonaticide and denial of pregnancy using data from judicial files. *Child Abuse & Neglect, 36*(7–8), 553–563.

Walker, N. (1968). *Crime and insanity in England: Volume 1, The Historical Perspective.* Edinburgh: Edinburgh University Press.

Ward, T. (1999). The sad subject of infanticide: Law, medicine and child murder 1860–1938. *Social & Legal Studies, 8*(2), 163–180.

Wessel, J., Endrikat, J., & Buscher, U. (2002). Frequency of denial of pregnancy: Results and epidemiological significance of a 1-year prospective study in Berlin. *Acta Obstetricia et Gynecologica Scandinavica, 81*(11), 1021–1027.

Wilczynski, A. (1997). *Child homicide.* London: Greenwich Medical Media Ltd.

6

Understanding Violent Women

Emma Milne and Jackie Turton

Introduction

In the 1990s, Liz Kelly called for feminists to be 'courageous enough' (1996, p. 47) to look at both male and female acts of violence, arguing that failure to develop a robust analysis of abuse by women risks leaving any discourse 'to the professionals and the media'. Importantly she emphasised that the lingering silence of feminist academics resulted in us failing, 'women and children who have suffered at the hands of women, and risk losing the clarity we need in order to hold on to what we have learnt and built in the last two decades' (1996, p. 35).

E. Milne (✉)
Department of Criminology and Sociology,
Middlesex University, London, UK
e-mail: e.milne@mdx.ac.uk

J. Turton
Department of Sociology, University of Essex,
Colchester, Essex, UK
e-mail: turtje@essex.ac.uk

© The Author(s) 2018
E. Milne et al. (eds.), *Women and the Criminal Justice System*,
https://doi.org/10.1007/978-3-319-76774-1_6

Kelly rightly pointed out that feminists had, for the most part, been reluctant to discuss violent women, for the very real fear it would undermine the hard-won battles secured by the campaigning and activism resulting from women's victimisation. While Kelly's article could be seen to break the silence within the feminist community, gathering data to develop an understanding and theoretical framework for women's violence has proved to be much more complex. Kelly was one of a small number of researchers who theorised about violent women before the millennium. Others included for example Renzetti (1992) who highlighted concerns about interpersonal violence within lesbian relationships; Cameron (1999) who presented an analysis of the female sexual murderer Rosemary West, drawing attention to the absence of feminist voices in the aftermath; and Wilczynski (1995, 1997) who probed sociocultural ambiguities around violent mothers.

This chapter briefly considers some of the data concerning women's violence, the public and professional responses to violent women and how researchers have attempted to understand violent behaviour by women. Unfortunately, we cannot do justice to all the progress that has been made so far in this area. Instead, we will limit our analysis to exploring important pockets of research concerning women's violence that focus around 'extreme' deeds, the pattern of violence that is most unusual for female offenders. In this regard, we intend to focus on two key violent crimes that have been documented in the literature—women who kill, and women who sexually abuse children—and use these to explore what we know about female violence and the significance of gender in both social and legal contexts. The difficulties for understanding female violence may in part lie with the questions asked. For instance, rather than seeking causes and solutions for why women commit acts of violence, the question should perhaps be why do women commit so little violence and when they do what is society's response? We consider these questions below.

In the first instance, while the focus of this chapter is on violent women, we should make clear the gender differences from the outset, as the amount of known violent crime committed by females is significantly less than that committed by their male counterparts (Babcock et al. 2003). This traditionally has led to a dearth of research interest in this area from academics and policy makers. Statistically, violent offences account for the largest portion of arrests of both men and women, but women comprised only 19% of violent offenders in England and Wales (Crime Survey for England and Wales 2016). Although in 2015/2016 'violence against the person' accounted for 38% of all female and 34% of male arrests (Ministry of Justice 2016, p. 48), overall only about 11% of those convicted for 'violence against the person' were women (Ministry of Justice 2017). Compared to men, women are less likely to be prosecuted and convicted for a violent offence and in part this is because female violence tends to be less frequent and less serious (Gelsthorpe and Wright 2015). However, on occasions (see below) the legal system may appear to take a more lenient approach. The violent crime figures captured in England and Wales are not unique. Data from the USA also demonstrates that rates of female perpetrated violent crime do not come close to that of their male perpetrators. The Uniform Crime Report (2017), which compiles official data in the USA published by the Federal Bureau of Investigation (FBI), showed that 244,197 men were arrested for a violent crime,[1] compared to 61,780 women in 2015. Therefore, statistically women commit only approximately 20% of recorded violent crime in the USA. Not only is the quantity of female violence different to that involving males, but it is also different in quality with significantly lower morbidity and mortality rates than male violence. Where violence is lethal, there are specific differences recorded, both in the USA and England, between male and female perpetrators. Victims of any lethal violence committed by women tend to be either family members or intimate partners; homicide victims of male perpetrators are more commonly strangers or acquaintances (Kruttschnitt et al. 2002).

Despite the fact that most female violence is restricted to the more private sphere, its control has been a social concern throughout history (Muncie 2015, p. 69), partly, as Muncie suggests, because it is 'underpinned by a strong desire to regulate females' independence and sexuality'. Recent apparent statistical rises in the rates of a more public form of female violence have fuelled media responses, as the presence of violent women is invariably perceived 'as an affront to the stability of society' (Koons-Witt and Schram 2003, p. 362). But on examination the evidence does not suggest a growing problem. Snyder and Sickmund (2006) report that rather than there being any dramatic changes in behaviour, it is new forms of regulation, surveillance, discipline and policing that have resulted in the higher statistical public profile for female offenders. Sharpe (2012) highlights the effects of changes in youth justice policy as a factor in the apparent increase in arrests of young women, and Gelsthorpe and Wright (2015) take this further by offering a more nuanced understanding of recorded female violence. The analysis of anecdotal evidence they gathered from senior police officers indicates that the rise in female arrests involving actual bodily harm generally only concerns minor violence, often occurring on the 'pubs and clubs' scene with cases invariably dismissed at an early stage. As such, perhaps this is an indication of the public and social visibility of particularly young women on the drinking scene rather than a growing trend in violent behaviour.

There has also been a rise in public and professional attention paid to women's violence within the private sphere specifically concerning domestic violence. This is an area of research where feminist scholarship has offered effective analysis,[2] illustrating the anomalies that can occur when using statistical data to understand the nature and form of women's violence and showing how the apparent increase in female violent offending can be explained by criminal justice policies. For example, in the USA, mandatory arrest policies implemented by the police in order to better respond to instances of intimate partner violence have resulted in a rise in female arrests in domestic violence cases, either as sole offenders or with their partners in dual arrests (Chesney-Lind 2002; Miller 2001). Many of these women are in fact also victims of domestic violence, and arrests have occurred without consideration of the context of violence that exists within the relationship, or the nature of the violence committed (see also Earle, this volume). There are specific concerns that many of these women may have acted out of self-defence (Melton and Belknap 2003; Muftić et al. 2007), in retaliation or as a form of resistance to male violence within the household. Feminists have been critical of research using the Conflict Tactics Scales (CTS) to draw conclusions that women use violence as frequently as men (Enander 2011). CTS research has received specific criticism for not measuring coercive tactics, which feminists have argued play a key part in abusive relationships. CTS studies have omitted sexual abuse, stalking and choking, and have not included violence committed after a relationship has ended (a time of increased danger for women). Furthermore, these studies have not considered the intensity, context, consequences or meaning of the violence (Taft et al. 2001). There is little doubt then that there are contextual factors that affect use of domestic violence by men and women, which need to be explored when analysing statistics on violent offending (Dasgupta 2002).

Both Dobash and Dobash (2004) and Johnson (2005) found that not only is domestic violence a gendered crime but where women are violent 'it is generally infrequent, is rarely "serious", results in few, if any injuries and has few, if any, negative consequences for men' (Dobash and Dobash 2004, p. 343). Hester's (2012) work looked at the ways heterosexual women in the UK were portrayed as perpetrators of domestic violence and concluded that in her sample women could not be considered as 'batterers' or 'intimate terrorists' (Johnson 2005) as very rarely do they invoke fear in their partners. So, as Johnson suggests, while we should not attempt to justify or minimise any female violence, we do need to understand the behaviour involved and the intentions behind the acts in order to develop appropriate theories, interventions and policies to support both perpetrators and their victims.

The problems in analysing the statistics concerning domestic violence, mentioned above, indicate the need for a more holistic approach, including a gendered perspective, to understanding crime. For instance, female violence does not exist in isolation and cannot be described solely as a result of patriarchal constraints or gendered identities. Therefore, especially in the context of female violence, we need to understand ways in which gender intersects and is affected by other social factors such as race, age, ethnicity, sexuality and circumstance. The need for a multidimensional focus is reinforced when we consider women who commit homicide and sexual abuse (as discussed below)—these women tend to have multiple social disadvantages as well as being judged against social gender norms and the mother role.

Women Who Kill

We know that women commit relatively little homicide. In England and Wales, between 2005/2006 and 2015/2016, women made up 14% of all homicide convictions and 9% of all murder convictions (Office for National Statistics 2017). However, as already noted, much of women's violent offending is against individuals with whom they are familiar. In relation to women who commit acts of homicide, their victims are often intimate partners and children (Peterson 1999). This is reflected in the available statistical data. Using the same homicide statistics from above, but only considering data relating to the killing of children aged under one year, the rate of female suspected offending increases to 26% (53% of suspects were male, 21% of suspects sex not recorded).[3] Other studies have found the rates of female perpetrators to be even higher. A Home Office report into homicide concluded that a female suspect was responsible for the killing in 47% of infant homicides (Brookman and Maguire 2003: 16–18; see also Wilczynski 1995). Children killed within the first 24 hours of life (neonates) are most likely to be killed by their birth mothers, and there are very few recorded instances of male offending in this area (see Brennan and Milne, this volume).

Consequently, while homicide is an unusual form of offending for women, when it occurs it is within a very specific, gendered context—women kill within the structures of their intimate relationships and family, and are very unlikely to kill strangers. This has influenced the way in which such acts of violence have been interpreted and responded to within both criminal justice and criminal law. Analysis of criminal justice interpretation of homicidal women continues to dominate feminist research concerned with the portrayal of the violent woman. Feminists have argued that women's violent offending is typically explained through narratives that construct women as 'good' or depicts them as 'mad', 'sad' or 'bad' (Morris and Wilczynski 1993; Morrissey 2003; Weare 2017). The portrayal of a woman as 'good' or 'bad' lies in the ability to align her behaviour with gender norms. If her behaviour (including her crime) can be recuperated back into the norms of femininity, then a lenient response may be available. If, however, her transgressions fall outside of the expected norms, then she is more likely to receive harsh punishment for her crimes. Such conclusions are not new; Carlen (1983), for example, makes this argument in relation to Scottish Sheriffs' practice of distinguishing between 'good' and 'bad' mothers when preparing for sentencing (see also Eaton 1986; Lloyd 1995). However, these narratives continue to operate as a theme within contemporary studies. For example, Weare (2017) argues that within the courtroom, narratives are constructed about women who kill their children, mitigating and nullifying the challenge their behaviour poses to the motherhood mandate and appropriate femininity. Weare, drawing on feminist theories, argues that motherhood is a central feature of the narrative of the 'good' woman and of appropriate femininity. Women who kill their children challenge this perception. Within the courtroom such women's actions are explained through narratives that construct women as 'bad', 'mad' or 'sad'. Each narrative removes a woman's agency by framing her action as a response to the characterisation assigned to her and used to explain her behaviour (see also Morrissey 2003).

Most feminists who identify these gendered constructions within narratives about female killers are critical of their use, arguing the negative consequences are twofold. Firstly, by constructing women as mad and thus facilitating lenient treatment, women's agency is removed and gender stereotypes are maintained and reinforced (Morrissey 2003; Weare 2013). Secondly, the gender construction individualises the problem of violent female offending to the woman who stands accused, consequently masking the social structures that, often, can be aggravating causes of violent offending. Ballinger (2007) makes this argument in her analysis of women who retaliated against violent husbands, resulting in their death. She argues that woman's homicidal actions are identified as stemming from the personal experience of being a victim of domestic violence. The consequence is that the heteropatriarchal social order, which facilitates interpersonal violence within intimate relationships, fails to be challenged. In the cases analysed by Ballinger, which were before the courts during the period 1900–1960, the structures of marriage that embody men's domination of women remain unchallenged and unrecognised as a cause of her violence. Instead, her fault as a defendant lies within her individual response to the situation, her inability to control herself and her decision to act violently in retaliation to her own victimisation. Consequently, the sociopolitical context that leads to and potentially causes women to violently kill abusive partners fails to be recognised or redressed.

The gender construction discourse has received substantial criticism. For example, Brennan (in press) suggests that the arguments presented by Ballinger (2007) are limited for two reasons. Firstly, Brennan challenges whether the court's perpetuation of gender norms through stereotypes impacts on societal perceptions of women. Brennan acknowledges that while perceptions of women outside of crime and criminal justice may affect responses to criminal women in terms of how they are understood and treated within the criminal justice system, she queries whether such interpretations of criminal women have any bearing on the general population. As women who break the law make up such as small proportion of all offenders, particularly those who are violent, the criminal woman may be viewed as 'different' regardless of the employment of gender stereotypes, and so how they are understood may have little bearing on how women in general are viewed. Furthermore, as gender stereotypes are seen to facilitate lenient legal treatment, which is often deemed to be warranted to mitigate punitive outcomes, Brennan asks whether we would actually want criminal justice to challenge existing gender norms, which could remove any recourse to a more lenient approach for women construed as 'good'? However, this argument would not, of course, relate to women constructed as 'bad'.

Secondly, Brennan challenges the feminist presumption that the law and criminal justice negates sociopolitical aspects of offending solely in the function of gender construction. Instead, she argues that, due to its wider theoretical foundations, the law does not recognise or take account of these factors with *any* offending. This includes cases relating to class, race and ethnicity. In order to allow for consideration of the sociopolitical context that may contribute to the actions of female offenders and, for example, increase the difficulties and demands of mothering a child, the foundational principles of criminal law would need to be overturned. Brennan is critical of feminist desires to have the wider sociocultural aspects of female offending recognised by the courts, simultaneously acknowledging women's agency in their offending behaviour, while still providing leniency. As Brennan argues, lack of, or reduced, agency is generally what is required under criminal law theory and doctrine to generate and defend lenient treatment.

The feminist critique of criminal justice responses to homicidal women and gender construction raises a number of interesting points. Firstly, it highlights the continued assumption that women are not violent and violence is not female. Courts continue to perceive individual character flaws in the behaviour of women who commit fatal acts of violence, to explain away their violent offending—a mental deficit, the 'mad'; an inability to cope, the 'sad'; or as monstrous and/or evil, the 'bad'. However, what is less clear from research is whether this gender construction is also applied to men who kill. Ballinger (2007) makes the point that gender constructions do not act on women alone. Furthermore, gender construction also needs to be considered if, when sentencing a man who has been convicted of murder, or any other form of homicide, a judge would declare that he was merely acting in line with the characteristics of his gender, albeit an extreme manifestation of masculinity. Further investigation into the construction of perceptions of homicidal men would be of use for this debate. Nevertheless, what continues to be a feature of criminal justice responses to homicidal women, and all female offenders, is that the closer they conform to the gender norm, the more likely they are to receive leniency (Carlen 1983; Eaton 1986; Morris and Wilczynski 1993; Weare 2013). This is problematic because it leads to the replication of gender norms within the courtroom. However, the situation as it stands is further compounded by the fact that those who are least able to conform to gendered norms, and therefore less likely to receive lenient treatment, are often the most vulnerable women in our society (Gartner and McCarthy 2006).

Women as Child Sexual Abusers

As with homicide, most perpetrators of child sexual abuse are male (Turton 2008; Russell and Finkelhor 1984), and recorded statistics suggest that women are responsible for an extremely small number of instances. Bunting (2005) identified that in England and Wales, women are responsible for approximately 5% of all sex crime including child abuse. There have been a number of estimates produced by researchers, and the most frequently quoted prevalence rates based on research findings indicate that female perpetrators are responsible for between 5% and 20% of all child sexual abuse (Saradjian 1996; Russell and Finklehor 1984). Of course, many cases go unreported. Of those cases that are reported, most do not reach criminal court, will not appear in any statistics and are often excluded from the research literature as victims remain silent. One way of identifying the rates of hidden crime is victim surveys, and the most useful for child sexual abuse is ChildLine.[4] In 2001/2002, the figures suggested that of over 8000 children counselled by ChildLine for sexual abuse, 13% cited a female abuser (Bunting 2005). While this figure again remains small compared to male perpetrators, it is a significant minority.

As suggested above, most perpetrators, including women who commit child sexual abuse, do not appear in the courts. So, unlike the discussion of women who kill, there is little evidence of any leniency in response. In fact where women do appear in court cases involving sexual abuse, the crimes tend to be extreme and as a consequence perpetrators have often been vilified as 'monsters' (e.g. Myra Hindley). However, the similarities with women who kill lie within the underlying concepts of gender roles that apply in terms of mothering and femininity. There has been considerable discussion in the literature revealing data in connection with issues of harm, cause and intent of female child sex abusers (Turton 2008; Bunting 2005; Denov 2004; Saradjian 1996), but what we want to do here is to highlight how the expectations of women's roles within society link to responses to violent behaviour. Women, especially mothers, are encouraged and expected to have close and loving relationships with children (Saradjian 1996), and in many ways, they share the universal nurturing role suggested by Glenn (1994). It is these traditional scripts that can provide the sociocultural basis for denial and prevent the identification of female perpetrators (Mellor and Deering 2010; Denov 2004). There are three key issues for concern that relate to gender expectations.

In the first instance, while all children who are sexual abuse victims find it difficult to disclose their abuse, the gendered model of the 'maternal' can silence victims of women, particularly in cases of maternal incest (Turton 2008; Rosencrans 1997; Mendel 1995). Partly this is because of the high risk of being disbelieved and shamed (Sgroi and Sargent 1993). In and of itself this is a problem, but also since the mother looms so large in the child's world, accusers risk making others feel uncomfortable by challenging stereotypes and the social mantra that 'all mothers love their children' (Turton 2010).

Secondly, the maternal idealisation that continues to be culturally endorsed excludes women who have ambivalent feelings towards their children. Women who have ambivalent feelings may have their concerns minimised or silenced because of the assumption that all mothers love their children and the belief that in cases where the 'bonding' process is delayed, they can learn to do so (Parker 1997). So, women concerned about their relationship with their child may be silenced and prevented from seeking help—shamed by the social idealisation of motherhood. On the other hand, female perpetrators who understand the expectations of the mothering role can hide any sexualised meanings to behaviour behind this stereotypical veneer.

> Such sexualised behaviour is often recognised by the victims but may go unobserved by onlookers or is minimised as over-enthusiastic child care or maybe excused as an exceptionally strong 'mother-love' bond. (Turton 2008, p. 32)

Finally, by idealising and universalising the mother role, we leave open the possibility of ignoring, minimising or denying abusive behaviour. The basic understanding that men are the sexual perpetrators in cases of child sexual abuse and that women are the nurturers creates a problem in cases of female perpetrators as 'when a woman sexually abuses a child it conflicts with society's gender schema' (Kite and Tyson 2004, p. 310).

It is the social gender patterning, therefore, that influences the public and professional response of denial and minimisation. Both of these responses, rather than challenging, create the ideal environment for the perpetrator, reinforcing the behaviour within the bounds of normality and acceptability. It is the unexpected reversal of gender norms that cause difficulties for professional practice and public recognition of women who sexually abuse children. While experienced professionals are developing changes within the child protection system, it remains difficult to escape the expected gendered narratives that remain entrenched in sociocultural scripts.

Understanding Gender Norms

The examples of homicide and female sexual abuse above indicate the ongoing importance of understanding the impact of cultural gender norms with regard to female offenders. Of course, it is too simplistic to explain such activity as simply reflecting the adoption of aggressive male behaviour in order to survive in a patriarchal environment, as suggested by some early scholars (Adler 1975). Some of the more contemporary literature, however, does reveal key areas that could be useful tools for developing a feminist framework for understanding violent women.

Firstly, the feminist literature has identified ways in which female offenders have been pigeonholed into male paradigms. Irwin and Chesney-Lind (2011), for instance, critique the work of Miller (2001) in identifying that much of the research surrounding women and violence focuses on *differences* and *similarities* between male and female offending, which tend to either essentialise/masculinise violent behaviour or at the very least ignore gender as a significant variable. These directions have been attempts to universalise the nature of crime in some way, explaining causation through a variety of contexts including family, school and neighbourhoods and often 'dropping' females into ready-made male frameworks (Irwin and Chesney-Lind 2011; Turton 2008). The major concern about this search for equivalence is the tendency to ignore the need for a gender consideration (Worrall 2002) leading to the masculinisation of female violent behaviour that draws on the stereotypical assumptions suggested above: violent offending is male and victimisation is female (Mendel 1995). This approach not only limits theoretical opportunities for understanding female criminality, but also denies women's agency—we need to move beyond the singular notion of crime as 'male' and offer a more considered interpretation of women's behaviour.

Secondly, the feminist literature privileges further recognition and emphasis regarding the importance of gender as pivotal for understanding female violence (Irwin and Chesney-Lind 2011; Worrall 2002; Carlen 2002; Smart 1995). This is vital, as it offers the opportunity to account for the continuing victimisation and undervaluing of girls and women as part of the context of their lives. Challenging the reproduction of the gendering process is important in order to avoid the pitfalls discussed above: reinforcing inequality and masculinising women's violence. Using this alternative analysis, we can suggest that rather than being seen as 'masculinised' behaviour, female violence could be viewed as a form of resistance to the disadvantages women experience within their gendered roles (Kruttschnitt and Carbone-Lopez 2006). For example, Irwin and Chesney-Lind (2011) suggest gender disadvantage offers women and girls little room for manoeuvre. Men who find themselves vulnerable through structures such as class or race still have a powerful outlet in the sex/gender system. On the other hand, women and girls dealing with their emotions in complex situations of inequality may well be punished for 'anti-feminine' behaviours strategies, sometimes including violence, that they employ to cope with their victimisation (Schaffer 2007). An issue has been illustrated by Melrose (2017) research concerning both the criminalisation and the sexual exploitation of girls in Rotherham and Rochdale.

Thirdly, the reproduction of gendered environments is not restricted to interpersonal relationships. Institutions such as the courts, the media and even some research programmes employ 'the dominant cultural narratives about women's violence' (Kruttschnitt and Carbone-Lopez 2006, p. 323). The recycling of gendered narratives of the 'good' and 'bad' homicidal woman, as outlined above, illustrates this point. Furthermore, the application of gender, and maternal, expectations by professionals working with children can lead to minimisation and sometimes denial of abusive behaviour (Turton 2008; Denov 2004). Or, as suggested in cases where the evidence is overwhelming, the de-feminisation process permits public vilification, as in the cases of Myra Hindley and Rosemary West.

Finally, gender is important as persisting inequalities place women at a constant disadvantage. However, we should recognise that this is only part of the picture and be wary of using gender as the *primary* consideration when exploring violent behaviour—especially if gender is prioritised. Gender differences need to be recognised within the context of other motives and meanings. A more consistent use of a multidimensional analysis—an intersectionality analysis—that includes gender as well as class, race, age, the environment and income has the possibility of furthering our understanding of female and male violence. This is important, as research suggests many of the women arrested and convicted of violent crime come from disadvantaged backgrounds (Gartner and McCarthy 2006).

Conclusion

The discussions above indicate that homicides and sexual crimes committed by women often challenge gender role boundaries in significant ways. For instance, the social rhetoric around child sexual abuse dictates that men are the perpetrators and women are the victims; Mendel (1995) labels this as the masculinisation of violence and the feminisation of victimhood. These accepted norms make the unexpected difficult to recognise. Maternal filicide is clearly different, but as a crime, it also implies an unnatural break with traditional ideas of what it is to be a mother and cultural notions of the mothering role. So, these violent acts are not just uncommon, but they break social norms and create difficulties for society. As we have demonstrated, this has considerable impact on the way such acts have been interpreted and understood within criminal justice and beyond. These violent crimes and their perpetrators challenge the social narratives of femininity and motherhood, which in turn has a direct impact on responses to female offenders in these circumstances. Scholars have long argued that professionals and researchers need to move beyond the mad/bad dichotomy (Morris and Wilczynski 1993; Morrissey 2003). However, as we show, this idea continues to operate within discourse relating to female offenders, specifically women who are convicted of homicide offences, assisting in explaining away their transgressions of gender norms. Not all female violent offending can be explained in this way, as analysis of child sexual abuse suggests. The case of female child sexual abusers illustrates a group of violent women whose experiences cannot be reincorporated into the narrative of femininity and womanhood. As such, their offending must be understood using a different mechanism—denial and minimisation. Underlying these explanations sits the premise that violent and sexually abusive women cannot be 'real' women. This is in contrast to male perpetrators whose behaviour might be measured along a line of a continuum of masculinity, as Kelly (1988) so neatly suggested. Therefore, developing a theoretical analysis to understand violent women does not fit a patriarchy/power axis. Instead, what is required is perhaps a more complex intersectionality approach, namely an understanding of the various structural and cultural influences on our emotional development and behaviour. That is not to say that such an approach is only of value in understanding female offenders. On the contrary, reviewing the framework for understanding violent women offers the opportunity to consider a more nuanced approach to male violence as well. However, as suggested, the caveat to an intersectionality approach to any analysis is the need to, not necessarily prioritise, but to include gender as a variable in any analysis. Otherwise, the narratives surrounding women who are violent are either subsumed into male paradigms or become embedded in professional discourse that inevitably leads to the reproduction of the gendered environments and roles illustrated above.

What can we take from this brief overview? Firstly, we can conclude that women commit significantly less violence than men and that it often takes different forms. This is certainly the case in instances of domestic violence as this generally occurs as resistance or retaliation. Analysis of women perpetrators of domestic violence illustrates how female violent crime cannot be accounted for by 'slotting' women into male theoretical frameworks. Furthermore, criminal justice and professional gender-neutral responses to such violence have significant consequences for women who are not the primary aggressor (Earle, this volume). The professional and criminal justice responses to women who commit neonaticide (see Brennan and Milne, this volume) or child sexual abuse appear to reproduce gendered forms. Women are expected to meet cultural expectations of motherhood and may have any violent behaviour denied or minimised, reinforcing idealised notions of femininity. By representing violent women, such as the homicidal mother, as either mad or bad, we not only limit the available interpretations of their actions, but also limit abilities to understand their motives.

So where can we go from here? We should ensure gender remains a fixed variable that is part of the mix in research analysis, professional practice and the criminal justice process when considering violent women. This is part of the package that will support not just female offenders but female victims as well. This does not mean forgoing accountability—it means contextualising women's violence while avoiding gender neutrality (Turton 2008); otherwise, women's violence will continue to be considered 'in terms of a male normative standard juxtaposed against stereotypes of respectable femininity' (Renzetti 1999, p. 44).

Notes

1. Violent crime is defined as offenses of murder and non-negligent manslaughter, rape, robbery and aggravated assault.
2. In relation to women who kill, even within domestically abusive relationships, and women who commit child sexual abuse, female offending remains very low compared to men's.
3. Data obtained from Homicide Index, Home Office. Data as of 14 November 2016; figures are subject to revision as cases are dealt with by the police and the courts, or as further information becomes available. Offences currently recorded as homicide where victims are under the age of one year by the sex of the principal suspect, 2002/2003–2015/2016. The term 'sex', as opposed to 'gender', is used by the Home Office.
4. ChildLine is a free confidential 24-hour helpline for children and young people. It was set up as a registered UK charity in 1986 and is now part of the National Society for the Prevention of Cruelty to Children (NSPCC).

References

Adler, I. (1975). *Sisters in crime*. New York: McGraw-Hill.

Babcock, J. C., Miller, S. A., & Siard, C. (2003). Toward a typology of abusive women: Differences between partner-only and generally violent women in the use of violence. *Psychology of Women Quarterly, 27*(2), 153–161.

Ballinger, A. (2007). Masculinity in the dock: Legal responses to male violence and female retaliation in England and Wales, 1900–1965. *Social & Legal Studies, 16*(4), 459–481.

Brennan, K. (in press). Murdering mothers and gentle judges: Paternalism, patriarchy and infanticide. *Yale Journal of Law and Feminism*.

Brookman, F., & Maguire, M. (2003). *Reducing homicide: A review of the possibilities* London: Home Office. Available at: http://webarchive.nationalarchives.gov.uk/20110218135832/http://rds.homeoffice.gov.uk/rds/pdfs2/rdsolr0103.pdf (Accessed 16 May 2014).

Bunting, L. (2005). *Females who sexually offend against children: Responses of the child protection and criminal justice systems*. London: Routledge.

Cameron, D. (1999). Rosemary west: Motives and meanings. *Journal of Sexual Aggression, 4*(2), 68–80.

Carlen, P. (1983). *Women's imprisonment: A study in social control*. London: Routledge.

Carlen, P. (2002). *Women and punishment*. Farnham, UK: Willan.

Chesney-Lind, M. (2002). Criminalizing victimization: The unintended consequences of pro-arrest policies for girls and women. *Criminology & Public Policy, 2*(1), 81–90.

Crime Survey for England and Wales. (2016). *Focus on violent crime and sexual offences: Year ending March 2015—Overview of violent crime and sexual offences*. Available at: https://www.ons.gov.uk/peoplepopulationandcommunity/crimeandjustice/compendium/focusonviolentcrimeandsexualoffences/yearendingmarch2015/chapter1overviewofviolentcrimeandsexualoffences—profile-of-offenders-involved-in-violent-crimes (Accessed 22 June 2017).

Dasgupta, S. D. (2002). A framework for understanding women's use of nonlethal violence in intimate heterosexual relationships. *Violence Against Women, 8*(11), 1364–1389.

Denov, M. (2004). *Perspectives on female sexual offending: A culture of denial*. Aldershot, UK: Ashgate.

Dobash, R. P., & Dobash, R. E. (2004). Women's violence to men in intimate relationships. *British Journal of Criminology, 44*, 324–349.

Eaton, M. (1986). *Justice for women?: Family, court and social control.* Milton Keynes: Open University Press.

Enander, V. (2011). Violent women? The challenge of women's violence in intimate heterosexual relationships to feminist analyses of partner violence. *NORA—Nordic Journal of Feminist and Gender Research, 19*(2), 105–123.

Gartner, R., & McCarthy, B. (2006). Maternal fillicide and the dark figure of homicide: Beyond the mad, the bad and the victim. In K. Heimer & C. Kruttschnitt (Eds.), *Gender and crime: Patterns in victimization and offending.* New York: New York University Press.

Gelsthorpe, L., & Wright, S. (2015). The context: Women as lawbreakers. In J. Annison, J. Brayford, & J. Deering (Eds.), *Women and criminal justice: From the Corston report to transforming rehabilitation* (pp. 39–59). Bristol: Policy Press.

Glenn, E. (1994). Social constructions of mothering. In E. Glenn, G. Chang, & L. Forcey (Eds.), *Mothering: Ideology, experience and agency* (pp. 1–29). London: Routledge.

Hester, M. (2012). Portrayal of women as inimate partner domestic violence perpetrators. *Violence Against Women, 18*(9), 1067–1082.

Irwin, K., & Chesney-Lind, M. (2011). Girls' violence: Beyond dangerous masculinity. In M. Chesney-Lind & M. Morash (Eds.), *Feminist theories of crime.* Farnham: Ashgate.

Johnson, M. (2005). Domestic violence: It's not about gender—Or is it? *Journal of Marriage and Family, 67*(5), 126–1130.

Kelly, L. (1988). *Surviving sexual violence.* Cambridge: Wiley.

Kelly, L. (1996). When does the speaking profit us? Reflections on the challenges of developing feminist perspectives on abuse and violence by women. In M. Hester, L. Kelly, & J. Radford (Eds.), *Women, violence and male power* (pp. 34–49). Buckingham: The Open University Press.

Kite, D., & Tyson, G. A. (2004). The impact of perpetrator gender on male and female police officers' perceptions of child sexual abuse. *Psychiatry, Psychology and Law, 11*(2), 308–318.

Koons-Witt, B., & Schram, P. (2003). The prevalence and nature of violent offending by females. *Journal of Criminal Justice, 31,* 361–371.

Kruttschnitt, C., & Carbone-Lopez, K. (2006). Moving beyond the stereotypes: Women's subjective accounts of their violent crime. *Criminology, 44*(2), 321–351.

Kruttschnitt, C., Gartner, R., & Ferraro, K. (2002). Women's involvement in serious interpersonal violence. *Aggression and Violent Behavior, 7,* 529–565.

Lloyd, A. (1995). *Doubly deviant, doubly damned: Society's treatment of violent women*. London: Penguin Books.

Mellor, D., & Deering, R. (2010). Professional response and attitudes toward female-perpetrated child sexual abuse: A study of psychologists, psychiatrists, probationary psychologists and child protection workers. *Psychology, Crime & Law, 16*(5), 415–438.

Melrose, M. (2017). Young people and sexual exploitation: A critical discourse analysis. In M. Melrose & J. Pearce (Eds.), *Critical perspectives on child sexual exploitation and related trafficking*. Basingstoke: Palgrave.

Melton, H. C., & Belknap, J. (2003). He hits, she hits. *Criminal Justice and Behavior, 30*(3), 328–348.

Mendel, M. (1995). *The male survivor: The impact of sexual abuse*. Beverley Hills, CA: Sage Focus.

Miller, S. L. (2001). The paradox of women arrested for domestic violence. *Violence Against Women, 7*(12), 1339–1376.

Ministry of Justice. (2016). *Women and the criminal justice system statistics 2015*. Available at: https://www.gov.uk/government/statistics/women-and-the-criminal-justice-system-statistics-2015 (Accessed 22 June 2017).

Ministry of Justice. (2017), May 18. *Criminal justice system statistics quarterly: December 2016: Prosecutions and convictions tool*. Available at: https://www.gov.uk/government/statistics/criminal-justice-system-statistics-quarterly-december-2016 (Accessed 8 October 2017).

Morris, A., & Wilczynski, A. (1993). Rocking the cradle: Mothers who kill their children. In H. Birch (Ed.), *Moving targets: Women, murder, and representation* (pp. 198–217). London: Virago.

Morrissey, B. (2003). *When women kill: Questions of agency and subjectivity. Transformations: Thinking through feminism*. London: Routledge.

Muftić, L. R., Bouffard, J. A., & Bouffard, L. A. (2007). An exploratory study of women arrested for intimate partner violence. *Journal of Interpersonal Violence, 22*(6), 753–774.

Muncie, J. (2015). *Youth and crime* (4th ed.). London: Sage.

Office for National Statistics. (2017). *Crime statistics, focus on violent crime and sexual offences, 2015/16*. Available at: https://www.ons.gov.uk/peoplepopulationandcommunity/crimeandjustice/compendium/focusonviolentcrimeandsexualoffences/yearendingmarch2015 (Accessed 12 April 2017).

Parker, R. (1997). The reproduction and purposes of maternal ambivalence. In W. Hollway & B. Featherstone (Eds.), *Mothering and ambivalence*. London: Routledge.

Peterson, E. (1999). Murder as self-help: Women and intimate partner homicide. *Homicide Studies, 3*(1), 30–46.

Renzetti, C. M. (1992). *Violent betrayal: Partner abuse in lesbian relationships.* Newbury Park, CA: Sage.

Renzetti, C. M. (1999). The challenge to feminism posed by women's use of violence in intimate relationships. In S. Lamb (Ed.), *New versions of victims: Feminists struggle with the concept* (pp. 42–56). New York: New York University Press.

Rosencrans, B. (1997). *The last secret: Daughters sexually abused by their mothers.* Brandon, VT: Safer Society Press.

Russell, D., & Finkelhor, D. (1984). Women as perpetrators. In D. Finkelhor (Ed.), *Child sexual abuse: New theory and research*. New York: Pergamon.

Saradjian, J. (1996). *Women who sexually abuse children.* Chichester: Wiley.

Schaffner, L. (2007). Violence against girls provokes girls' violence. *Violence Against Women, 13*(12), 1229–1248.

Sgroi, S., & Sargent, N. (1993). Impact and treatment issues for victims of child sexual abuse by female perpetrators. In M. Elliott (Ed.), *The last taboo.* London: Longman.

Sharpe, G. (2012). *Offending girls: Young women and youth justice.* Abingdon: Routledge.

Smart, C. (1995). *Law, crime and sexuality.* London: Sage.

Snyder, H., & Sickmund, M. (2006). *Juvenile offenders and victims: 2006 National Report* (NCJ 178257). Washington, DC: US Department of Justice, Office of Justice Programs, Office of Juvenile Justice and Delinquency Prevention.

Taft, A., Hegarty, K., & Flood, M. (2001). Are men and women equally violent to intimate partners? *Australian and New Zealand Journal of Public Health, 25*(6), 498–500.

Turton, J. (2008). *Child abuse, gender and society. Routledge research in gender and society.* New York: Routledge.

Turton, J. (2010). Female sexual abusers: Assessing the risk. *International Journal of Law, Crime and Justice, 38*(4), 279–293.

Uniform Crime Reports. (2017). *2015 crime in the United States: Ten-year arrest trends by sex, 2006–2015.* Available at: https://ucr.fbi.gov/crime-in-the-u.s/2015/crime-in-the-u.s.-2015/tables/table-33 (Accessed 22 June 2017).

Weare, S. (2013). "The mad", "the bad", "the victim": Gendered constructions of women who kill within the criminal justice system. *Laws, 2*(3), 337–361.

Weare, S. (2017). Bad, mad or sad? Legal language, narratives, and identity constructions of women who kill their children in England and Wales. *International Journal for the Semiotics of Law, 30*(2), 1–22.

Wilczynski, A. (1995). Risk factors for parental child homicide-results of an English study. *Current Issues in Criminal Justice, 7*(2), 193–222.

Wilczynski, A. (1997). Mad or bad? Child-killers, gender and the courts. *British Journal of Criminology, 37*(3), 419–436.

Worrall, A. (2002). Rendering women punishable: The making of a penal crisis. In P. Carlen (Ed.), *Women and punishment: The struggle for justice* (pp. 47–66). Cullompton: Willan.

Part II

The Criminal Justice System: Failing or Improving?

7

Sentencing Women in the Transformed Probation Landscape

Gemma Birkett

Introduction

In 2013, the government promised that new reforms would 'deliver better outcomes for women offenders' (Ministry of Justice 2013b, p. 16). This was a bold statement and a laudable ambition. However, this strategy—called and aimed at Transforming Rehabilitation—will only be successful if sentencers are aware of (and support) the options that new providers put in place to achieve its goals. This chapter considers current levels of awareness of the new reforms among magistrates. Highlighting reservations about the suitability of community provision, and a lack of awareness about developments under Transforming Rehabilitation, it emphasises the lack of information that magistrates receive on this issue. Supplementing the findings of a recent research project conducted with 168 magistrates (see Birkett 2016), this chapter

G. Birkett (✉)
Department of Sociology, City, University of London,
London, UK
e-mail: Gemma.birkett.1@city.ac.uk

© The Author(s) 2018
E. Milne et al. (eds.), *Women and the Criminal Justice System*,
https://doi.org/10.1007/978-3-319-76774-1_7

provides a post-Transforming Rehabilitation 'update', drawing on 24 semi-structured interviews and a survey of 86 magistrates sitting across England and Wales. As such, it places particular focus on developments that followed the implementation of the Offender Rehabilitation Act 2014,[1] the legislative measures underpinning the government's flagship Transforming Rehabilitation policy agenda.

Gender and Sentencing

The decision-making process in court is understandably complex, but it is perhaps even more so when sentencing women. For some sentencers, treating women differently jars with the fundamental principles of the Judicial Oath.[2] This view is understandable and highlights concerns that in treating some defendants in a 'special' way (based only on arbitrary characteristics), others will be disadvantaged. Recent research by Marougka (2012) highlighted the contradictory nature of judicial attitudes on this topic; while many sentencers had an understanding of the distinctive needs of women and were willing to take these into consideration, they also insisted that they 'treated everyone the same'. Other research debates similar tensions (see Birkett 2016; Gelsthorpe and Sharpe 2015; Criminal Justice Joint Inspection 2011).

It is important to highlight, however, the stream of legislative and (international) policy developments that advocate (or legally require) sentencers to engage with the specific needs of women offenders. In 2010, the United Nations General Assembly passed a resolution to create the Rules for the Treatment of Female Prisoners and Non-Custodial Measures for Women Offenders (known as the 'Bangkok Rules'). The rules were designed to provide guidance for governments and sentencing authorities to reduce the use of unnecessary imprisonment for women (particularly mothers) and ensure the suitable treatment of those incarcerated. The UK Equality Act of the same year introduced a 'gender equality duty' (section 149) which requires public authorities (including prisons, probation and court staff) to promote equality of opportunity between women and men (and combat discrimination in all areas of public services). In this legislation, the government publicly acknowledged that the principle of equal treatment should not necessarily lead to *identical* treatment (Cavadino et al. 2013, p. 302).

Judicial and sentencing bodies in England and Wales advocate a similar stance. In addition to guidance produced by the Sentencing Advisory Panel in 2009 (which recommended that judicial principles may need to be 'slightly adjusted to allow for the particular vulnerabilities of women offenders'), the Sentencing Council incorporated the mitigating factor of 'sole or primary carer for dependent relatives' into the Sentencing Guidelines for England and Wales in 2011. The Judicial College Equal Treatment Bench Book further states that,

> ...sentencers must be made aware of the differential impact sentencing decisions have on women and men including caring responsibilities for children or elders; the impact of imprisonment on mental and emotional well-being; and the disproportionate impact that incarceration has on offenders who have caring responsibilities if they are imprisoned a long distance from home. (2013, p. 11)

Such requirements sit alongside previous (New Labour's commitment to the Corston agenda) and current (the Coalition/Conservative Strategic Objectives for Female Offenders) government policies which continue to stress the need for sentencers to consider women's specific needs when passing sentence. This approach has widespread support among the wider criminal justice community, from penal reform charities (such as *Women in Prison*, the *Prison Reform Trust* and the *Howard League*) to those representing sentencers. The *Magistrates' Association*, for example, has publicly stated its intention 'to increase awareness among magistrates of the factors which may need to be considered when sentencing women, and the effects of custody on them and their families' (in Prison Reform Trust 2015: 1). Recent developments under the Offender Rehabilitation Act 2014 (section 10) place further requirements on sentencers to take into consideration women's specific needs in relation to community punishments. Yet despite such legislative requirements and a general political consensus, research continues to highlight a level of unease among some sentencers in relation to the principle of differential treatment for women (see Hedderman and Barnes 2015; Birkett 2016).

On the whole, previous research has demonstrated that magistrates recognise that the pathways into male and female offending can be different. Those offences traditionally regarded as 'female' (such as stealing food, welfare fraud and theft from employers) have been viewed as having a lesser degree of harm. Studies have revealed that magistrates understand that such forms of offending are often linked to domestic or family responsibilities (including victimisation or experiences of abuse), which they have tended to regard as a mitigating factor (see Eaton 1986; Farrington and Morris 1983; Gelsthorpe and Loucks 1997; Worrall 1990). Research in this area has also exposed the clear distinctions made by magistrates in relation to those they regard as 'troubled' versus those they consider to be 'troublesome', the former in need of supported interventions, the latter requiring punishment (see Eaton 1986; Carlen 1983; Heidensohn 1985). Several studies have pointed to the existence of 'patriarchal chivalry' in the courtroom that in believing 'troubled' women would benefit from a custodial sentence (for help with mental health problems, drug or alcohol addictions or for their own safety), magistrates may be engaging in 'up-tariffing' by sending too many non-violent women to prison unnecessarily (see Carlen 1983; Gelsthorpe 1992; Heidensohn 1985; Horn and Evans 2000; Hedderman 2004). Indeed, some have even called for magistrates' sentencing powers to be curtailed (see Hedderman 2011, 2012).

It is important to consider the important role played by court reports (in particular pre-sentence reports) in this regard. Research has demonstrated that magistrates strongly tend to agree with reports submitted to the court by probation (75% according to the CJJI report of 2011 and 73% according to Ministry of Justice data (2016)) and are unlikely to deviate from their recommendations (although they are permitted to do so). The delivery of court reports has changed substantially in recent years. Ministry of Justice data demonstrate that since 2012 the overall proportion of standard pre-sentence reports has declined for males and females by around fifteen percent, to be replaced by faster, often oral, reports (2016, p. 78). While traditional pre-sentence reports are more comprehensive in nature and based on a full risk assessment, fast delivery (oral or written) reports are usually completed on the day of request.[3] Such reports are only deemed suitable where the case is of low or medium seriousness and the court has indicated that a community sentence is being considered.[4]

While adhering to the government's commitment to swift and sure justice, there are concerns that such developments may not afford probation officers the time to assess defendants fully (of particular importance for vulnerable defendants who may be deemed as 'low risk'), resulting in inadequate information for sentencers. Several commentators have called for pre-sentence (or certainly more detailed) reports to be used as the 'norm' for women who often fall into the vulnerable defendant category (see Prison Reform Trust 2015; Minson 2015; Howard League 2014). It is concerning that a recent inspection of women's community services conducted by Her Majesty's Inspectorate of Probation (HMIP) found that 'insufficient effort was made by [court] probation [staff] to understand and explain the gender-specific needs of women in two in three cases' (HMIP 2016, p. 24). The report repeated recommendations made by others (see CJJI 2011; Marougka 2012; Minson 2015) that the NPS should 'have structures in place to provide timely information to sentencers about the needs of women who offend and the interventions available locally' and to 'make sure that pre-sentence reports take account of the specific needs of women who offend' (HMIP 2016, p. 11).

Providing information to sentencers is a key. Research studies continue to highlight the limited knowledge that magistrates possess on community provision for women (see Birkett 2016; Gelsthorpe and Sharpe 2015; HMIP 2016; Radcliffe and Hunter 2013). This is despite the government's promise *a full decade ago*, that sentencers would be 'better informed about community provision for women, what is available in their areas and how it can address women's needs more effectively than custody' (Ministry of Justice 2007, p. 6). One of the most recent studies in this area revealed that magistrates' limited knowledge of specialist provision for women has a clear impact on levels of confidence in community sentences (Birkett 2016). As very few magistrates in England and Wales have received training on the circumstances surrounding women's offending, such results are understandable. Previous research has demonstrated the direct correlation between levels of training and preparedness to consider more creative sentencing options (see Lemon 1974). If the government is serious about increasing the number of non-violent women punished in the community, then increased training options (financial implications notwithstanding) are a sensible way forward (see also Gelsthorpe and Sharpe 2015).

Policy and Legislative Developments

This chapter does not have capacity to provide a comprehensive synopsis of developments in women's penal policy (see Birkett 2017; Seal and Phoenix 2013; Hedderman 2011); however, it is worth noting that the very first strategy for women—aimed at reducing their numbers in custody—was published nearly twenty years ago. In promising 'a cross-government, comprehensive, targeted and measurable Women's Offending Reduction Programme' (Home Office 2001, p. 1), the Home Office stated its intention to support projects that would divert women from custody, aid resettlement after release from prison and provide community-based non-custodial supervision (Corcoran 2011). In 2006–2007, the Home Office launched Together Women, a programme of holistic provision for women who had offended (or were at risk of offending) across five demonstrator sites in northern England (Seal and Phoenix 2013, p. 170; see Gelsthorpe et al. 2007; Hedderman et al. 2008). Together Women incorporated a variety of women's centres that provided 'one-stop-shop' services to help prevent women from entering the criminal justice system or to help with their post-custodial resettlement (Seal and Phoenix 2013, p. 170).

The publishing of the Corston Report in 2007 represented a watershed moment in revealing the specific needs of women offenders to a wider audience, however. Consistent with the wealth of research in this area, Corston categorised the main vulnerabilities faced by women offenders as domestic (including parenting and childcare), personal (including mental health, low self-esteem and substance misuse) and socioeconomic (including poverty and unemployment). In highlighting the difficult experiences faced by many women in prison (who presented no real risk to the public), Corston called for an extension of the network of holistic women's centres to enable more women to be punished in the community where appropriate. The newly formed Ministry of Justice accepted the majority of Corston's proposals and provided time-specific funding (£15.6 million in 2009–2010[5]) for the establishment of additional centres along with a Ministerial 'Champion' to drive forward the reforms. While the status of women's penal policy was affected by the election of the Conservative-led Coalition in 2010 (there being no strategy until 2013), the current plan (outlined in a document entitled *Strategic Objectives for Female Offenders*) adopts flavours of Corston to advocate the widespread use of community punishments for women.

Given the refreshed focus (including regular meetings of an expert Advisory Board), it is regrettable that women were only mentioned in one paragraph of the original Transforming Rehabilitation document which stated that future provision should meet their 'specific needs and priorities' (2013a; see Annison et al. 2015). Despite an official recognition of this omission—where the department promised that the reforms would deliver 'better outcomes for women offenders' (2013b, p. 16)—the initial format of the Offender Rehabilitation Bill, the legislation enshrining Transforming Rehabilitation, contained no specific mention of women. A later amendment (to become section 10 of the Act) stated that the supervision and rehabilitation of women must comply with section 149 of the Equality Act 2010 and identify anything that is intended to meet their 'particular needs'. The resulting contracts with the twenty-one new providers of probation services, the Community Rehabilitation Companies (CRCs), were kept deliberately broad so that each organisation could interpret 'particular needs' as it saw fit. A fundamental 'rub' occurs, however, when considering that the majority of the new probation providers are private for-profit companies who are focused on achieving maximum efficiency,[6] a concept that runs counter to the holistic, needs-based approach advocated by Corston and the network of women's community service providers.

The Offender Rehabilitation Act 2014 also made amendments to the range of community sentencing options available to the courts. The Rehabilitation Activity Requirement (RAR) replaced the Specified

Activity Requirement (SAR) to give greater flexibility to probation to determine the rehabilitative interventions delivered to offenders. A recent report on the introduction of the RAR by HMIP explained that a key government objective was to 'encourage innovative work' (2017) by the new CRCs. While court orders used to specify the nature of the activity and the number of days required to complete it, now only the maximum number of days can be specified. Activity days can range from a short session of one hour to a whole working day, depending on the nature of the programme. The types of activities that constitute a RAR have been kept deliberately broad (and differ according to the provision available in each CRC area), but can include workshops for alcohol or drug misuse, victim awareness courses, help with employment, training and education (ETE) and help with finances. RARs have become an extremely popular sentencing option, taking 'centre stage in community sentencing for rehabilitation' (HMIP 2017, p. 7). Ministry of Justice data (2016) reveal that 29% of community and suspended sentence orders made in 2015/2016 contained a RAR, compared to 8% for an Accredited Programme and 8% for an Alcohol/Drug/Mental Health Treatment intervention.[7]

While it is too early to provide an assessment of the effectiveness of RARs (nor is it the focus of this chapter), the HMIP report (2017) highlighted a range of teething troubles from concerns about sentencer information and confidence, to a lack of guidance for practitioners. Proper systems of evaluation for RAR activities have also not yet been established (of particular importance considering that much of this work is outsourced), exacerbating concerns about the wide divergence in provision across England and Wales (a situation of 'postcode lottery justice'). Given the issues around sentencer confidence in relation to *existing* community options (see Birkett 2016), such findings are particularly concerning. The HMIP report outlined the pressure on CRCs to plan suitable activities for those sentenced to a RAR and deliver them within the specified timeframe. It revealed, however, 'significant shortcomings and a noticeable lack of impetus or direction in a good proportion of cases' and concluded that there were 'early signs of a reduction in sentencer confidence' (HMIP 2017, p. 4). The report went on to highlight the 'uncomfortable tension… between the making of the order and what is delivered, with the system leaving sentencers to assume services they are not fully confident about' (HMIP 2017, p. 4). Although going beyond statutory requirements—as sentencers are not required to know the exact nature of activities that offenders may undertake—it is acknowledged that the more information they receive on a service, the more likely they are to have confidence in its appropriateness to deliver the necessary outcome(s).

While many experts welcomed the greater involvement of probation in women's sentence plans, there is a concern that the changes could impact negatively on existing arrangements. Some areas had previously offered a gender-specific option (the Female-Only Specified Activity Requirement or FOSAR) which enabled women to be automatically placed in female-only environments to complete parts of their order (often within the environs of a women's centre). While the RAR provides probation officers with greater autonomy to work with women according to their needs, the broad definition of 'rehabilitation activity' means that some officers may choose to work with women on an individual basis and not refer them to existing services. A recent thematic inspection of women's community services conducted by HMIP revealed that:

> Many responsible officers and sentencers remained unclear as to what provision for women existed in their communities. In some areas, RAR was delivered by the women's centre, and this was seen as a positive approach by sentencers. Sentencers, however, generally felt they had insufficient information on the availability of RAR provision in the community, and that there were very few activities specifically for women. (2016, p. 24)

The HMIP report also highlighted sentencers concerns about information relating to women's compliance with their orders. Such concerns are exacerbated by the growing disconnect between the NPS and the CRCs, particularly striking in the courts where the CRCs have no presence. The new process requires the NPS to prepare all court reports, with the provision of specific activities (such as RARs) to be determined by the CRC. If the offender breaches their order, the CRC must refer their case back to the NPS who will then decide whether to pursue it further. If they do, it is the NPS that will prepare the breach report and recommend the necessary penalty to the court. There is growing concern (and indeed frustration) among sentencers and practitioners about the lack of three-way communication in this regard. Given the high rates of sentencer compliance with court reports, it is crucial that the CRCs communicate their (developing) provision to the NPS, their own officers and any partner agencies so that the court reports can reflect this (HMIP 2016, p. 8). While it is acknowledged that new working practices will take time to embed, the situation must improve to avoid continued confusion around sentence planning and delays in the commencement (or amendment) of orders.

Methods and Data

This chapter forms part of a much larger project on the sentencing and punishment of women under the new Transforming Rehabilitation arrangements. The data referred to in this chapter relate to 24 semi-structured interviews and a survey of 86 magistrates sitting across three areas in England and Wales during the period 2015–2016. While the areas have been anonymised, it is important to note that Area 1 covers a large metropolitan area, Area 2 covers urban and rural areas and Area 3 covers some urban areas but is mostly rural. Magistrates were recruited through the Magistrates' Association, and as such, the results cannot be generalised to the magistracy at large (not all magistrates are members of the Association, although many are). A call for interview participants was sent in a Magistrates' Association email newsletter, and individuals were asked to make contact. The survey questionnaire was sent to all Magistrates Association members sitting in the three areas under review. It is important to note that while including the same questions, survey data are likely to generate different responses from in-depth interview data. Several 'free text' boxes were included in the survey to allow respondents the space to articulate their views as much as possible, and all participants were encouraged to make contact if they wished to add further comments. All names have been changed to ensure participant anonymity.

Findings

Both interviewees and survey respondents were asked a number of questions relating to their consideration of women offenders (and whether this was different from men); their views on the flexibility of the sentencing framework and developments with the RAR; their knowledge of community provision for women and the suitability of certain requirements (in particular unpaid work).

Sentencing Women Differently?

Consistent with previous literature (see Gelsthorpe and Sharpe 2015; Gelsthorpe and Loucks 1997; Hedderman 2004; Birkett 2016), participants were divided about the flexibility of the sentencing framework for the purposes of punishing women. Most survey respondents (57 out of 86) felt that they had sufficient flexibility, with several highlighting their judicial power to move beyond the guidelines if they felt it necessary. As outlined in similar research by Hedderman and Barnes (2015), such respondents made no distinction between *equal* treatment and the *same* treatment:

> If both genders are truly equal, both should receive parity of treatment. (Survey Respondent 83, Female, Area 3)

One respondent explained that they had not come across occasions where they had needed 'extra measures' for women (Survey Respondent 37, Female, Area 3), although others stated the opposite, however, and believed that their inability to differentiate in sentencing could have a disproportionately negative impact on women. For those that felt the sentencing framework was too constrained, concerns mainly focused on motherhood and childcare responsibilities:

> [The guidelines make] no allowance for the impact on children if the woman is a single parent. (Survey Respondent 3, Female, Area 3)

[The guidelines need] to recognise the different impact sentences have on them and their effect on their pivotal roles in family life. (Survey Respondent 30, Female, Area 3)

Interviews raised similar themes, with mixed views expressed in all three research areas, although there was a much stronger feeling among magistrates in Area 2 that women and men should be considered in exactly the same way. 'Rob' (Area 2, Interview) felt that it was important not to get 'sentimental' about women offenders and that 'in these days of equality, we can't differentiate between a woman offender and a man offender'. 'Yvonne' (Area 2, Interview) similarly stressed that 'equal is equal' and that 'sometimes we can make too many excuses for mothers'. 'Sam' (Area 2, Interview), however, expressed frustration with the sentencing framework and explained that the current set-up didn't allow her to take into account that 'often women's circumstances are different from men's'. As far as she was concerned, 'it needs to be far more flexible' as the guidelines were 'written for a man'. 'Sam' acknowledged that only a few of her colleagues were aware of a distinct strategy for women, and that there needed to be:

Much more work, much more attention, given that what little I know having read the Corston Report and all the rest of it, the training, that women's circumstances are very different.

'Sandra' (Area 1, Interview) agreed that the guidelines did not have the 'flexibility' to work around 'the challenges of motherhood'.

Several magistrates recognised that many of the women that came before them lived in vulnerable or chaotic situations. 'Mary' (Area 1, Interview) explained that 'when you have a woman before you in court and you're sentencing her, you've got a feeling at the back of your mind that you're dealing with somebody who might be a victim of crime as well as a perpetrator of crime'. 'Chris' (Area 3, Interview) stressed the need to consider whether 'they may have... abusive partners, so there can be certain aspects to it which you need to bear in mind'. 'George' (Area 1, Interview) similarly felt that as women offenders were often victims, 'the sentence should, I would hope, give access to try to sort out the other problems as well'. Such views were reflected in the survey, with one respondent acknowledging that 'women sometimes or often commit crimes due to the fear of domestic abuse or other coercion' (Respondent 85, Male, Area 1).

The general consensus among all participants was that women did not respond well to overly punitive sentences and were more likely to benefit from targeted rehabilitative interventions. 'Susan' (Area 1, Interview) felt that 'particularly [with] women, maybe the focus should be on the carrot than the stick', while Survey Respondent 76 (Female, Area 1) similarly stated that 'women need more help rather than punishment'. As highlighted in previous studies, most magistrates could not recall the last time they had sentenced a woman to custody, and several were keen to stress their extreme reluctance to do so (see Hedderman and Barnes 2015).

Developments Under the Offender Rehabilitation Act

Interviewees were asked about sentencing developments under the Offender Rehabilitation Act 2014 (and in particular the introduction of the RAR) and whether they viewed these as an improvement from the existing arrangements (notably the SAR). Many expressed unease when discussing the new legislation as they were unaware of the specific changes it introduced, and only a few had read official documents relating to the Transforming Rehabilitation agenda. While some participants were comfortable with the increased autonomy that the ORA afforded to probation, others expressed concern that the new legislation had taken away the small amount of influence they had previously been able to exert. One survey respondent viewed the changes as a positive development:

> RAR activities are more likely to be the most effective element of a community sentence in the case of women because they seem to respond more to them than punitive elements. (Survey Respondent 74, Male, Area 3)

'Mike' (Area 1, Interview) was also supportive of the changes and stressed that 'probation are there to devise the most appropriate means of fulfilling all the aspects of sentencing… I think that magistrates who want to interfere in that are just wrong'.

'Susan' (Area 1, Interview) was concerned about developments, however, and expressed a 'feeling that we're handing [power] over to somebody else'. 'Mary' (Area 1, Interview) went further to outline her dislike of the new system on the basis that 'it takes away a level of decision-making from the sentencers, which is inappropriate, because sentencing is public, and open, and transparent'. 'Jeremy' (Area 2, Interview) simply felt that:

We've lost, if you like, the power to say 'this is what we want'.

In addition to the perceived inability to influence proceedings, and echoing the concerns around sentencer confidence highlighted by a recent HMIP report (2017), some participants were apprehensive that they had no control over the number of RAR days (or hours) that offenders would subsequently undertake. 'Mary' (Area 1, Interview) explained that 'when you specify that you're sentencing somebody to a RAR, all you're saying is the maximum number of days that they have to do. If the CRC decides not to do anything with them, there's nothing we can do about it'. 'Elizabeth' (Area 1, Interview) expressed similar frustration that there was 'not enough information about what they're doing, the 60 days, if you say, or it's 20 days, whatever, it's a maximum, not a minimum, there's no guarantee that… [they'll do it]'. While resigned to the new sentencing process, some were clear that colleagues should not refrain from 'expressing a view' about their expectations for the order. 'Mary' explained that she tried to persuade colleagues to make comments in court 'so that it's in our sentencing remarks, and that it may be filtered through in the form of some kind of guidance'.

Knowledge of Gender-Specific Provision

Consistent with the findings of previous research, thirty-one of the survey respondents had no idea whether there existed any gender-specific services for women in their area (see Radcliffe and Hunter 2013; Jolliffe et al. 2011; Birkett 2016). While twenty-nine said that they were aware of provision, they were unable to name specific organisations when questioned and provided general answers such as:

Probation offer women specific courses. (Respondent 32, Male, Area 1)

A women's hub. (Respondent 4, Female, Area 1)

Interviews produced similar results; the majority of magistrates could not name specific provision and were keen to learn about what was available. Such findings are particularly disappointing considering that many sat in courts serviced by several women's centres. 'Mary' (Area 1, Interview) admitted that she had limited knowledge of local provision but felt that:

From the point of view of what probation, and now the CRCs are offering women, I think it's pretty limited. If you said to me, 'name me a woman-specific programme' I couldn't.

Several of the interviewees had heard about gender-specific provision 'through the grapevine'. 'Rob' (Area 2, Interview) thought that he had heard of the local women's centre (when prompted), while 'Jeremy' (Area 2, Interview) said he had visited the service, yet was unable to provide any specific information about what it offered. 'Chris' who sat in Area 3 was also unable to name any of the services that worked with women, although when prompted, he recalled that he had heard about the women's service which was 'apparently very successful'. Several participants expressed frustration with this situation. 'Steven' (Area 1, Interview) admitted that he had 'no real idea about what happens', with 'David' (Area 1, Interview) expressing a similar concern that probation was not responsive to questions from magistrates who 'don't know enough about what goes on behind the scenes'.

Only a few participants had knowledge of the gender-specific strategies that were being developed by the CRCs in their areas. CRC1, for example, had recently introduced a new policy that female offenders could only be supervised by female probation officers. While some magistrates in Area 1 were supportive of this development, most viewed it as a retrograde step. The most common concerns related to gender equality and the belief that women needed to mix with men (particularly male probation officers with whom they could build positive relationships). 'Steven' (Area 1, Interview) felt the new policy 'doesn't do a great deal for equality', while 'Alice' (Area 1, Interview) believed the arrangements simply provided a 'cocoon' for women who needed to 'live in the real world'. 'Jeremy', a magistrate in Area 2, also expressed unease with the gender-specific approach. He believed that it amounted to 'segregation' and a return to 'Victorian thinking that only women can be dealt with by women'. He believed gender-specific policies were problematic because 'that's not the way the world is'. The general consensus among all participants was that 'one size doesn't fit all' ('David', Area 1, Interview) and that women should be able to decide whether they wanted to take part in female-only strategies. Several survey respondents believed that there was a general tendency to overuse custody for women, and blamed this on the lack of appropriate community-based sentencing options (see Hedderman and Barnes 2015).

Consistent with previous findings (see Birkett 2016), most participants (including 55 of 86 survey respondents) said that they would welcome more gender-specific provision for women in their local area. Survey respondents overwhelmingly focused on greater levels of support for female victims of domestic violence, services that provided support for mothers and additional services for drug and alcohol addictions. Suggestions ranged from a bail hostel (Survey Respondent 5, Female, Area 2), a residential service for mothers and children (Survey Respondent 14, Female, Area 2), a women's refuge (Survey Respondent 82, Female, Area 2), more interventions to help with issues such as low self-confidence (Survey Respondent 2, Female, Area 3), housing, parenting, relationships and domestic abuse (Survey Respondent 10, Female, Area 3), and self-harm and PTSD (Survey Respondent 79, Female, Area 3). Many recognised that women responded to structured forms of support, with less focus on punitive elements.

Interviewees provided similar responses. Many outlined the importance of adopting a holistic approach for women (although they did not frame their responses in such language). 'George' (Area 1, Interview) wanted to see greater levels of non-statutory provision made available (such as help with benefits, housing, self-esteem and empowerment) and felt that women benefitted from an 'environment where those things were available'. 'Claire' (Area 1, Interview) also placed great importance on such factors and felt that:

> Building up their knowledge, building their skill sets, building up the confidence is key to everything... these are key things that will help keep them out of courts.

'Rob' (Area 2, Interview) agreed that a female-only environment was 'bound to be beneficial, because it takes away a problem, perhaps, because if they are victims of violent partners, then they need to be taken into a safe, secure environment for them to be able to relax'.

'Natasha', a magistrate who sat in Area 3, felt that there needed to be 'much more sharing of other services that are available'. She requested more feedback from the local women's service, to include 'the number of women who have been referred... a very, very brief precis of some of the issues, totally anonymised obviously, and how they're working towards rehabilitating, and the results they've had'. 'Natasha' was aware that many women before the courts had suffered a history of abuse and felt strongly that women offenders should be supervised by female practitioners. The emphasis, as far as she was concerned, should be on 'the caring bit'. Such concerns were highlighted in the survey, with one respondent remarking that 'the only feedback we get is if someone is returned to court in breach of their community order. We rarely get to know of the success stories' (Survey Respondent 43, Female, Area 3).

The Suitability of Unpaid Work Requirements

In addition to the newly introduced RAR (which provides the 'reha-bilitative' element), unpaid work is available to satisfy the 'punitive' element of community orders (if appropriate). The research revealed a perception among probation officers that there has been a rise in this requirement for women. Some participants expressed an awareness that, due to their often vulnerable circumstances, unpaid work could be difficult for many women to complete. The requirement to impose a punitive element (and the need to impose high-level community orders in order to avoid a short term in custody) made this a particular dilemma. 'Rob' (Area 2, Interview) explained that more obstacles arose with 'single women, single parents, who are unable, perhaps because of their commitments, to get the release of the hours to be able to serve them'.

None of the participants had any real idea of the types of activities that women undertook as part of their unpaid work requirement, and no information about the suite of options offered (see Birkett 2016). While the majority had not considered this in any detail, there was a consensus that any unpaid work should be suitable (i.e. nothing too physical) and that mixed groups might not always be appropriate for particularly vulnerable women. 'Susan' (Area 1, Interview) was concerned that mixed groups 'would be an issue… from the point of view of the task that they're asked to do, firstly, and secondly because of the kind of interaction between the different people'. 'Mary' (Area 1, Interview) was happy for women to be involved in gentler groups such as arts and crafts, as it was far better than 'sending women into a situation where they may feel threatened'. While 'Sam' (Area 2, Interview) said that she 'would insist [unpaid work] was female-only', she went on to admit that she wasn't sure if this option even existed.

Overall, however, participants did not view mixed groups as a bad thing unless the women were particularly vulnerable (and therefore unsuitable for this requirement in the first place). 'Pete' (Area 2, Interview) felt that groups should continue to be mixed to allow women to undertake work in a positive male environment. 'Yvonne' (Area 2, Interview) similarly agreed that women needed to 'learn the hard way' and stand up for themselves in male-dominated environments. The issue of mixed groups for unpaid work purposes seemed less of an issue for participants in Area 3. 'Chris' (Area 3, Interview) recalled that he had 'never heard any adverse comments regarding unpaid work… At least not for many, many years'. 'Natasha' (Area 3, Interview) admitted that due to the rurality of the region it was 'difficult to get women together, because of the sparsity of women offenders around'.

Reflection Points

This 'update' has revisited and addressed many of the points high-lighted in past research (in relation to magistrates' attitudes to the sentencing of women and knowledge of gender-specific provision in the community), but also raised some new concerns following the introduction of the Offender Rehabilitation Act in 2014. Consistent with previous studies, most magistrates were clear that they did not treat women differently and considered *equal* treatment to mean the *same* treatment. This situation persists despite official guidance to the contrary, and it is clear that official bodies (including the Ministry of Justice, NOMS, the Judicial Office and the Magistrates' Association) should work to ensure that sentencers are aware of policy develop-ments (see also Hedderman and Barnes 2015; Gelsthorpe and Sharpe 2015; Birkett 2016). It is important to stress, however, that while per-haps not considering women differently, most magistrates were clear that they took the relevant mitigating factors (particularly parenting responsibilities and childcare) into account when sentencing women (see Marougka 2012; Gelsthorpe and Loucks 1997; Birkett 2016). As such, sixty-six percent of survey respondents and the majority of interviewees felt that the sentencing framework was sufficiently flexi-ble in this regard. Thirty-four percent of survey respondents did not, however, and continued to express frustration that the current frame-work did not allow them to take into consideration the specific needs of women.

As reflected in other studies, most magistrates expressed frustration with the lack of information they received about suitable community options for women. The vast majority (including sixty-two percent of survey respondents) had no idea about what happened on community sentences or the precise activities that women undertook. Particular concerns related to the introduction of the RAR. Magistrates' con-cerns in this regard, also highlighted in a number of reports published by HMIP, must be prioritised if it is to develop into the 'flagship' rehabilitative element of community orders. While acknowledging that information about the *exact* activities that offenders undertake is beyond the sentencing requirements, studies have demonstrated that sentencer knowledge of provision and confidence in it are entwined. This point is an important one, given the current government objectives for magistrates to make full use of community sentencing options for women. This research therefore emphasises a message already delivered by past studies—the importance of sentencer information on community sentencing options, something that magistrates themselves have expressed a desire for. Information should be provided on a national scale but must also be communicated by the CRCs via local channels so that magistrates have a greater awareness of provision in their area.

Sufficient information also needs to filter through court reports. Magistrates are clearly influenced by their content (see Minson 2015), now completed by NPS court staff. It is concerning that a recent report by HMIP revealed that the lack of information included in court reports 'did not always enable the court to make a judgement about the most suitable community sentence' (2017, p. 18). While it is not possible to prove whether the information included in court reports has deteriorated following the implementation of the Offender Rehabilitation Act, it is clear that magistrates need to have sufficient confidence that the two agencies of offender management (the NPS and the CRCs) are working closely together and in the best interests of their shared clients. The ability for CRCs to demonstrate the suitability and enforceability of rehabilitation activities (through the development of clear lines of communication with external providers, such as women's centres) to sentencers (via the NPS) must also be addressed.

A final area of reflection relates to unpaid work. Given their financial incentive to ensure that women comply with the terms of their order, it makes logical sense for CRCs to develop unpaid work placements that are more suited to the needs of women (making greater use of single placements, allowing women to undertake work in female-only groups or providing more flexible forms of part-time work to take place). If magistrates are to support the government's intentions to punish more non-violent, low-risk women in the community, then the sentencing options available to do this must work for women as well as men. Such a strategy is not radical, but simply reflects the government's expectations for women under the Transforming Rehabilitation reforms.[8]

Notes

1. Following the implementation of the Offender Rehabilitation Act 2014, the existing Probation Trusts were split into two. The National Probation Service (NPS) remains under government control and is responsible for managing the most 'high'-risk offenders in the community (and providing services in the courts). The 21 new Community Rehabilitation Companies (CRCs) are responsible for managing those deemed to be 'low' or 'medium' risk in the community. Most are run by private companies and, in addition to a block sum, receive some of their funding via a system of payment by results.
2. Which requires sentencers to 'do right to all manner of people after the laws and usages of this realm, without fear or favour, affection or ill will'.
3. These reports may also include a full risk assessment of the offender.
4. Oral reports are used for less complex cases where the sentencing court requires only a limited amount of information.
5. Specific funding for women's community services under the Coalition government totalled £5.2 million (jointly funded by the independent Corston Independent Funders Coalition) in 2010–2012, £3.78 million by NOMS in 2012–2013 and £3.78 million in 2013–2014 through Probation Clusters (National Audit Office 2013: 5).
6. The CRCs receive funding in two parts. They receive a fee for their 'through the gate' services and delivering the sentences of the courts. They receive additional funding according to their ability to reduce reoffending rates (Payment by Results).
7. It is important to note that the requirements are not mutually exclusive and some orders many contain a RAR as well as an accredited programme, drug and/or alcohol treatment requirement.
8. The Ministry of Justice (2014) has stated its expectation that the CRCs should make provision for women to be supervised by female officers, attend probation in women-only settings and no longer complete unpaid work in mixed groups *where practicable.*

References

Annison, J., Brayford, J., & Deering, J. (Eds.). (2015). *Women and criminal justice: From the corston report to transforming rehabilitation*. Bristol: Policy Press.

Birkett, G. (2016). 'We have no awareness of what they actually do': Magistrates' knowledge of and confidence in community sentences for women offenders in England and Wales. *Criminology and Criminal Justice, 16*(4), 497–512.

Birkett, G. (2017). *Media, politics and penal reform: Influencing women's punishment*. Basingstoke: Palgrave Macmillan.

Carlen, P. (1983). *Women's imprisonment*. London: Routledge and Kegan Paul.

Cavadino, M., Dignan, J., & Mair, G. (2013). *The penal system: An introduction* (5th ed.). London: Sage.

Corcoran, M. (2011). Dilemmas of institutionalization in the penal voluntary sector. *Critical Social Policy, 31*(1), 30–52.

Criminal Justice Joint Inspection. (2011). *Thematic inspection report: Equal but different? An inspection of the use of alternatives to custody for women offenders*. Manchester: HM Inspectorate of Probation.

Eaton, M. (1986). *Justice for women*. Milton Keynes: Open University Press.

Farrington, D., & Morris, A. (1983). Sex, sentencing and reconviction. *British Journal of Criminology, 23*(3), 229–248.

Gelsthorpe, L. (1992). Social inquiry reports: Race and gender considerations. *Research Bulletin, 32*, 17–22.

Gelsthorpe, L., & Loucks, N. (1997). Magistrates' explanations of sentencing decisions. In C. Hedderman & L. Gelsthorpe (Eds.), *Understanding the sentencing of women* (Home Office Research Study 170). London: Home Office.

Gelsthorpe, L., & Sharpe, G. (2015). Women and sentencing: Challenges and choices. In J. Roberts (Ed.), *Exploring sentencing practice in England and Wales*. Basingstoke: Palgrave Macmillan.

Gelsthorpe, L., Sharpe, G., & Roberts, J. (2007). *Provision for women offenders in the community*. London: Fawcett Society.

Hedderman, C. (2004). Why are more women being sentenced to custody? In G. McIvor (Ed.), *Women who offend: Research highlights in social work 44* (pp. 82–92). London: Jessica Kingsley.

Hedderman, C. (2011). Policy developments in England and Wales. In R. Sheehan, G. McIvor, & C. Trotter (Eds.), *Working with women offenders in the community* (pp. 26–44). Abingdon: Willan.

Hedderman, C. (2012). *Empty cells or empty words? Report for the criminal justice alliance*. London: Criminal Justice Alliance.

Hedderman, C., & Barnes, R. (2015). Sentencing women: An analysis of recent trends. In J. Roberts (Ed.), *Exploring sentencing practice in England and Wales* (pp. 93–117). Basingstoke: Palgrave Macmillan.

Hedderman, C., Palmer, E., & Hollin, C. (2008). *Implementing services for women offenders and those 'at risk' of offending: Action research with together women*. London: Ministry of Justice.

Heidensohn, F. (1985). *Women and crime*. Basingstoke: Macmillan Press.

Her Majesty's Inspectorate of Probation. (2016). *Thematic inspection of the provision and quality of services in the community for women who offend*. Manchester: HMIP.

Her Majesty's Inspectorate of Probation. (2017). *The implementation and delivery of rehabilitation activity requirements*. Manchester: HMIP.

Home Office. (2001). *The government's strategy for women offenders*. London: The Stationery Office.

Horn, R., & Evans, M. (2000). The effect of gender on pre-sentence reports. *Howard Journal of Criminal Justice, 39*(2), 184–197.

Howard League for Penal Reform. (2014). *Mitigating motherhood: A study of the impact of motherhood on sentencing decisions in England and Wales*. London: The Howard League.

Jolliffe, D., Hedderman, C., Palmer, E., & Hollin, C. (2011). *Re-offending analysis of women offenders referred to Together Women (TW) and the scope to divert from custody*. London: Ministry of Justice.

Judicial College. (2013). *Equal treatment bench book*. Available at: https://www.judiciary.gov.uk/wp-content/uploads/JCO/Documents/judicial-college/ETBB_all_chapters_final.pdf.

Lemon, N. (1974). Training, personality and attitude as determinants of magistrates' sentencing. *British Journal of Criminology, 14*(1), 34–48.

Marougka, M. (2012). *Sentencing women: Considering the factors that influence decision-making*. Available at: http://www.thegriffinssociety.org/system/files/papers/fullreport/griffins_research_report_2012-03_final.pdf.

Ministry of Justice. (2007). *The government's response to the report by Baroness Corston of a review of women with particular vulnerabilities in the criminal justice system*. London: The Stationery Office.

Ministry of Justice. (2013a). *Transforming rehabilitation: A strategy for reform*. London: Ministry of Justice.

Ministry of Justice. (2013b). *Transforming rehabilitation: A strategy for reform* (Response to Consultation CP(R) 16/2013). London: Ministry of Justice.

Ministry of Justice. (2014). *Update on delivery of the government's strategic objectives for female offenders*. London: Ministry of Justice.

Ministry of Justice. (2016). *Offender management caseload statistics*. London: Ministry of Justice.

Minson, S. (2015). Sentencing and dependents: Motherhood as mitigation. In J. Roberts (Ed.), *Exploring sentencing practice in England and Wales* (pp. 137–153). Basingstoke: Palgrave Macmillan.

National Audit Office. (2013). *Funding of women's centres in the community: Briefing for the justice select committee*. London: National Audit Office.

Prison Reform Trust. (2015). *Sentencing of mothers: Improving the sentencing process and outcomes for women with dependent children*. London: Prison Reform Trust.

Radcliffe, P., & Hunter, G. (2013). *The development and impact of community service for women offenders: An evaluation*. London: ICPR, Birkbeck College.

Seal, L., & Phoenix, J. (2013). Raw deal: The curious expansion of penal control over women and girls. In A. Dockley & I. Loader (Eds.), *The penal landscape: The howard league guide to criminal justice in England and Wales* (pp. 167–188). Abingdon: Routledge.

Sentencing Advisory Panel. (2009). *Advice to the sentencing guidelines council: Overarching principles of sentencing*. London: Sentencing Advisory Panel.

Worrall, A. (1990). *Offending women: Female law breakers and the criminal justice system*. London: Routledge.

8

Why Training Is Not Improving the Police Response to Sexual Violence Against Women: A Glimpse into the 'Black Box' of Police Training

Elizabeth A. Stanko OBE and Katrin Hohl

Introduction

Few allegations of rape are reported to police. Even fewer rape allegations reach court, and even fewer still result in the conviction of the alleged suspect (CPS 2016). This outcome is replicated throughout the world. Characterised as the 'justice gap' (see, for instance, Horvath and Brown 2009), the process of investigating rape allegations was the subject of a ten-year inquiry inside the London Metropolitan Police Service (MPS). Two full months' data in 2012 was the focus of more detailed analysis (Hohl and Stanko 2015). This analysis showed that victim withdrawal of complaints accounts for almost half of the attrition of the 587 sample cases studied. The next largest contribution to

E. A. Stanko OBE (✉) · K. Hohl
Department of Sociology, City, University of London,
London, UK

K. Hohl
e-mail: Katrin.Hohl.1@city.ac.uk

© The Author(s) 2018
E. Milne et al. (eds.), *Women and the Criminal Justice System*,
https://doi.org/10.1007/978-3-319-76774-1_8

167

attrition was the police decision to take no further action, *accounting for 67% of attrition in non-withdrawn allegations.* These decisions are rarely scrutinised by anyone outside of policing. Analysis shows that there are three critical factors present in decisions to proceed in the allegation data recorded by police: the availability of independent evidence of the incident, the identification of a suspect who is a 'credible criminal', and the assessment that a complainant is 'credible'. All of these strengthen the likelihood that an allegation will result in a charge by the Crown Prosecution Service (CPS).

The Angiolini Review found that rape myths still influenced the way police manage rape complaints, and that the officers who were in roles to support rape victims perceived victims as 'not telling the truth' (2015: 76). The enquiry concluded that there was a compelling case for improvement in the police management of rape and sexual assault. There is growing acceptance, from the Angiolini Review to Her Majesty's Inspectorate of Constabulary (HMIC) (an independent police oversight body in England and Wales), that victims who report rape to police in London are more likely to be highly vulnerable (see also Stanko and Williams 2009), more likely to know their assailant, and only occasionally involve a complete stranger attacking a victim without warning. Four key vulnerabilities dominate rape allegations reported in London over the decade of the MPS study: the complainant is young (under 18) at the time of the rape; drugs and alcohol mis-/overuse are present (either for the victim, the assailant or both); the complainant has mental health issues; and there is a domestic abuse/violence context. Police investigation, as the consensus of research and the conclusions from a raft of enquiries point out, needs to be viewed through the lens of how vulnerable victim experiences sexual assault/exploitation (Horvath and Brown 2009; Brown and Walklate 2011; Hohl and Stanko 2015; Williams and Stanko 2016). What seems to be continuously frustrating to activists, scholars and government officials is how little seems to have improved in the justice outcomes for those who report rape to the police despite decades of scrutiny.

Debates—seemingly endless—about why these institutional changes have *not* resulted in incremental improvement across the board in the policing of sexual violence against women often return to the mantra that police officers need to be provided with more *training*. But *why* should training lead to improvement in police decision-making and action? Training, as a lever (or theory) of change, is expected to be a mechanism to change police actions and responses but thinking about training as a mechanism of change too often removes it from the culture and structures within which police decisions are made (see Hoyle 1998). While police culture, societal expectations and personnel are continuously changing over time, police training is largely hermetically sealed within the core culture of policing, one that continues to be criticised for its macho culture, lack of diversity and command and control ethos. Few outsiders see training in action. Essentially, police train police, and any insight from scholarship and/or research, and even force performance or HMIC inspections, is generally kept at arms' length from the training school preparations because there is no active mechanism to address these concerns from within. This observation is important for activists and campaigners working on policing improvement to understand because they too call for more and better training. The growing impact of a feminist critique has been felt inside policing: few police forces would for instance not recognise the fact that the overwhelming majority of victims of domestic abuse and rape and sexual assault are women and girls. But how has this recognition permeated into the way police are trained to respond to these demands for policing intervention? And what does the evidence tell us about the link between training, learning and improvement? What kind of insight from the feminist research on sexual violence against women and girls needs to permeate the way 'the police train the police'?

This chapter aims to stimulate critical debate about police training in the area of sexual violence against women. It draws on the authors experience of working with two police forces, as part of a Police Knowledge Fund (PKF) project, to co-produce an evidence-informed training package for Sexual Offences Investigative Trained (SOIT) officers, and the lead author's experience in working inside a police force for 15 years.

What we present in this chapter are personal observations and reflections based on these experiences—a glimpse into the 'black box' of police training. Fully opening the 'black box', i.e. a systematic analysis of police training in the area of sexual violence against women and girls, would require a level of transparency and openness to outside scrutiny that at present does not exist.

The remainder of the chapter is structured as follows. First, we discuss why police training is a popular solution suggested to improve police response to sexual violence against women and girls. Then, based on our observations of working with training units, we outline some defining features of police training that we believe are crucial in understanding how police training is carried out in practice, and the barriers they present to improving police response to wider violence against women through training. In particular, we reflect on the challenges of academic-police collaborations aimed at introducing an evidence-informed element to police training on sexual violence and engaging with victims of sexual violence. The final section asks, through the conceptual framework of 'craft vs. science' in policing (Willis 2013) and the adult learning literature, how training might improve officer decision-making in 'messy' domestic abuse and complex sexual offences cases involving vulnerable victims.

Training as the Solution?

The continuous search for improvement in the policing of violence against women has largely pinned its hopes on the influence of 'better' police training. At the same time, changes in organisational practice or the role of inspection presume that the 'best' training is available, and as such bespoke specialist roles have been developed in some forces to deal specifically with domestic abuse or rape victims. The recognition of rape, sexual assault and domestic abuse, as key performance improvement areas in strategic force-wide plans and performance regimes, has been prompted by the active monitoring by HMIC of the operationalisation of the policing practice to help and to support domestic abuse and sexual assault victims (HMIC 2017).

Despite the rather sparse evidence base, there is a stubborn insistence in putting forward recommendations that presume that training leads to improvement. The available knowledge about the policing of domestic abuse—far more studied than the policing of rape—is used here as an example of the problems of 'training' better police officers by police officer trainers. The College of Policing's (CoP) own research on the impact of training on coercive control aimed to measure change in the police officer's understanding of domestic abuse (Wire and Myhill 2016). Wire and Myhill set out to test whether first responder training on coercive control in one force in England improves police officer knowledge and understanding. There is an assumption in this training package that better understanding will lead to better action and response. The authors test for this using a questionnaire developed specifically for this evaluation. This experimental training package was applied within the current model of 'training' delivery to police officers within their organisations. The findings suggest that the training had 'no impact on officers' general attitudes to domestic abuse' but had some positive effects for some (but not all) indicators of knowledge and understanding of coercive control. In other words, training per se is not a silver bullet or 'solution' to the issues identified by researchers and by the HMIC for changing the practice of policing domestic abuse.

In order to understand why training might not work as intended, the following section outlines some key features of police training in practice as we have observed them in working with police training units and in observing police training on rape and sexual offences. These are personal observations of the authors in working with police forces and, in the case of the first author, working inside a police force for 15 years.

Understanding Police Training in Practice

Handing Down the Craft

Police training has been delivered largely by former operational police officers who bring with them a view about *the way things work from experience in policing and particularly here*. Trainers—at least those in

England and Wales—undergo certification in order to become 'trained trainers' who understand how adults learn. The approach recognises that handing down the *craft* from one officer to another often relies on tacit knowledge (not academic knowledge) to share good practice. Some of this craft is highly specialised and has a tradition of 'perfected practice' in areas such as homicide investigation, advanced driving, public order policing or firearms training. Professional skill development—especially for police officers seeking to learn a different operational role such as a sexual assault liaison officer—takes place *inside policing* and rests on police internal knowledge, taking little account of other sources of information (and particularly independent academic evidence). The approaches and techniques that are being handed down have rarely been tested and are not challenged by those outside the police, least of all from academic research, because the world of in-house training is largely hermetically sealed to outside eyes and ears.

Insulation from Academic Evidence and Scrutiny

Because police training is largely sealed off from outside scrutiny, there is little transparency, educational review or accountability for what is being taught. What we found working with police forces on the sexual assault liaison officer course was that reviews of learning material take place internally, behind closed doors. There is a platform for online learning but not for sexual assault liaison officers. There was neither scrutiny from outside the police service of the sexual assault liaison officer course material nor any way to assess whether the learning approach helps 'improve' police response or is compatible with science or systematic academic research evidence on rape and sexual assault. Course attendance for officers choosing this role typically requires 'abstraction' from operational duties, meaning the learner attends the training in person, with little written training material available for the learners to take home, review and to refresh (with the exception of the written law on sexual assault and rape). A largely oral culture of training, with little written documentation, limits the practical ways in which training units can be scrutinised and held to account. The COP has, in part, been created to set national standards for training and professional practice. For sexual offence investigation, including the SOIT role, there currently exists no national standard or nationally accredited training, and no Authorised Professional Practice (APP)[1] guide to enable police force training units to tether their training to what is considered to be best practice.

There is currently almost total reliance on craft-based, police officer trainers who have had little exposure to the evolving academic knowledge about the impact of sexual violence on victims and their contact with police. At present, the influence of 'research and evidence-based practice' is extremely limited; police training units write and prepare their own lesson and learning plans in-house, or use those from the COP (which for sexual assault do not exist). Training units often do not have the capacity or resources to access, evaluate, and use academic research fully. To give one example of the practical barriers to using outside evidence from the PKF project, police IT firewall settings meant officers were not able to receive academic articles on the topic of rape or sexual violence via email due to those words ('sexual' or 'rape') being contained in the text.

Unfortunately too, there is little scientific research on how police training *works* to change behaviour (i.e, what is the mechanism for change?). There is sparser evidence on how best to 'train' for investigating complexity and complex situations involving vulnerable victims, such as in cases of sexual assault and domestic abuse. Development and delivery of training are split and often conducted by separate teams of officers, with training materials passed on to the officers who deliver the training. Trainers and training developers are supposed to be 'experts' in *training*, able to deliver for any topic; they are not subject area experts. The prevailing assumption is that 'police trainers' can deliver any training package by reading out and following the instructions of the training package itself; that trainers do not need to be experts in the subject matter they are delivering. This is flawed. If we expect police officers to be critically thinking, problem-solving professionals who are evidence informed, a different approach to training is urgently needed; one that encourages better learning about what the (scholarly) evidence says about successful interventions *with victims* so that this thinking can be applied to complex situations encountered when responding to domestic abuse, and allegations of rape and sexual assault.

Reproducing Localised Organisational Procedure

Police officer trainers who train police officers for new roles draw upon their own experience of 'doing the role' to inform the substance of the ways of working they wish other police officers to follow; as well as knowledge about the local, social, legal and organisational context for 'best practice' from their operational experience. Police trainers may also rely on 'command' to provide an invisible funnel through which new information is assimilated into police action. 'This is the way we do things around here' is an expression used to convey a host of hierarchical and unspoken conventions about ways of working. Within the UK policing network, there is an acceptance that process and procedure will differ between forces (e.g. forms or the way officers tape evidence bags may differ). Within a police force, knowing local convention conveys competence, especially important for new joiners to operational units. Understanding how things work locally may also imply knowledge about how a particular commanding officer or a particular unit requires operational officers to conduct investigations, consult the officer in charge or share information. Developing a lesson plan on what constitutes a problem and how to manage it (as police action, process and procedure) is constructed through the lens of localised, organisational process. Telling trainees 'what to do' turns the job into using *process and procedure* as an anchor for deciding how to respond to a situation, event or report of a crime. However, if training is to provide access to knowledge which is validated outwith the police culture, then an officer needs to be exposed to that information. In theory, this information could influence practice and act as a buffer to traditional ways of working and promote iterative improvement from within.

Police training though is largely overshadowed by local force process and procedure, an invisible institutional framework to exclude knowledge that is generated outside policing itself. These differences loomed large in the work conducted with forces described below. Much time and effort was expended working through individual force procedure to enable the two forces collaborating with the project to identify common ground on which learning could be improved. Regardless of where an operational officer works, each individual police officer (who is providing vital support to sexual assault victims) is continuously confronted by having to make informed (and defensible) decisions about very complex situations. Routinely accounting for how policing decisions are made (when, why and often under some form of supervision) invisibly underpins traditional training. We also found that the work of the training unit is not routinely informed by the police force's way of accounting for its success in its business. There is—at least in these training units—no internal in-house feedback loop to assess whether what the police trainers are training officers to do 'works', or make any difference in the performance of a police force in terms of delivering 'good enough policing.'

The Status of Training Within the Organisation

Working within a police training unit, preparing the next generation of officers for their role, does not confer much status within the police organisation. Too often training is considered a 'dead zone', where officers who have grown weary of front-line work, or officers who are burnt out and 'need a rest', or who can't find a role in the rest of the organisation, train others to do what they no longer wish to do. These training officers may have been out of operations for a long time. They may not have been the best practitioners either. They are seldom developed professionally as learning specialists. While these issues have been recognised in a number of HMIC reviews (HMIC 2002; Neyroud 2010), they remain a significant organisational barrier to improvement to learning within the police service.

Police-Academic Co-production of SOIT Training

This chapter draws on learning from a police-academic collaboration funded through the UK's PKF. The project translated academic research on the policing response to rape into a new training programme designed for sexual assault liaison police officers (SOITs) in two forces in England. The process of creating a new approach to improving sexual assault liaison officer training was informed by research evidence mentioned earlier and published in 2015 in the London study of rape allegations (see Hohl and Stanko 2015). The lessons learnt from the academic-police collaboration's creation of a new training course in the two partner forces can be shared with other police forces at home here in the UK and abroad.

In order for innovative, evidence-infused police training 'to be understood and relevant', there must be a broad alignment of what is considered to be 'good policing' (HMIC 2014) or 'good enough policing' (Bowling 2007) shared across borders. These reflections here will largely focus on the grounding of 'what is meant by good training' or 'good enough' training, so that policing is better (after all, that is the purpose of training—improving professionalism). This explicitly means that somehow—and over time—the impact of the training should be able to be measured, transparent, and experienced by victims who report sexual assault as 'good enough'.

Sexual assault liaison policing is a specialist role inside the police service in England and Wales, differing among the forty-four police forces. Some of the roles combine victim support with sexual assault investigation; other forces separate the two roles. The approach to a force's policing role and the place of policing of sexual assault within this may differ between forces. 'Training' officers for this role is largely in-house, in-force. Force police training approaches should be compatible with national training standards set by the COP so sexual assault training modules should abide by learning objectives specified by the College but these do not yet require that the specific information within any module aligns with the available (best) evidence according to *academic* standards. Training on how to interview *witnesses and particularly suspects* has been influenced by psychology. Cognitive interviewing, whose evidence base is largely influenced by its research with university student samples, frames the section of the course devoted to interviewing practice. Although drawing on the academic evidence that demonstrates that victims report feeling 'not believed' or 'being blamed' for the sexual assault, our study found there was no course material that set out the problem of sexual assault offending as a problem of exploiting vulnerability (the evidence is presented in Hohl and Stanko 2015). Preparation of any training delivered to officers desiring a new role is largely undertaken by training units within individual police forces, and as outlined above, the 'evidence' basis for what an officer 'does' and how she/he 'does it' is largely managed through in-house *craft-based* skill development and rarely observed in situ by anyone other that police practitioners. At present, there is a gap in academic knowledge about the impact of such training on police practice across the country and in the force itself. There is also a gap in exploring whether what is being taught accords with the academic evidence about the nature of rape and sexual assault, a criticism found in much of the academic literature on the experience of victims.

A Review of Sexual Assault Liaison Officer Training

The PKF project's theory of change draws on what the research evidence says about factors that contribute to victim outcomes for rape allegations. The research (Hohl and Stanko 2015) highlights the vulnerabilities of victims through an analysis of allegations reported to a local police force and demonstrates the influence of these vulnerabilities on outcomes. This theory of change suggests that better evidence-informed training (officers attuned and better informed about victim vulnerabilities and the implications for criminal investigations) would strengthen (or at least align) police training with improving the justice outcomes of rape allegations. An evidence-informed course would set out to develop explicitly an appreciative inquiry approach to putting victim vulnerability at the heart of sexual liaison police officer training and require the trainees to think differently in order to make decisions informed by victim need. Although only a partial 'fix' to 'whole system' improvement in the investigation of rape allegation (e.g. there needs to be more work regarding the interviewing skills of officers who are, after all, interviewing highly vulnerable victims), the project provides new insight into the process of academic-police collaboration on police training.

The PKF project opened the discussion in the two forces' training units about how the needs of the complainant of rape and the needs of the investigation are often in tension. These needs are not fixed, and learning to balance these should be part of the core competency of a successfully trained specialist officer. The needs of the complainant are framed by the kinds of vulnerabilities complainants 'bring with them' when reporting a rape. As noted above, understanding the nature of these vulnerabilities should enable officers to prepare in advance how they will manage these vulnerabilities within the investigation window. These should be made explicit, as these are common issues officers will be managing in their roles. What we found in the discussions was that while academics on the project foregrounded 'victim vulnerability', police trainers had previously put this in the background, with legal definitions, process and procedures being prioritised over the under-standing of how vulnerability is important in recorded allegations of rape.

Co-producing Sexual Assault Liaison Officer Training

Working with two forces meant that there were two different approaches to the policing roles that 'support victims' and 'lead investigations', and thus there were different in-house training designs for that support. The project working group (comprising academics and police officers) agreed to two key changes to the previous training course that were critical to better delivery. First, there was the inclusion *as a core part of the lesson plan* of the use of case studies reflecting the kinds of vulnerabilities that those who allege rape have. Second, the training package addressed 'well-being' needs of the police officers themselves, as officer resilience is often stretched when working with victims with serious vulnerabilities. The PKF project found that sexual assault liaison officers struggled to reconcile the conflicting demands of the police investigation and safeguarding the victim's well-being, as well as keeping the victim 'on board' and engaged in the investigation. One common example that liaison officers would give is that while an exhausted and traumatised victim is likely to be desperate to shower and sleep, and ask to be taken home, the investigating officer might instruct the officer to interview the victim and take forensic evidence regardless, so the investigation can commence and potential arrests can be made. The training package aimed to equip officers with the understanding and skills to negotiate these situations and also be mindful of their own well-being.

Both forces have now pledged to use the new training materials, harnessing the information on victim vulnerabilities (e.g. proportion of victims who are underage, used drugs or alcohol prior to the attack, or have a current or previous intimate relationship with the perpetrator) and use cases dealt with by the local police force as case study materials. It took a lot of effort to shift 'the way we do things around here' for just one course.

Conceptualising Police Training: Craft vs. Science

Reflecting on our observations of police training practice, and the co-production of the SOIT training package in particular, Willis's (2013) distinction between *craft-based* and *science-based* skill development appears a useful framework to apply to the current approach to training (see also Willis and Mastrofski 2016). Willis discusses policing as a profession through a framework characterising police knowledge as influenced by 'craft' (experience) versus 'science' (academic research/ evidence informed). He suggests that *science-based* (or even *science-informed*) approaches are less prevalent. Willis further proposes that improvement in policing would and should enable a more scientific-aligned way of working that does sit comfortably alongside the historical craft-based way of working. This framework has implications for the way we think about police training.

Policing as a *craft-based profession* would approach training and the acquisition of policing skills in supporting rape victims and investigating rape through the lens of 'perfecting craft'. A craft is acquired and improved through practice and is taught by fellow craftspeople (police officers) who *know* about good practice of refined policing skills through their experience of field operations. Applied to the case of sexual assault liaison policing, *craft as 'trained knowledge'* would be prepared and delivered by police officer trainers for police officer trainees, designed to show the trainees how to respond to, for example, a rape victim, using in-house force approved tools[2]—emphasising the legal provisions, legal processes and internal police procedures. There may or may not be input from victim support workers. Improvement in craft may be measured in the refinement of applying force procedure and protocols to better practice, *but the training itself may not challenge traditional ways of knowing, thinking and working in the field.*

Craft-based knowledge is infused within *police force cultures* within which craft is acquired (Chan 1997; Bacon 2014). In any police force, it is impossible to avoid this wider cultural context. For a craft savvy police officer, the closer the officer adheres to the process or procedure, the better. Improvement in officer performance is typically measured through looking at the process or procedure, *not by the outcome, nor by how well treated victims feel.* Performance measurement would need to capture, too, whether police were managing the high vulnerability of victims of sexual assault better as a consequence of training. Given the research that now exists about the gap between knowledge regarding domestic abuse and coercive control, and policing action and training (Vigurs et al. 2016; Robinson et al. 2016; Wire and Myhill 2016), it is time to think differently about how to measure the success of training itself. Training alone is not a single solution, but one linked to a full raft of supportive organisational self-awareness that provides systematic feedback to supervisors as well as operational staff. This is the purpose of continuous professional development, critical for any profession.

Improving Complex Decision-Making Through Training

There is limited or no evidence in policing on which to base any chosen approach for the mode or method of training (see Wheller and Morris 2010 for a review). According to Mugford et al. (2013: 312) 'what is currently absent in the police training literature are concrete empirically supported instructional strategies that can be incorporated into training to promote the long-term retention and transfer of learned skills and knowledge.' This has implications for police training practitioners—the approaches taken to improve their trainees' actions on the job are not yet evidence informed, simply because this evidence does not yet exist. Instead, police trainers largely rely on what they 'did' when they were operational officers. As a result, police forces are unable to rely on police trainers who are knowledgeable about the latest academic evidence and developments in the professional skills they are passing on.

Recent HMIC inspections on public protection, domestic abuse and child sexual exploitation indicate that police forces have not yet delivered a *significant* and sustained change in practice (HMIC and HMCPSI 2012; HMIC 2015). Nor has the police service agreed on what constitutes 'success'—is this in the victim's eyes (good and fair treatment regardless of criminal justice outcome), the police officer's eyes (an investigation accepted as a charged case by the CPS) or some combination of organisational performance outcomes? Nor has the police service yet delivered a 'good enough' police training response in the policing of domestic abuse (Bowling 2007). There is little evidence-based knowledge about how training might change police behaviour and action (see Neyroud 2010). A theory of change might make transparent the issues that may be contributing to the continued 'confusion' around what to do when responding to a domestic and/or sexual assault incident. As Mugford et al. remind us (2013: 317) 'in "naturalistic" scenarios, information on what actions to take draw on a multiplicity of knowledge that must be brought together in a collective way to address a complex issue'. Put simply, complex *decision-making requires applying knowledge, improving knowledge and reflectively reviewing practice as a consequence.*

In situations of rape and sexual assault, police officers have complex decisions to make and thus would benefit from ongoing, iterative social science insight to guide their organisational responses. The research on violence against women documents its complex nature (Kelly 2002; Kelly et al. 2005; Hohl and Stanko 2015). A large volume of literature explores female victims' responses to men's violence, and these responses are also complex and include coping mechanisms which make any policing investigation tricky (Stanko 1985; Kelly 1988; Jordan 2008). As police officers are expected to assess the victim's need to trigger legal interventions (criminal as well as civil), the more assistance police officers have in understanding female victims' coping mechanisms, the better. Indeed, these are not just the lessons of female victims—the complexities of gender loom large in sexual violence of men and boys too (Davies 2002). But these complexities also deserve a gender-based approach in scholarly knowledge unpicking how men and boys are exploited sexually.

Returning to sexual offences training, a training session rarely starts with a clear analysis of what the victims are telling police about the problem of sexual assault *locally*. What are the circumstances presented by those who report sexual assault or rape, and how do these circumstances challenge the application of law? What most police services will admit is that most victims know their offenders, and that the circumstances of applying law require unpicking tricky issues of consent, force and exploitation of vulnerability in these pre-existing relationships. This is not easy. For forces using practitioner trainers, a focus on applying procedure and law does not help steer trainees' skills towards gathering (best) evidence of what happened and how that evidence might demonstrate a violation of law. The impact of 'messy' cases on high demand for limited resources requires far more attention and time, and in the age of austerity, often causes frustration and/or officers' stress and burnout inside policing. The ability to *train* police officers requires police officers to acknowledge the business they manage ('messy cases'), *learn* how to manage 'messiness' differently using insights from scholarly research on victims' vulnerability to exploitation, adapt the learning to enable officers to understand the business of sexual assault allegations, and apply their practice and problem-solving skills to the kinds of rape allegations that actually are reported to their local police service.

Concluding Remarks

Just over half of London victims turn away from justice after they contact police (Hohl and Stanko 2015). These victims disengage. This does not mean that the rape allegations they report are unfounded;

what we know about these victims is that the majority are highly vulnerable at the time of the assault. These incidents deserve much more understanding so that we might improve victims' experience *and* victims' strength to challenge assailants. There is academic research that tells us why vulnerability might cause victims to back away from justice, *but not what to do differently as a consequence of knowing this.* If the UK has learned anything in the past five years from the scandals of historical sexual abuse allegations, it is that few victims felt they were taken seriously, felt that they were believed or felt that they had the strength to push back against 'rape myths' seeping into their exchanges with authorities (see Chapter 10, this volume). Linking police training with an analysis of the situation of victims who report rape allegations locally requires the police service to know what kinds of sexual allegations come to their attention and how to respond best to the kinds of vulnerabilities these victims bring with them when they turn to the police for help.

There remains a gulf between academic language and practitioner language, and this communication gap hinders the integration of 'academic/outside the force' knowledge into training, procedures and understanding inside the police force. Police forces should invite academics with subject matter expertise and expert operational practitioners to participate, to observe and to help transform training. Both must be willing to understand the evidence and the insight from both perspectives, to value both craft and science. The co-production of the content and the approach to the training will be uncomfortable and irritating at times but the space within which the police 'train their own' has tended to be a closed shop for too long.

Notes

1. APP is developed and owned by the COP (the UK professional body for policing). APP is authorised by the COP as the official source of professional practice on policing. Police officers and staff are expected to have regard to APP in discharging their responsibilities.
2. Since 2009 all UK police forces are expected to use the Domestic Abuse, Stalking and Harassment (DASH) tool.

References

Angiolini, E. (2015). *Report of the independent review into the investigation and prosecution of rape in London*. London: CPS. Available at: http://www.cps.gov.uk/publications/equality/vaw/dame_elish_angiolini_rape_review_2015.pdf (Accessed 14 June 2017).

Bacon, M. (2014). Policing culture and the new policing context. In J. Brown (Ed.), *The future of policing*. London: Routledge.

Bowling, B. (2007). Fair and effective policing methods: Towards 'good enough' policing. *Journal of Scandinavian Studies in Criminology and Crime Prevention, 8*(1), 579–619.

Brown, J., & Walklate, S. (Eds.). (2011). *Handbook on sexual violence*. London: Routledge.

Chan, J. (1997). *Changing police culture: Policing in a multicultural society*. Cambridge: Cambridge University Press.

Crown Prosecution Service (CPS). (2016). *Violence against women and girls. Crime report 2015–2016*. Available at: http://www.cps.gov.uk/publications/docs/cps_vawg_report_2016.pdf (Accessed 14 June 2017).

Davies, M. (2002). Male victims of sexual assault: A selective review of the literature and implications for support services. *Aggression and Violent Behavior, 7*(3), 203–214.

Her Majesty's Inspectorate of Constabulary (HMIC). (2002). *Training matters*. London: Her Majesty's Government. Available at: https://www.justiceinspectorates.gov.uk/hmic/media/training-matters-20020101.pdf (Accessed 22 June 2017).

Her Majesty's Inspectorate of Constabulary (HMIC). (2014). *Everyone's business: Improving the police response to domestic abuse*. Available at: https://www.justiceinspectorates.gov.uk/hmic/wp-content/uploads/2014/04/improving-the-police-response-to-domestic-abuse.pdf (Accessed 14 June 2017).

Her Majesty's Inspectorate of Constabulary (HMIC). (2015). *Increasingly everyone's business: A progress report on the police response to domestic abuse*. Available at: http://www.justiceinspectorates.gov.uk/hmic/wp-content/uploads/increasingly-everyones-business-domestic-abuse-progress-report.pdf (Accessed 14 June 2017).

Her Majesty's Inspectorate of Constabulary (HMIC). (2017). *Rape Monitoring Group*. London: Her Majesty's Government. Available at: https://www.justiceinspectorates.gov.uk/hmic/about-us/working-with-others/rape-monitoring-group/ (Accessed 14 June 2017).

Her Majesty's Inspectorate of Constabulary (HMIC) and Her Majesty's Crown Prosecution Service Inspectorate (HMCPSI). (2012). *Forging the links: Rape investigation and prosecution. A joint inspection by HMCPSI and HMIC.* London: HMCPSI and HMIC. Available at: https://www.justiceinspectorates.gov.uk/hmic/media/forging-the-links-rape-investigation-and-prosecution-20120228.pdf (Accessed 14 June 2017).

Hohl, K., & Stanko, E. (2015). Complaints of rape and the criminal justice system: Fresh evidence on the attrition problem in England and Wales. *European Journal of Criminology, 12*(3), 324–341.

Horvath, A., & Brown, J. (Eds.). (2009). *Rape: Challenging contemporary thinking.* Cullompton: Willan.

Hoyle, C. (1998). *Negotiating domestic violence: Police, criminal justice and victims.* Oxford: Oxford University Press.

Jordan, J. (2008). *Serial survivors: Women's narratives of surviving rape.* Annandale: The Federation Press.

Kelly, L. (1988). *Surviving sexual violence.* Cambridge: Polity.

Kelly, L. (2002). *Routes to (in)justice: A research review on the reporting, investigation and prosecution of rape cases.* London: Her Majesty's Crown Prosecution Service Inspectorate.

Kelly, L., Lovett, J., & Regan, L. (2005). *A gap or a chasm? Attrition in reported rape cases* (Home Office Research Study No. 293). London: HMSO.

Mugford, R., Corey, S., & Bennell, C. (2013). Improving police training from a cognitive load perspective. *Policing: An International Journal of Police Strategies & Management, 36*(2), 312–337.

Neyroud, P. (2010). *Review of police leadership and training.* London: Home Office. Available at: www.gov.uk (Accessed 22 June 2017).

Robinson, A., Pinchevsky, G., & Guthrie, J. (2016). A small constellation: Risk factors informing police perceptions of domestic abuse. *Policing and Society, 28*(2), 189–204. https://doi.org/10.1080/10439463.2016.1151881.

Stanko, E. (1985). *Intimate intrusions: Women's experience of male violence.* London: Routledge.

Stanko, B., & Williams, E. (2009). Reviewing rape and rape allegations in London: What are the vulnerabilities of the victims who report to the police? In A. Horvath & J. Brown (Eds.), *Rape: Challenging contemporary thinking* (pp. 207–228). Cullompton: Willan.

Vigurs, C., Wire, J., Myhill, A., & Gough, D. (2016). *Police initial responses to domestic abuse.* London: College of Policing. Available at: http://whatworks.college.police.uk/Research/Documents/Police_initial_responses_domestic_abuse.pdf (Accessed 14 June 2017).

Wheller, L., & Morris, J. (2010). *Evidence reviews: What works in training, behaviour change and implementing guidance?* London: NPIA. Available at: http://whatworks.college.police.uk/Research/Documents/What_Works_in_Training_and_Behaviour_change_REA.pdf (Accessed 14 June 2017).

Williams, E., & Stanko, B. (2016). Researching sexual violence. In M. Brunger, S. Tong, & D. Martin (Eds.), *Introduction to policing research: Taking lessons from practice* (pp. 121–136). Abingdon, Oxon: Routledge.

Willis, J. (2013). *Improving policing: What's craft got to do with it?* Washington, DC: Police Foundation.

Willis, J., & Mastrofski, S. (2016). Improving policing by integrating craft and science: What can patrol officers teach us about good police work? *Policing and Society, 28*(1), 27–44. https://doi.org/10.1080/10439463.2015.1135921.

Wire, J., & Myhill, A. (2016). *Domestic abuse matters. Evaluation of first responder training.* London: College of Policing. Available online: http://www.college.police.uk/News/Collegenews/Documents/Domestic_Abuse_Matters.pdf (Accessed 14 June 2017).

9

Why Focus on Reducing Women's Imprisonment?

Jenny Earle

Introduction

The Prison Reform Trust (PRT) is an independent UK charity working to create a just, humane and effective penal system by inquiring into the workings of the system; providing information to prisoners, staff and the wider public; and by influencing Parliament, government and officials and making the case for reform. The organisation has two principal objectives which are: to reduce unnecessary imprisonment and promote community solutions to crime; and improve treatment and conditions for prisoners and their families.

The Trust provides an Advice and Information service to women and men in prison, is secretariat to the All-Party Parliamentary Group on Penal Affairs and publishes the biannual Bromley Briefing Prison Fact File, recognised as an authoritative source of information about the criminal justice and prison systems.

J. Earle (✉)
Prison Reform Trust, London, UK
e-mail: jenny.earle@prisonreformtrust.org.uk

© The Author(s) 2018
E. Milne et al. (eds.), *Women and the Criminal Justice System*,
https://doi.org/10.1007/978-3-319-76774-1_9

Since 2012, the Trust has been pursuing a programme to reduce women's imprisonment.[1] In this chapter, I set out the objectives and rationale underpinning the *Transforming Lives* strategy, consider opportunities for progress and setbacks encountered. I focus in particular on the intersection where women may be both victim and offender and argue that the impact of histories of trauma, abuse and grief, and involvement in coercive relationships with men, are particularly salient for women's offending. This is a key gender difference—while family and relationships are important protective and supportive factors for men in the criminal justice system, the opposite is more often the case for women.

Background

The PRT has long called for a reduction in women's imprisonment and a step change in how the criminal justice system responds to women. It is over ten years since publication of the Corston Report (2007) on Women with Particular Vulnerabilities in the Criminal Justice System and five years since the Commission on Women Offenders in Scotland (2012), chaired by Dame Angiolini. These and many other inquiries and reports have all concluded that prison is rarely a necessary, proportionate or effective response to women who get caught up in the criminal justice system (PRT 2011; House of Commons Justice Committee 2015). However, because women are such a small minority of the prison population, they are often overlooked. They comprise less than five percent of the prison population and around 15% of those supervised in the community. Criminal justice policies, processes and agencies generally assume that offenders are male and women have therefore been described as 'correctional afterthoughts' (Gobeil et al. 2016). This neglect may be regarded by some as benign, but the evidence is rather that women can be subject to double standards, harsh judgements and punitive responses with often devastating consequences for themselves and their families. 'Criminal women' do not conform to traditional stereotypes and are often regarded as 'other'—other than normal women, other than real criminals and perhaps most significantly—other than real victims (Carlen and Christina 1985). The criminal justice system relies heavily on a 'clear differentiation between the totally innocent victim and the totally guilty offender' (Rumgay 2010, p. 49), a distinction routinely reinforced by popular media. However, there is mounting evidence that many women in prison have been victims of much worse crimes—including physical or sexual abuse during childhood, domestic violence or sexual exploitation as adults—than those they may have committed. A significant proportion of foreign national women in prison have been trafficked into offending (Hales and Gelsthorpe 2012). This needs to be better recognised and understood. The purpose of this chapter is to demonstrate the significance of the linkages between women's exposure to male violence, coercion and abuse and their own offending behaviour. This is not to argue that there is always a direct causal link, or that women lack agency, but that a vicious circle of victimisation and criminal activity can develop, creating a toxic lifestyle that is extremely difficult to escape (Rumgay 2010; Loveless 2010).

Objectives of the Transforming Lives Programme

For the reasons elaborated in this chapter, the PRT's *Transforming Lives* programme set out to reduce the number of women sent to prison UK-wide. To achieve this goal, the organisation has been working with others to:

- Improve the governance of women's justice across the UK, which requires dedicated leadership and cross-government co-ordination informed by a robust economic case;
- Strengthen the pathways into mental health and social care services for vulnerable women caught in the criminal justice system;
- Increase awareness of the links between women's experience of domestic abuse and their offending;
- Reduce the use of custodial remand unless the seriousness of the offence or the protection of the public demands it;
- Promote non-custodial options particularly for mothers of dependent children;

- Reduce the number of foreign national and black and ethnic minority women in custody;
- Work intensively in local high-custody areas to foster greater use of early intervention, out-of-court disposals and community orders for women.

In 2014, the PRT published the Transforming Lives report in partnership with the UK Programme Action Committee of Soroptimist International Great Britain and Ireland, a women's voluntary organisation committed to inspiring action and improving the lives of women and girls in the UK and worldwide. The organisation has consultative status at the United Nations. In the report's foreword, leading Soroptimist Dr. Kay Richmond notes that,

> Preventing violence against women has been at the core of Soroptimist project work for many years, and having learnt that it is so often an underlying factor in women's offending, we welcomed this opportunity to provide a voice for women who, very often, are victims themselves. (PRT 2014a, p. i)

The report's recommendations for a rebalancing of criminal justice responses to women are based on the action research conducted by local Soroptimist Clubs across the UK (PRT 2013a). Although punitive responses to minor offending are often justified in the name of public opinion, in fact attitudes to crime and punishment can be more nuanced than tabloid political discourse allows. A YouGov opinion poll conducted by the PRT revealed strong support for public health measures to tackle women's offending. Treatment for drug addiction, help to stop alcohol misuse and mental health care were the top three solutions to get public backing for reducing offending by women who commit non-violent crimes (PRT 2017a, p. 11).

Women's Imprisonment—An Overview[2]

The women's prison population in England and Wales more than doubled between 1995 and 2010—from under 2000 to over 4000 women. The numbers subsequently declined by over 10%—from 4279 women in April 2012 to 3821 in April 2016 (PRT 2017a, p. 1). But the UK still has one of the highest rates of women's imprisonment in Western Europe, and in 2017, there were over 4000 women in prison at any one time.[3]

Prison statistics can be confusing, and it is important to understand the difference between a 'snapshot' of the prison population and the total intake (receptions) of individuals into prison over the course of a year. In England and Wales, there are usually fewer than 4000 women in prison at any one time, but around 9000 women are received into prison over the course of a year, either on remand or under sentence, or on recall. The former 'snapshot' figure will have a higher proportion of those on longer sentences, while the latter annual receptions figure includes all those who have been sent to prison even for very short periods. A total of 8562 women were sent to prison in the year to June 2016, including those remanded into custody and those serving a sentence (MoJ 2016a).

Reflecting the less serious nature of their offending, most women entering prison serve very short sentences. In the year to June 2016, 63% of sentenced women entering prison were serving six months or less compared to 47% of men (MoJ 2016a). The use of these very short sentences for women increased by 6% between 2015 and 2016, while the use of community sentences dropped by around a third between 2006 and 2015 (MoJ 2016b). There has also been a significant decline in the use of out-of-court disposals for women and an increase in the use of suspended prison sentences (MoJ 2016c).

Of the women who were sentenced to imprisonment, 84% had committed a non-violent offence compared to 76% of men in prison. More women are sent to prison for theft than for violence against the person, robbery, sexual offences, fraud, drugs and motoring offences combined, and 80% of female theft offences were for shoplifting. Women are twice as likely as men to be in prison for a first offence—22% of women compared to 12% of men have no previous convictions or cautions when first sent to prison (PRT 2017a, p. 2).

Furthermore, there is a continuing over-representation of black and minority ethnic women in prison as they comprise 19% of the women's prison population compared to 14% of the general women's population. Black British women make up 10% of the women's prison population—over three times higher than the 3% they comprise of the general women's population. Analysis conducted for the Lammy Review (2017) of Black, Asian and Minority Ethnic (BAME) representation in the Criminal Justice System found that black women were twice as likely as white women to receive a custodial sentence in the Crown Court for drugs offences. Asian and other minority ethnic women were over 40% more likely than white women to be convicted at magistrates' court (PRT 2017c; Cox and Sacks-Jones 2017).

Gender Differences in Offending, Offenders and Imprisonment

There are a number of key differences in the drivers and patterns of offending between women and men and in the characteristics of female and male offenders, which are reflected in the prison population. These are set out below and provide a compelling evidence base for requiring a distinct, gender-aware criminal justice response to women in contact with the criminal justice system and reduced use of imprisonment.

Abuse and Coercive Relationships

More than half of women in prison (53%) report having experienced emotional, physical or sexual abuse as a child compared to just over a quarter (27%) of men (PRT 2017a, p. 3). In the Offender Assessment System (OASys), the government's operational database that is used to assess the risks and needs of eligible offenders in prison and on probation, 57% of women report having been victims of domestic violence (PRT 2017a, p. 3).[4] Because many women are reluctant to admit or disclose abuse, both these figures are likely to be an underestimate. Inspectorate reports on women's prisons include surveys of the women resident at the time of the inspection, and these confirm high levels of prior victimisation. For example, in HMP Bronzefield, the largest women's prison in the UK since the closure of HMP Holloway, 58% of the women surveyed said they had experienced domestic abuse, and 34% of the women said they were experiencing it at the time they were sent to prison (HMIP 2016, p. 59).

Indeed, women's offending is much more likely than men's to be prompted by their relationships. Nearly half of women in prison (48%) questioned for the *Surveying Prisoner Crime Reduction* survey reported having committed offences to support someone else's drug use compared to 22% of men (Light et al. 2013, p. 16). Women can become trapped in a vicious cycle of victimisation and criminal activity. Their situation is often worsened by poverty, substance dependency or poor mental health. Leaving an abusive relationship can be risky—the period when a woman is planning or making her exit is often the most dangerous for her and her children (Sev'er 1997).

The vulnerability of women to domestic abuse and the impact this can have on their offending have been recognised by national and international organisations. The UN Special Rapporteur on Violence Against Women commented following her mission to the UK,

> It is crucial to develop gender-specific sentencing alternatives and to recognise women's histories of victimisation when making decisions about incarceration. Most women in prison do not present a threat to society and the consequences of their incarceration includes enormous personal, economic and social costs. Creativity in sentencing decisions could lead to more orders of a non-custodial nature. (Manjoo 2014)

She recommended that the UK government should

> Establish specific safeguards to ensure that women's histories of victimization and abuse are taken into consideration when making decisions about incarceration, especially for non-violent crimes. (OHCHR 2015, p. 23)

Women's offending is closely related to their involvement in abusive relationships. In collaboration with User Voice and various women's service providers in England, Wales and Scotland, PRT has discussed with women their experience of committing offences on behalf of or to protect a partner, to support a partner's drug use, under pressure from a partner or otherwise in connection with domestic abuse, including coercive and controlling behaviour. Several women commented that they had committed offences on many occasions and over prolonged periods of time to support a partner's drug use, including by shoplifting, by selling drugs and by committing offences which they did not feel comfortable discussing. They said they felt trapped in these unhealthy relationships.

In general, the women felt that the police were rarely sympathetic or helpful to them as victims of domestic abuse and did not demonstrate an understanding of the dynamics of abusive relationships. Research has confirmed that women encounter a culture of disbelief in the criminal justice system about the violence and exploitation to which they may have been exposed (Hales and Gelsthorpe 2012). Women said they did not have confidence in the police to identify the primary aggressor and protect them as victims. A number of women said it was common for them to be arrested by the police in relation to incidents of domestic violence in which they had not been the primary aggressor. Linked with this was the unwillingness of the women in most cases to support proceedings against their abusive partner. This might be for a variety of reasons including: fear of retaliation from their abusive partner; in order to keep the family together for the sake of the children; because of dependence on their partner for money or a home; because of worries that social services might become involved and they might lose their children; or because they had come to believe that the violence was their fault. As one woman reported in a discussion with PRT, 'You're too scared to charge him because you know you'll get a worse time when he gets out'.

Economic Disadvantage as a Driver

Women's economic disadvantage also plays a part in their offending—both because it is an obstacle to financial independence from men and because it makes them more vulnerable to welfare spending cuts which have come thick and fast in the past decade. A Cabinet Office study of women offenders found that 28% of women's crimes were financially motivated compared to 20% of men's (Cabinet Office Social Exclusion Task Force 2009, p. 15). Earlier research on mothers in custody found that 38% attributed their offending to 'a need to support their children', single mothers being more likely to cite a lack of money as the cause of their offending than those who were married (Caddle and Crisp 1997). There is some evidence that sanctioning of those on Jobseeker's Allowance is contributing to women's debt (Ryan 2016; Kirby 2016). One example that PRT was made aware of by a probation officer involved a mother of young children who was doing unpaid work in a local charity shop as part of the terms of a community order. Between fulfilling the requirements of the unpaid work order, caring for her children and difficulties accessing a computer because she did not own one, she had failed to apply for the specified number of jobs. As a result, her benefits were suspended for several weeks, meaning she could not provide for her children and was at serious risk of reoffending as she felt shoplifting was the only way she could put food on the table. Probation staff were intervening on her behalf to appeal the decision and restore her benefit income. Elsewhere, an evaluation of community services for women offenders found that these services were important for supporting women who had debts arising from fines and social fund loans that were being deducted from their benefits. Other women had borrowed money from loan companies and were being threatened by bailiffs and in these cases support workers needed to arrange realistic repayment terms to reduce the risk of women reoffending because they had an urgent need for cash (Radcliffe and Hunter 2013; see also Sheehan et al. 2011). The National Offender Management Service has in principle recognised that 'long-term poverty, debts and loans with high interest are the reality for many women offenders' (NOMS 2012, p. 36), but 'offender management' in practice can be oblivious to such pressures.

Gendered Impacts of Imprisonment

Imprisonment itself is experienced very differently by women and men, and women are detained at higher security levels than their offences generally warrant because the prisons have not been designed for women's risk profile. A disturbing reflection of the gendered impact of incarceration is the fact that women are much more likely than men to harm themselves while in prison, accounting for 19% of self-harm incidents despite women comprising just 5% of the prison population (PRT 2017a, p. 6). The reasons for this include women's histories of sexual abuse and trauma, and for mothers their guilt, grief and distress at separation from their children, and mental illness. Because women in prison—especially if they are mothers—are regarded as having offended against gender norms as well as against the law, they are liable to experience more intense shame, social exclusion and stigma (Lloyd 1995; Hudson 2002; Crewe et al. 2017). Women are almost twice as likely as men in prison to be identified as suffering from depression (65% compared to 37%) and more than three times as likely as women in the general population (19%). Just less than a third of women in custody (30%) had a psychiatric admission prior to entering prison, and nearly, half of all women prisoners (46%) report having attempted suicide at some point in their lives. This is twice the rate of male prisoners (21%) and more than seven times higher than suicide attempts amongst the general population (6%) (PRT 2017a, p. 4). Prison inspectorate reports confirm the vulnerability of many incarcerated women. For example, an inspection of HMP Eastwood Park in Gloucestershire found that 'over three quarters reported mental health or emotional well-being issues…Many of the women continued to report a history of abuse, rape, domestic violence and involvement in prostitution' (HMIP 2017, p. 5). A further indication of their vulnerability is that nearly a third of women in prison (31%) spent time in care as children compared with a quarter (24%) of male prisoners (PRT 2016, p. 3).

Women are generally imprisoned further from home than men because there are fewer women's prisons and these have wider catchment areas. They therefore receive fewer visits from family and friends which adversely affects their ability to maintain relationships and family contacts and compounds the difficulties of resettlement. A report on HMP Eastwood Park found 52% of women prisoners said it was difficult or very difficult for family and friends to visit, and at the time of inspection, over a quarter of the women had received no visits (HMIP 2017, p. 20).

The high rate of self-harm is further testament to the acute toll prison takes on women. In 2016 and 2017, 30 women died in prisons in England—of these, over half were self-inflicted deaths. The twelve self-inflicted deaths in 2016 were the highest in a year since 2004 (IAP 2017, p. 10). Women's deaths in prison have escalated at a greater rate than men's, prompting an urgent inquiry by the Independent Advisory Panel on Deaths in Custody. The inquiry's Working Paper and the report from the Prisons and Probation Ombudsman (2017) drew attention to factors including reductions in staffing levels combined with the loss of experienced, trusted staff; vacancies in mental health teams, unmet mental health, drug and alcohol treatment needs; an increase in illicit drug use, intimidation, bullying and debt in custody; a marked decrease in use of release on temporary licence; an increased likelihood of homelessness on release; and a high number of recalls. The Independent Advisory Panel also noted the knock-on effect of the hasty closure of Holloway prison including increased distance from home for women sent to prison and pressure on other prisons combined with the closure of critical women-only support services in the community (IAP 2017, p. 3).

Reflecting on the evidence received in response to the Panel's call for evidence, its chair Juliet Lyon said in her Foreword:

> There was a clear consensus that a sustained effort must be made to imprison fewer women by investing in preventative work, mental health treatment, social care, treatment for addictions, and developing a range of community sentences in which courts could remain confident. (IAP 2017, p. 4)

This support for measures to reduce women's imprisonment is grounded in evidence of its disproportionate impact. In considering how to ensure a gender equitable criminal justice system, the particular pains that prison causes women need to be understood. These include the pains of 'failed motherhood'.

Mothers in Prison

As in the wider society, women in prison are far more likely than men to be primary carers of children. A lack of data collection about the primary care responsibilities of women in the criminal justice system both reflects and reinforces policy failures in this area. The Surveying Prisoner Crime Reduction Survey (William et al. 2012) found that six in ten women in prison had (on average) two dependent children. One-fifth were lone parents before imprisonment, and the proportion was higher amongst black women (Lammy Review 2017; PRT 2017c). Women's imprisonment results in an estimated 17,240 children being separated from their mothers each year (Wilks-Wiffen 2011). For eight out of ten children, it is the first time they have been separated from their mother for more than a day or so (Vallely 2012). It has been estimated that annually in England and Wales around 3000 children aged 0–2 years are affected by their mothers' imprisonment (Galloway et al. 2014, p. 7). Fewer than one in ten children are cared for by their father when a mother goes to prison, 40% are cared for by grandparents or other family members, and only 5% remain in their own home. By contrast, when a father is imprisoned, his children almost invariably remain with the mother—only 2% of children with a father in prison were in other kinship care (HMIP 1997; see also PRT 2017a). A report by the Prisoners Advice and Care Trust found that up to 6000 children a year are 'being forgotten by the system when their mother is sent to prison' (PACT 2011, p. 1). A survey of 1400 women serving a first sentence in Holloway prison revealed that 42 women (3% of those interviewed) had no idea who was looking after their children and that 19 children under the age of 16 were looking after themselves (Revolving Doors Agency 2004, p. 40). As a number of commentators have noted, the fact of being imprisoned renders a woman a 'bad mother' and women feel the shame keenly (Baldwin 2015; Baldwin and Epstein 2017).

Women who have new babies or give birth while imprisoned may apply for a place in a prison mother and baby unit (MBU). In March 2016, 35 babies were with their mothers in a prison MBU. However, 29% of women were refused admission to an MBU in 2015/16 compared to 16% refused the previous year (Sikand 2017). The reasons for this are not entirely clear, but administrative obstacles and delays seem to be part of the problem rather than a shortage of available places. Research also highlights lack of awareness of MBUs amongst women who may be eligible and their advocates, as well as shortcomings and delays in the decision-making process that can result in women being unnecessarily separated from their babies.

The impact on children of parental imprisonment can be traumatic: they are twice as likely as their peers to have poor mental health (Murray et al. 2009) and are more at risk of poverty, poor health and insecure housing and finances (Smith et al. 2007). Their educational outcomes are adversely affected, and the risk of antisocial behaviour in children trebles.

Sentencing of Mothers

The PRT discussion paper *Sentencing of Mothers* (Minson et al. 2015) sets out the law and guidance that courts should apply when sentencing a person with primary care responsibilities. These make it abundantly clear that,

> …non-custodial sentences are preferable for women with dependent children, with custodial sentences to be considered when the offence is serious or violent or the woman represents a continuing danger. Even then a custodial sentence should only be given after considering the best interests of the child or children, whilst ensuring that appropriate provision has been made for their care. (2015, p. 10)

The paper notes evidence of and concern about the inconsistent application of the relevant principles and recommends that the Sentencing Council consider issuing an Overarching Principle setting out the court's duty to investigate and accord due weight to a defendant/offender's sole or primary caring responsibilities (Minson et al. 2015, p. 15). Although the Guidelines do recognise sole or primary caring responsibilities as a mitigating factor, there is little guidance given on how this should be considered or weighed in the balance (see Sentencing Council 2015). A Criminal Justice Joint Inspection review of resettlement recommended more focus on the specific needs of women as parents. While acknowledging that 'sometimes an offender's family may be the victims of their crime and sometimes they may be a negative influence', the report 'absolutely confirms the central importance of an offender's family and friends to their successful rehabilitation' (CJJI 2014, p. 7). Unless the court is properly informed about an offender's caring responsibilities—through the pre-sentence report—these and the specific consequences for her children cannot be considered. Ensuring the provision of accurate information to the court is vital if outcomes for children and their mothers are to be improved.

Mind the Gap—Between Rhetoric and Reality

In the light of the evidence presented thus far, it is not surprising that there is widespread political consensus on the need to reduce women's imprisonment. What is more surprising is that little sustained progress has been achieved. One reason for this is a lack of consistent leadership and governance. Four different Secretaries of State for Justice between 2012 and 2017 have expressed commitment to adopting a more gender-informed response to women's offending. Giving evidence to the Justice Committee in March 2016, Michael Gove (2016) said 'we need to think hard about alternatives to custody for a section of the female prison cohort'. Dr. Philip Lee MP who was the third chair, in as many years, of the government's Ministerial Advisory Board on Female Offenders said in Justice Questions (2016) 'I think it is important that we have a gender specific approach to women' and,

> Women who commit crimes are often some of the most vulnerable in our society... We want to see fewer women in custody and to promote a greater focus on early intervention, diversion and multiagency approaches to ensure that the justice system can take proper account of the specific needs of women. (Hansard HC Deb. 2016)

However, the *Transforming Lives* (PRT 2014a, p. 5) report found that 'gender-specific approaches are the exception but should be the rule' and expressed concern that,

> There seems to be a common view amongst many working in criminal justice agencies that men and women must be treated the same, albeit as individuals. Guidance on the application of the public sector equality duty is clear that treating people equally does not mean treating them the same. (2014a, p. 20)

This is neither a new nor a simple problem. In her 2005 Longford Trust Lecture, Baroness Hale DBE, the only woman on the Supreme Court, pointed out that 'equality is a complicated subject. It is now well-recognised that a misplaced conception of equality has resulted in some very unequal treatment for the women and girls who appear before the criminal justice system' (Hale 2005). In a recent case in the Supreme Court (R. [on the application of Coll] v Secretary of State for Justice (2017) 1 WLR 2093), she took the opportunity to spell this out in relation to the lack of provision of Approved Premises for women, finding that this constitutes direct sex discrimination as it adversely affects women's resettlement prospects.

The law is clear that where the underlying circumstances of women and men are different, distinct approaches may be needed to achieve equitable outcomes. The provisions of the Equality Act 2010 reflect this—for example allowing women-only or women-specific services. Indeed, the gender equality duty requires public services, including those delivered by the private and voluntary sector, to assess and address the different needs of women and men. Because of the mounting evidence that this was not being achieved in the criminal justice system, and following pressure from the PRT, Soroptimists and others, the Offender Rehabilitation Act 2014 was amended during its passage through Parliament to include an express obligation on the Secretary of State for Justice to ensure that the distinct supervision and support needs of women offenders are identified and addressed.[5]

This new legislative provision reflects the requirements of the United Nations (2010) Bangkok Rules on women offenders and prisoners to which the UK is signatory. These give guidance to policy makers, legislators, sentencing authorities and prison staff about reducing the unnecessary imprisonment of women, especially those with children, and on how to identify and respond to the specific needs of women in contact with the criminal justice system.

In its scrutiny of offender management, the Criminal Justice Joint Inspection report *Equal but Different* found that,

> …in nearly three quarters of all the cases and reports examined, the woman involved was seen as vulnerable in some way. Most of these women were or had been a victim of domestic abuse. Some were subject to sexual exploitation. There were concerns about self-harm in around a third of all cases and of suicide in around one quarter of the cases. They are therefore a very needy group of offenders who clearly required both careful monitoring and active input during supervision. (CJJI 2011, p. 57)

However, the government's Transforming Rehabilitation 'revolution', which took effect in 2015, resulted in a dramatic reorganisation of key elements of the criminal justice system and paid scant regard to the distinct needs of women offenders. With the stated aim to reduce high rates of post-release reoffending, the probation service was split into a National Probation Service retained in the public sector with responsibility for supervising high-risk offenders, providing information to courts, and enforcement, while the 35 probation trusts were repackaged into 21 Community Rehabilitation Companies. These were put out to tender to supervise low- and medium-risk offenders. Although the MoJ stated that it was committed to addressing the factors associated with women's offending, including domestic violence, sexual abuse, substance misuse and homelessness (MoJ, cited in PRT 2013b, p. 2), this did not translate into practice.

The Offender Rehabilitation Act 2014 extended, for the first time, statutory post-release probation supervision to short-sentenced offenders—even if they were imprisoned for only a few days. The PRT

(2013b) and others warned that this would have significant implications for women as they are disproportionately likely to be on a short sentence and would now be subject to a 12-month licence on release even if they had only served a few days or weeks in custody (see also Epstein 2016). As PRT said in evidence to the MoJ consultation on the Transforming Rehabilitation outsourcing proposals:

> It is clear from a wealth of research and inquiries that a gender-sensitive approach offers the best hope of a reduction in women's reoffending. In designing the new commissioning system, it must be acknowledged that because the causes of reoffending for women are particularly complex and interrelated, working with them is often time-consuming and demanding, requiring high levels of teamwork, mutual support and supervision, and multiagency co-operation. (PRT 2013b, p. 3)

The House of Commons Committee on Public Accounts (2016) confirmed the fears of many that the reforms would be counterproductive. In its initial assessment of the promised 'rehabilitation revolution', in their report they noted that,

> ...one of the biggest challenges in delivering successful probation and resettlement services in custody and community is giving offenders access to services beyond the direct control of the justice system... We heard that the offender housing problem is deteriorating, with 42% of service users participating in research carried out for the National Audit Office feeling that help with housing has got worse since the probation reforms. (2016, p. 6)

The incidence and impact of homelessness are especially marked for women at risk of offending. As the House of Commons Communities and Local Government Committee (2016, p. 27) report on Homelessness noted, there is a 'close connection between offending and homelessness' and 'particular challenges for homeless women who are at greater risk of sexual violence, prostitution, or engaging in unhealthy relationships in order to access accommodation' (2016, p. 30). Reports of women leaving prison with nothing but a sleeping bag, together with other evidence of the chronic shortage of suitable housing options for women who offend, prompted the PRT and Women in Prison (2016) to publish *Home truths: housing for women in the criminal justice system.* This made detailed recommendations to national and local government as well as criminal justice agencies to improve the provision of safe, secure and affordable housing for women.

Despite warnings that if the new post-custody supervision regime was not introduced with care it would drive up the short-sentenced prisoner population, this is precisely what happened (PRT 2017a, p. 6). Prior to the Offender Rehabilitation Act 2014, which came into effect on 1 February 2015, no woman serving under 12 months was recalled to prison. Since women are more likely to serve short prison sentences than men, they have been disproportionately adversely affected by the changes despite Section 10 of this Act. In this sense, the changes to supervision and recall represent the latest example of 'net widening' whereby 'administrative changes result in a greater number of individuals being controlled by the criminal justice system' (Guiney 2016). A measure justified on rehabilitative grounds has instead rein-forced the revolving door of prison, breaches and recalls back into custody, with significant cost to the Ministry of Justice and repercus-sions for local services. Despite the statutory safeguards and senti-ments expressed by successive Secretaries of State for Justice, reports from the House of Commons Public Accounts Committee (2016) and the HM Inspectorate of Probation (2016) have highlighted the nega-tive impact that the Transforming Rehabilitation reforms have had on women's services, family support, housing and employment outcomes. Perversely, these are all protective factors that are known to reduce reoffending.

Recognising the Links: Early Intervention

The cross-government strategy to end violence against women and girls now explicitly recognises the vulnerability of women offenders who are affected by domestic abuse. Improvements in the police response to domestic abuse are underway following the 2014 inspection report

Everybody's Business by Her Majesty's Inspectorate of Constabulary (HMIC 2014), and the College of Policing is taking steps to improve police understanding of the dynamics of domestic abuse, including controlling and coercive behaviour. Also welcome are the measures to tackle human trafficking and modern slavery, such as establishing the new Anti-Slavery Commissioner, statutory guidance for agencies to improve their identification of victims, reforms to the National Referral Mechanism and the new statutory defence for victims who have been compelled to commit an offence as a consequence of trafficking or slavery. Sentencing guidance has been amended to recognise coercion as a factor reducing culpability (see Sentencing Council 2015).

Intervention at the point of arrest provides a unique opportunity to link some of the most vulnerable women in the community to support that could, for example, help them escape violent and coercive relationships and establish independent lives, reducing their risk of offending. Following a consultation in 2015, the Home Office published the *Ending Violence against Women and Girls Strategy 2016–2020*. The new strategy recognises the need to 'support female offenders affected by domestic abuse' and makes clear that:

> …the only way we can achieve real, sustainable progress is if national and local government, local partners and agencies, and every community work together to prevent women and girls from becoming victims in the first place and make sure those who have experienced abuse receive the support they need to recover. Tackling VAWG is everybody's business. (HM Government 2016, p. 8)

Problem-solving approaches like police triage schemes can break down the sometimes false dichotomy between 'victim' and 'offender' and, working in partnership with VAWG services, provide women with a chance to disclose and address the way domestic abuse and coercive relationships may drive their offending. As one police inspector involved in trialling a Women's Triage scheme put it, 'I have been astounded by the number of female offenders who are victims of domestic abuse and how that is a significant trigger to their offending' (cited in Guiney and Earle 2017, p. 8).

The concept of triage was adapted by youth justice initiatives from hospital accident and emergency departments, enabling local youth offending teams to undertake a rapid assessment of the individual's needs and circumstances. Where appropriate, assistance was offered to the young person and their family by way of an out-of-court disposal. Triage schemes took a graduated approach: in cases of the most minor offending triage primarily consisted of restorative measures such as letters of apology to the victim. For medium-level offences, young people had access to supportive interventions, such as for substance misuse or anger management. For the most serious offences, young people were fast-tracked and given support as their prosecution progressed through the youth justice system.

PRT has advocated greater use of such approaches for women at the point of arrest in cases where the harm caused by an offence is low but the needs of the individual may be multiple and/or complex (Guiney and Earle 2017). This report draws on detailed research and interviews with police, probation staff and women's voluntary-sector providers and showcases how problem-solving approaches have been used to break the cycle of women's offending, encourage multiagency working and manage the changing demands on police resources at a time when money is short. A number of initiatives have been or are undergoing independent evaluation and are showing positive results—including reduced arrest and custody rates (Guiney and Earle 2017; Gray et al. 2016).

The need for these initiatives has grown with a significant decline in the use of out-of-court disposals for women in recent years—peaking in 2007 at 96,457 women, falling at a significant rate to 36,239 in 2015, a decrease of over 62% (PRT 2017a, p. 7). It is also important to note that while many women appear in court following arrest and charge a great many more women are prosecuted by other means. This includes TV licence evasion, welfare fraud, fare evasion and sanctions relating to the non-attendance of children at school. Because these cases are not dealt with by the police, there is no option but to use an out-of-court disposal. TV licence evasion accounted for 36% of all prosecutions for women, but only 6% for men. In 2015, 70% of all the 189,349 defendants prosecuted for this offence were women (PRT 2017a, p. 2).

Women can end up in prison for these offences, although a custodial sentence is in theory unlawful (Epstein 2016).

What Works: The Role of Women's Centres and Gender-Specific Services

There is a considerable international literature on 'what works for women' (Sheehan et al. 2011). A focus on how successful schemes can be replicated across England and Wales and on removing barriers to early intervention and diversion into support services is overdue. For example, in some areas, women who are prosecuted for domestic abuse offences are automatically excluded from diversion schemes, but these women may well be victims of domestic abuse, who have used reactive violence against a primary aggressor and need referral to specialist services.

The available evidence suggests that prison is rarely a necessary, appropriate or proportionate response to women who come into contact with the justice system and that women's centres can be far more effective in tackling the drivers to women's offending and their unmet health and support needs. While reduced reoffending is a narrow and a crude measure by which to assess effectiveness, it is the one of most salience to the Ministry of Justice.

In 2015, the Justice Data Lab assessed the impact on reoffending of support provided to female offenders by women's centres throughout England. The one-year proven reoffending rate for 597 offenders who received support provided by women's centres throughout England was 30%, compared with 35% for a matched control group of similar offenders from England (MoJ 2015, p. 1). This was based upon analysis of information that has been supplied by 39 women's centres throughout England to the National Offender Management Service (NOMS).

A careful analysis by Hedderman and Jolliffe (2015) found that women released from prison are twice as likely to reoffend as a comparable cohort of women given community orders. Propensity score matching using information on over 3000 women's current offence and criminal history was used to create a sample of 320 women who had been sentenced to prison who were equivalent on all measured variables to 320 women who received a community sentence. Twelve months after release, those from prison were found to have committed significantly more and more costly offences and also to be more likely to be sent back to prison. The overall additional cost of prison in this sample was conservatively estimated to be £3.6 million.

There is also evidence from the NOMS that women are more likely to comply with a community order or period of licence supervision than men, which justifies confidence that many will engage constructively with an out-of-court disposal order with conditions (NOMS 2014, p. 22). However, the most recent data shows a decline in women's compliance rates which needs further investigation (NOMS 2015, p. 20, 2016, p. 35).

The economic case for justice reinvestment is compelling. The annual cost of housing a woman in prison for a year is in the region of £38,000 to £46,000, and in contrast, the average cost of a community order is £2800 and approximately £1500 for support in a women's centre (NOMS 2012, p. 8). Recent analysis by the Women-Centred Working project has found that a women's centre providing holistic, gender-informed services is likely to be attractive to Local Authorities, NHS England/Public Health England and independent trusts and foundations supporting the voluntary and community sector. The analysis below *excludes* the avoided cost of prison custody, but still shows savings of around £32,000 annually per woman (Table 9.1).

Closure of HMP Holloway and the Unmet Need for Women's Services

Ironically perhaps, the closure of HMP Holloway—the largest women's prison in Western Europe and the only women's prison in London—both exposed and exacerbated the chronic dearth of support services for women. The announcement in November 2015 that it was being closed down, its actual closure in June 2016, and planning consultations for the site's use, all provided fresh impetus to the call for more women's

Table 9.1 Cost-benefit calculation for investing in women's centres. *Source* Women-centred working: Taking forward women-centred solutions (Carroll 2016, p. 17)

Costs per woman over two years		Local authority savings over two years	
Engagement, advocacy and support work	£2852	Drugs misuse services	£4541
Supervision, risk assessment and management	£412	Retaining custody of child (avoiding care)	£52,676
Women centre overhead	£640	Domestic violence-related services	£11,824
Freedom programme	£200		
Multiagency steering group	£16		
Total costs	£4120	Total savings	£69,041

centres, including one situated on the site. There have been growing calls to ensure that the site's development should honour the legacy of this institution (where in a previous guise suffragettes were incarcerated and force-fed) by providing for women's access to gender-specific holistic support services. Following the PRT's original proposal to convert the visitors' centre into a women's centre, other women's and criminal justice organisations have become engaged in efforts to ensure a positive outcome to this prison closure. Although not its primary purpose, 'the prison played a valuable social role both within the borough and beyond in supporting women within the criminal justice system' (Islington Borough Council 2017, p. 13). The now empty prison sits on a large area of public land in Islington, the most densely populated area in the UK with some of the highest housing costs. The redevelopment of the site provides a unique opportunity to meet women's needs and benefit the local community (Centre for Crime and Justice Studies 2017).[6]

Conclusion—Political Will Needed to Deliver Women's Justice

The case for reducing the number of women imprisoned for relatively minor offences is overwhelming and successive governments have accepted this in theory. The challenge is to secure consistent political leadership and drive to put in place the measures necessary to achieve the goal. Law and policy in the UK make clear that applying the equality principle requires consideration of women's specific needs, as well as an awareness of the historic and present patterns of disadvantage that women face. However, for women offenders, this principle is more often honoured in the breach. As this chapter has shown, the current framework does not deliver justice for women who are often simultaneously victims and offenders and suggests underlying confusion about what gender equality means. According to a Women's Aid (2011, p. 15) report, women offenders 'might experience double discrimination: their needs might not be taken into consideration within the criminal justice system and their victimhood is undermined by them being offenders'. In its 2016 White Paper on Prison Safety and reform, the government promised a strategy for women offenders—so far this has not been delivered. In the tenth anniversary year since publication of the Corston review, it is long overdue.

Acknowledgements This article reflects the efforts of my PRT Transforming Lives programme colleagues—especially Katy Swaine Williams, Tom Guiney, Zoey Litchfield and Lauren Nickolls—who tirelessly interrogate Ministry of Justice data and myriad other sources to shed light on gender differences and inequalities in the criminal justice system and how to remedy them. I would also like to thank Emma Milne who has provided invaluable comments on earlier drafts and persevered with a non-academic author!

Notes

1. This work was initially supported by the Pilgrim Trust and subsequently by the Big Lottery Fund.
2. Unless otherwise stated, all the data in this section are taken from Ministry of Justice statistics and can also be found in the PRT (2017b), Bromley Briefing Prison Fact File and in the women's briefings on the Prison Reform Trust website www.prisonreformtrust.org.uk/women.
3. Most of the data here are for England and Wales, as criminal justice is devolved in Scotland and Northern Ireland. For a comparative account see Full Fact (2017) and Travis (2017). See also Allen and Watson (2017).
4. For a gendered critique of OASys see, for example, Caulfield (2010).

5. Section 10 of the *Offender Rehabilitation Act 2014* places a duty on the Secretary of State for Justice to ensure that arrangements for the supervision or rehabilitation of offenders identify specific provision for women.

References

Allen, G. & Watson, C. (2017). *UK prison population statistics* (House of Commons Briefing Paper SN/SG/04334). Available at: http://researchbriefings.files.parliament.uk/documents/SN04334/SN04334.pdf (Accessed 21 September 2017).

Baldwin, L. (Ed.). (2015). *Mothering justice: Working with mothers in criminal and social justice settings.* Hampshire: Waterside Press.

Baldwin, L., & Epstein, R. (2017). *Short but not sweet: A study of the impact of short custodial sentences on mothers and their children.* Leicester: De Montfort University.

Cabinet Office Social Exclusion Task Force. (2009). *Short study on women offenders.* London: Ministry of Justice. Available at: http://webarchive.nationalarchives.gov.uk//, http://www.cabinetoffice.gov.uk/media/209663/setf_shortstudy_womenoffenders.pdf (Accessed 22 September 2017).

Caddle, D., & Crisp, D. (1997). *Imprisoned women and mothers* (Home Office Research Finding No. 162). London: Research and Statistics Directorate, Home Office.

Carlen, P., & Christina, D. (1985). *Criminal women: Autobiographical accounts.* Cambridge: Polity Press.

Carroll, N. (2016). *Taking forward women centred solutions.* Women Centred Working. Available at: http://www.womencentredworking.com/wp-content/uploads/2016/04/Women-Centred-Working-Taking-Forward-Women-Centred-Solutions-report-Embargoed-until-18_4_16.pdf (Accessed 22 September 2017).

Caulfield, L. (2010). Rethinking the assessment of female offenders. *Howard Journal of Crime and Justice, 49*(4), 315–424.

Centre for Crime and Justice Studies. (2017). *Justice matters for Holloway.* Available at: https://www.crimeandjustice.org.uk/tags/justice-matters-holloway (Accessed 22 September 2017).

Commission on Women Offenders Scotland. (2012). *Chaired by Dame Elish Angiolini.* Available at: http://www.gov.scot/Topics/archive/reviews/commissiononwomenoffenders (Accessed 21 September 2017).

Corston, J. (2007). *The Corston report: A report by Baroness Jean Corston of a review of women with particular vulnerabilities in the criminal justice system.* London: Home Office. Available at: http://www.justice.gov.uk/publications/docs/corston-report-march-2007.pdf (Accessed 21 September 2017).

Cox, J., & Sacks-Jones, K. (2017). *"Double disadvantage": The experiences of Black, Asian and minority ethnic women in the criminal justice system.* London: Women in Prison.

Crewe, B., Hulley, S., & Wright, S. (2017). The gendered pains of life imprisonment. *The British Journal of Criminology,* (azw088), 1–20.

Criminal Justice Joint Inspection (CJJI). (2011). *Equal but different? An inspection of the use of alternatives to custody for women offenders.* London: CJJI. Available at: http://www.justiceinspectorates.gov.uk/probation/wp-content/uploads/sites/5/2014/03/womens-thematic-alternatives-to-custody-2011.pdf (Accessed 21 September 2017).

Criminal Justice Joint Inspection (CJJI). (2014). *Resettlement provision for adult offenders: Accommodation and education, training and employment.* London: CJJI. Available at: https://www.justiceinspectorates.gov.uk/cjji/wp-content/uploads/sites/2/2014/09/Resettlement-thematic-for-print-Sept-2014.pdf (Accessed 21 September 2017).

Epstein, R. (2016). Through the gate: The view is bleak. *Criminal Law and Justice Weekly,* 180 (47). Available at: https://www.criminallawandjustice.co.uk/features/Through-Gate-View-Bleak (Accessed 21 September 2017).

Full Fact. (2017). *Women in prison: How does the UK compare?* Available at: https://fullfact.org/crime/women-prison-how-does-uk-compare/ (Accessed 4 July 2017).

Galloway, S., Haynes, A., & Cuthbert, C. (2014). *An unfair sentence, all babies count: Spotlight on the criminal justice system.* London: NSPCC. Avaliable at: https://www.nspcc.org.uk/services-and-resources/research-and-resources/2014/all-babies-count-unfair-sentence/ (Accessed 8 October 2017).

Gobeil, R., Blanchette, K., & Stewart, L. (2016). A meta-analytic review of correctional interventions for women offenders: Gender-neutral versus gender-informed approaches. *Criminal Justice and Behaviour, 43*(3), 301–322.

Gove, M. (2016). *Oral evidence, prison reform HC859, Michael Gove in reply to Q34 from Victoria Prentis MP.* London: Justice Committee, House of Commons.

Gray, P., Simmonds, L., & Annison, J. (2016, November 18). *The resettlement of women offenders: Learning the lessons.* Plymouth University. Available at: https://www.plymouth.ac.uk/uploads/production/document/path/8/8608/Women_s_Research_Project_FINAL_REPORT_13_Feb_2017.pdf (Accessed 21 September 2017).

Guiney, T. (2016). Total recall: Why more women are being returned to prison than ever before. *The Justice Gap*. Available from: http://thejusticegap.com/2016/11/total-recall-women-returned-prison-ever/ (Accessed 21 September 2017).

Guiney, T., & Earle, J. (2017). *Fair cop? Improving outcomes for women at the point of arrest*. London: Prison Reform Trust. Available at: http://www.prisonreformtrust.org.uk/Portals/0/Documents/Women/Fair%20Cop.pdf (Accessed 8 October 2017).

Hale, B. (2005, December 5). The sinners and the sinned against: Women in the criminal justice system. *The Longford Trust*. Available at: https://www.longfordtrust.org/longford-lecture/past-lectures/lectures-archive/brenda-hale-the-sinners-and-the-sinned-against-women-in-the-criminal-justice-system/ (Accessed 22 September 2017).

Hales, L., & Gelsthorpe, L. (2012). *The criminalisation of migrant women*. Cambridge: Institute of Criminology, University of Cambridge. Available at: http://www.crim.cam.ac.uk/people/academic_research/loraine_gelsthorpe/criminalreport29july12.pdf (Accessed 8 October 2017).

Hedderman, C., & Jolliffe, D. (2015). The impact of prison for women on the edge: Paying the price for wrong decisions. *Victims and Offenders, 10*(2), 152–178.

Her Majesty's Government. (2016). *Ending violence against women and girls strategy 2016–2020*. Home Office: London. Available at: https://www.gov.uk/government/uploads/system/uploads/attachment_data/file/522166/VAWG_Strategy_FINAL_PUBLICATION_MASTER_vRB.PDF (Accessed 21 September 2017).

Her Majesty's Inspectorate of Constabulary (HMIC). (2014). *Everybody's Business: Improving the police response to domestic abuse*. Available at: https://www.justiceinspectorates.gov.uk/hmicfrs/wp-content/uploads/2014/04/improving-the-police-response-to-domestic-abuse.pdf (Accessed 21 September 2017).

Her Majesty's Inspectorate of Prisons (HMIP). (1997). *Women in prison: A thematic review*. Available at: https://www.justiceinspectorates.gov.uk/hmiprisons/wp-content/uploads/sites/4/2014/07/WOMEN-IN-PRISON-1996.pdf (Accessed 21 September 2017).

Her Majesty's Inspectorate of Prisons (HMIP). (2016). *Report on an unannounced inspection of HMP & YOI Bronzefield*. Available at: https://www.justiceinspectorates.gov.uk/hmiprisons/wp-content/uploads/sites/4/2016/04/Bronzefield-web2015.pdf (Accessed 21 September 2017).

Her Majesty's Inspectorate of Prisons (HMIP). (2017). *Report on an unannounced inspection of HMP Eastwood Park*. Available at: https://www.justiceinspectorates.gov.uk/hmiprisons/wp-content/uploads/sites/4/2017/03/Eastwood-Peastark-Web-2016.pdf (Accessed 21 September 2017).

Her Majesty's Inspectorate of Probation. (2016). *A thematic inspection of the provision and quality of services in the community for women who offend.* Available at: https://www.justiceinspectorates.gov.uk/hmiprobation/wp-content/uploads/sites/5/2016/09/A-thematic-inspection-of-the-provision-and-quality-of-services-in-the-community-for-women-who-offend.pdf (Accessed 27 September 2016).

House of Commons Communities and Local Government Committee. (2016). *Homelessness, third report of session 2016–2017.* Available at: https://publications.parliament.uk/pa/cm201617/cmselect/cmcomloc/40/40.pdf (Accessed 21 September 2017).

House of Commons Justice Committee. (2015). *Women offenders: Follow-up, thirteenth report of session 2014–15.* Available at: https://publications.parliament.uk/pa/cm201415/cmselect/cmjust/314/314.pdf (Accessed 21 September 2017).

House of Commons, Justice Questions, Hansard Vol. 616, col. 767, 1 November 2016.

House of Commons Public Accounts Committee. (2016). *Transforming rehabilitation, seventeenth report of session 2016–17.* Available at: https://publications.parliament.uk/pa/cm201617/cmselect/cmpubacc/484/484.pdf (Accessed 21 September 2017).

Hudson, B. (2002). Gender issues in penal policy and penal theory. In P. Carlen (Ed.), *Women and punishment: The struggle for justice* (pp. 21–46). Willan: Cullompton.

Independent Advisory Panel on Deaths in Custody (IAP). (2017). *Preventing the deaths of women in prison—Initial results of a rapid information gathering exercise by the independent advisory panel on deaths in custody.* Available at: http://iapdeathsincustody.independent.gov.uk/wp-content/uploads/2017/08/IAP-rapid-evidence-collection-v0.3-preventing-the-death-of-women.pdf (Accessed 21 September 2017).

Islington Borough Council. (2017). *Holloway prison: Draft Supplementary Planning Document (SPD).* Available at: https://www.islington.gov.uk/~/media/sharepoint-lists/public-records/planningandbuildingcontrol/publicity/publicconsultation/20172018/20170815hollowayprisondraftspd.pdf (Accessed 27 September 2017).

Kirby, D. (2016, May 11). Benefit sanctions are pushing some people towards "survival crime". *I News Online.* Available from: https://inews.co.uk/essentials/news/uk/benefit-sanctions-pushing-people-towards-survival-crime/ (Accessed 29 June 2016).

Lammy, D. (2017). The Lammy review: An independent review into the treatment of, and outcomes for, Black, Asian and minority ethnic individuals in the criminal justice system. Available at: https://www.gov.uk/government/uploads/system/uploads/attachment_data/file/643001/lammy-review-final-report.pdf (Accessed 21 September 2017).

Light, M., Grant, E., & Hopkins, K. (2013). *Gender differences in substance misuse and mental health amongst prisoners results from the Surveying Prisoner Crime Reduction (SPCR) longitudinal cohort study of prisoners.* London: Ministry of Justice. Available from: https://www.gov.uk/government/uploads/system/uploads/attachment_data/file/220060/gender-substance-misuse-mental-health-prisoners.pdf (Accessed 22 September 2017).

Lloyd, A. (1995). *Doubly deviant, doubly damned: Society's treatment of violent women.* London: Penguin Books.

Loveless, J. (2010). Domestic violence, coercion and duress. *Criminal Law Review, 2,* 93–108.

Manjoo, R. (2014). Special rapporteur on violence against women country mission to the United Kingdom and Northern Ireland, United Nations Human Rights: Office of the High Commissioner. Available at: http://www.ohchr.org/EN/NewsEvents/Pages/DisplayNews.aspx?NewsID=14514 (Accessed 21 September 2017).

Minson, S., Nadin, R., & Earle, J. (2015). *Sentencing of mothers.* London: Prison Reform Trust. Available at: http://www.prisonreformtrust.org.uk/Portals/0/Documents/sentencing_mothers.pdf (Accessed 21 September 2017).

Ministry of Justice (MoJ). (2015). *Justice data lab re-offending analysis: Women's centres throughout England.* Available at: https://www.gov.uk/government/uploads/system/uploads/attachment_data/file/427388/womens-centres-report.pdf (Accessed 21 September 2017).

Ministry of Justice (MoJ). (2016a). *Prison receptions: Q2 2016 (Table 2.1), offender management statistics quarterly: April to June 2016.* Available at: https://www.gov.uk/government/statistics/offender-management-statistics-quarterly-april-to-june-2016 (Accessed 21 September 2017).

Ministry of Justice (MoJ). (2016b). *Sentencing (pivot table) criminal justice system statistics sentencing: December 2015.* Available at: https://www.gov.uk/government/statistics/criminal-justice-system-statistics-quarterly-december-2015 (Accessed 21 September 2017).

Ministry of Justice (MoJ). (2016c). *Out of court disposals (pivot table) criminal justice system statistics sentencing: December 2015.* Available at: https://www.gov.uk/government/statistics/criminal-justice-system-statistics-quarterly-december-2015 (Accessed 21 September 2017).

Murray, J., Farrington, D. P., Sekol, I., & Olsen, R. F. (2009). Effects of parental imprisonment on child antisocial behaviour and mental health: A systematic review. *Campbell Systematic Reviews, 4,* 1–105.

National Offender Management Service (NOMS). (2012). *A distinct approach: A guide to working with women offenders.* London: Ministry of Justice National Offender Management Service. Available at: https://www.justice.gov.uk/downloads/publications/noms/2012/guide-working-with-women-offenders.pdf (Accessed 21 September 2017).

National Offender Management Service (NOMS). (2014). National offender management service offender equalities annual report 2013/14. London: Ministry of Justice National Offender Management Service. Available at: https://www.gov.uk/government/uploads/system/uploads/attachment_data/file/380129/noms-offender-equalities-annual-report-2013-14.pdf (Accessed 28 September 2017).

National Offender Management Service (NOMS). (2015). National offender management service offender equalities annual report 2014/15. London: Ministry of Justice National Offender Management Service. Available at: https://www.gov.uk/government/uploads/system/uploads/attachment_data/file/571996/annual-report.pdf (Accessed 28 September 2017).

National Offender Management Service (NOMS). (2016). National offender management service offender equalities annual report 2015/16. London: Ministry of Justice National Offender Management Service. Available at: https://www.gov.uk/government/uploads/system/uploads/attachment_data/file/479966/noms-offender-equalities-annual-report-2014-15.pdf (Accessed 28 September 2017).

Office of the High Commissioner for Human Rights (OHCHR). (2015). *Report of the Special Rapporteur on violence against women, its causes and consequences, on her mission to the United Kingdom of Great Britain and Northern Ireland (31 March–15 April 2014).* Geneva: OHCHR. Available at: http://www.ohchr.org/EN/NewsEvents/Pages/DisplayNews.aspx?NewsID=14514& (Accessed 21 September 2017).

Prison Advice and Care Trust (PACT). (2011). *Protecting the welfare of children when a parent is imprisoned.* London: Prison Advice and Care Trust (PACT). Available at: http://childhub.org/sites/default/files/library/attachments/1174_Protecting_children_original.pdf (Accessed 21 September 2017).

Prisons and Probation Ombudsman (PPO). (2017, March 28). Learning lessons bulletin fatal incidents investigations issue 13: Self-inflicted deaths among female prisoners. Available at: http://www.ppo.gov.uk/app/uploads/

2017/03/PPO-Learning-Lessons-Bulletin_Self-inflicted-deaths-among-female-prisoners_WEB.pdf (Accessed 21 September 2017).

Prison Reform Trust (PRT). (2011). *Reforming women's justice: Final report of the women's justice taskforce.* London. Available at: http://www.prison-reformtrust.org.uk/Portals/0/Documents/Women%27s%20Justice%20 Taskforce%20Report.pdf (Accessed 21 September 2017).

Prison Reform Trust (PRT). (2013a). *Soroptimist international Great Britain and Northern Ireland action pack: Reducing women's imprisonment.* Available at: http://www.prisonreformtrust.org.uk/Portals/0/Documents/ Soroptimist%20Action%20Pack_online.pdf (Accessed 21 September 2017).

Prison Reform Trust (PRT). (2013b). Transforming women's justice response to Ministry of Justice consultation on transforming rehabilitation. Available at: http://www.prisonreformtrust.org.uk/Portals/0/Documents/ Transforming%20Rehabilitation%20Women%20FINAL.pdf (Accessed 21 September 2017).

Prison Reform Trust (PRT). (2014a). *Transforming lives: Reducing women's imprisonment.* Available at: http://www.prisonreformtrust.org.uk/Portals/0/ Documents/Transforming%20Lives.pdf (Accessed 21 September 2017).

Prison Reform Trust (PRT). (2016). *In care, out of trouble.* Available from: http://www.prisonreformtrust.org.uk/Portals/0/Documents/In%20care%20 out%20of%20trouble%20summary.pdf (Accessed 21 September 2017).

Prison Reform Trust (PRT). (2017a). *Why focus on reducing women's imprisonment?* Available at: http://www.prisonreformtrust.org.uk/Portals/0/ Documents/Women/why%20women_final.pdf (Accessed 21 September 2017).

Prison Reform Trust (PRT). (2017b). *Counted out: Black, Asian and minority ethnic women in the criminal justice system.* Available at: http://www.prison-reformtrust.org.uk/Portals/0/Documents/Counted%20Out.pdf (Accessed 21 September 2017).

Prison Reform Trust (PRT) and Women in Prison (WIP). (2016). *Home truths: Housing for women in the criminal justice system.* Available at: http:// www.prisonreformtrust.org.uk/Portals/0/Documents/Women/Home%20 Truths%20Updated.pdf (Accessed 21 September 2017).

R (Coll) v Secretary of State for Justice. (2017). UKSC 40.

Radcliffe, P. & Hunter, G. (2013). *The development and impact of community services for women offenders: An evaluation.* London: The Institute for Criminal Policy Research. Available at: http://www.icpr.org.uk/media/34025/ReportNuffieldfinal.pdf (Accessed 8 October 2017).

Revolving Doors Agency. (2004). *Bad girls? Women, mental health and crime.* London: Revolving Doors Agency.

Rumgay, J. (2010). When victims become offenders: In search of coherence in policy and practice. *Family & Intimate Partner Violence Quarterly, 3*(1), 47–64.

Ryan, F. (2016, May 11) Benefit sanctions are now hitting 'hardworking' families. *The Guardian Online.* Available at: https://www.theguardian.com/society/2016/may/11/benefit-sanctions-hurting-low-paid-vulnerable-people (Accessed 29 June 2017).

Sentencing Council. (2015). *Theft offences: Definitive guidelines.* Available at: https://www.sentencingcouncil.org.uk/wp-content/uploads/SC-Theft-Offences-Definitive-Guideline-content_FINAL-web_.pdf (Accessed 21 September 2017).

Sev'er, A. (1997). Recent or imminent separation and intimate violence against women: A conceptual overview and some Canadian examples. *Violence Against Women, 3*(6), 566–589.

Sheehan, R., McIvor, G., & Trotter, C. (Eds.). (2011). *Working with women offenders in the community.* Cullompton: Willan.

Sikand, M. (2017). *Lost spaces: Is the current procedure for women prisoners to gain a place in a prison mother and baby unit fair and accessible?.* London: The Griffins Society.

Smith, R., Grimshaw, R., Romeo, R., & Knapp, M. (2007). *Poverty and disadvantage among prisoners' families.* York: Joseph Rowntree Foundation.

Travis, A. (2017, March 14). England and Wales have highest imprisonment rate in western Europe. *The Guardian Online.* Available at: https://www.theguardian.com/society/2017/mar/14/england-and-wales-has-highest-imprisonment-rate-in-western-europe (Accessed 4 July 2017).

United Nations. (2010). *United Nations rules for the treatment of women prisoners and Non-custodial measures for women offenders (the Bangkok Rules).* Resolution 2010/16. Available at: http://www.un.org/en/ecosoc/docs/2010/res%202010-16.pdf (Accessed 8 October 2017).

Vallely, P. (2012, September 19). Mothers and prison: The lost generation. *The Independent.* Available at: www.independent.co.uk/news/uk/crime/mothers—prison-the-lost-generation-8157387.html (Accessed 22 September 2017).

Williams, K., Papadopoulou, V., & Booth, N. (2012). *Prisoners' childhood and family backgrounds*. London: Ministry of Justice. Available at: https://www.gov.uk/government/uploads/system/uploads/attachment_data/file/278837/prisoners-childhood-family-backgrounds.pdf (Accessed 21 September 2017).

Wilks-Wiffen, S. (2011). *Voice of a child: A report on the impact that a mother's imprisonment has on a child*. London: Howard League for Penal Reform.

Women's Aid. (2011). *Supporting women offenders who have experienced domestic and sexual violence*. Bristol: Women's Aid Federation of England and Wales.

10

Women, Crime and Criminal Justice: Tales of Two Cities

Loraine Gelsthorpe

Baroness Corston's report, *A review of women with particular vulnerabilities in the criminal justice system*, made a series of recommendations to bring about improvements in relation to the treatment of women in the criminal justice system. Now, some six years after her report, we found that it is well recognised that women face very different hurdles from men in their journey towards a law abiding life, and that responding appropriately and effectively to the problems that bring women into the criminal justice system requires a distinct approach.

(Justice Select Committee report *Women Offenders: After the Corston Report July, 2013: 3*)

L. Gelsthorpe (✉)
Institute of Criminology, University of Cambridge, Cambridge, UK
e-mail: lrg10@cam.ac.uk

© The Author(s) 2018
E. Milne et al. (eds.), *Women and the Criminal Justice System*,
https://doi.org/10.1007/978-3-319-76774-1_10

Introduction

Baroness Corston's (2007) report represented a significant staging post in the long journey to give greater recognition to women offenders in the criminal justice system. There has been increased interest in women offenders since the early 1980s in particular, with exposure of world-wide interconnecting systems of racism, patriarchy, colonialism and economic injustice and more global conversations about gender and justice and identification of steps forwards and backwards both across and within different continents (Barbaret 2014). Evidence from a recent publication of the world prison population list shows that more than 714,000 women and girls are held in penal institutions throughout the world (6.9% of the global population; Walmsley 2017), but with wide variation across countries in terms of imprisonment and vacillation in regard to awareness and acknowledgement of women's distinctive needs. It is this phenomenon of vacillation, steps forwards and backwards within England and Wales in particular, which provides the focus for this chapter. There have been some positive developments in terms of policy and practice in regard to women offenders. In England and Wales, the rate of imprisoning women has declined from 8.4 women per 100,000 of the population in 2005 to 6.7 women per 100,000 in 2015; in 2017 women comprised 4.6% of the total prison population (3974 women) compared with 5.9% in 2005.[1] We have seen the development of community-based initiatives and services in the last twenty years. The publication of the Corston Report on vulnerable women in the criminal justice system in 2007 in England and Wales was seen to be a watershed development, marking steps forwards. But there are also some challenges and reverses to prompt concern and critical reflection. Indeed, we can find 'a tale of two cities' in regard to developments.

A Tale of Two Cities (1859) is a novel by Charles Dickens, set in London and Paris before and during the French Revolution. It ranks among the most famous works in the history of fictional literature. The novel depicts the plight of the French peasantry demoralized by the French aristocracy in the years leading up to the revolution, the corresponding brutality demonstrated by the revolutionaries toward the former aristocrats in the early years of the revolution, and many unflattering social parallels with life in London during the same time period; rich and poor divided, affluence and aspiration and poverty and gloom compared. The aim of this chapter is to explore these 'two cities' in relation to reforms relating to women and criminal justice.

In 1862, a prison matron wrote of her charges:

> As a class, they are desperately wicked [...] deceitful, crafty, malicious, lewd and devoid of common feeling...in the penal classes of the male prisons there is not one man to match the worst inmate of our female prisons. (A Prison Matron 1862, p. 46)

Fast forward a century and we find Ann Smith (1962) painting a much more sympathetic picture of the lives of women in prison in her book, *Women in Prison*. Whilst women had remained somewhat invisible in writings and theories or had been portrayed in stereotypical pathological terms in the intervening period, this was about to change. Frances Heidensohn (1968) challenged the invisibility of women in the study of crime and deviance and foreshadowed an early critique.[2] The publication of Carol Smart's *Women, Crime and Criminology* in 1976 marked a step change and posed serious questions as to why so many women were being imprisoned for relatively small crimes. Combined with messages from second wave feminism in the late 1960s and early 1970s it became clear that responses to women law breakers could not be separated off from the study of how *all* women are defined and controlled in society. Ideas and stereotypes about women abound in regard to sexuality, motherhood, prostitution, abortion, alcoholism, and retirement, for instance, in all societies. There was an awakening that women and girls are disciplined, managed, corrected and punished as prisoners, partners, patients, mothers, and victims, through imprisonment, medicalization, secure care, and cultural stereotypes (Hutter and Williams 1981; Cain 1989).

Thus there has been a journey of discovery, challenging theoretical work within criminology to recognise women, making visible women's victimisation (particularly in the areas of sexual assault and domestic violence, including offenders' victimisation) and exposing discriminatory practices within the criminal justice system (Heidensohn and Silvestri 2012; Burman and Gelsthorpe 2017), but leading to contrasting perspectives.

Tale 1: A City of Positive Developments and Optimism

As early as 1990 Pat Carlen indicated concern about the increasing number of women being sent to prison each year, and that little was known about alternatives to custody for women, or community support for ex-offenders. She reviewed existing provision for women at the time, identified innovative projects in other countries, and outlined the impediments (both ideological and political) to reducing the number of women in prison. Carlen (1990) produced what might be described as a blueprint for the abolition of women's custody, arguing that what was needed was a specialist legal service for women prisoners (to advise on concerns about medical treatment and child custody issues in particular), the creation of a network of half-way houses for imprisoned addicts and their babies, the provision of a 'welcoming' visitors' centre in every women's prison, and the need for a 'feminist jurisprudence' and 'women-wise penology'—both of which relate to the need to recognise women's needs in a system so clearly designed for men. A central tenet of the message here was that realistic alternatives to custody could be used for women.

The Conservative Government's addition of s.95 to the Criminal Justice Act 1991 which made explicit a requirement to collect data was hard fought for by various pressure groups, but the result—a requirement to collect statistical information on women and on race (though separately rather than together)—was received as an important symbolic victory. The first s.95 report on women was published by the Home Office in 1992. There were no further editions until 1999 but there have been editions every two or three years since, the most recent publication being in 2015 (Ministry of Justice 2016). When the Labour Government came to power in 1997 with a large majority there was expectation that new ideas could be put into practice. There were some discernible differences between this new government and its predecessor. There was interest in 'what works', there was recognition of 'social' dimensions of pathways into crime as well as 'individual' pathways, and there was acknowledgement of the need to look at research evidence in dealing with offenders. Thus the 'prisoncentricity' which had dominated Conservative Government thinking in earlier years came

to be surrounded by new ideas to perhaps emphasise that imprisonment needed to be made more effective. Much hope was placed in the
Labour Government's Social Exclusion Report (2002) *Reducing Re-
Offending by Ex-Prisoners* and indeed, in the Foreword to the Report,
Prime Minister Tony Blair explained that it was not that too many men
and women were in prison, but that there had been 'a failure to capi-
talise on the opportunity prison provides to stop people offending for
good' (Social Exclusion Unit 2002: 3). However, at the same time, the
Report acknowledged that women's needs were often greater than men's
but were often felt to be overlooked or dealt with in a system designed
for male offenders (Social Exclusion Unit 2002: 139). There was also
recognition that the women's prison population was growing at a greater
rate than that of men notwithstanding a lack of evidence to suggest
that more women were committing crime or more serious crime (see
Gelsthorpe and Morris 2002). The Report outlined the prospect of a
Women's Offending Reduction Programme (WORP) and Action Plan
which boldly stated:

> Statistics show that the courts have been using custody more frequently
> for women over the last few years, even though the nature and seriousness
> of their offending has not, on the whole, been getting worse…The evi-
> dence suggests that courts are imposing more severe sentences on women
> for less serious offences. (Home Office 2004: 3)

Its aims were especially welcomed by academics and practitioners in the
field who knew these things so well:

> Its purpose is to reduce women's offending and the number of women
> in custody, by providing a better tailored and more appropriate response
> to the particular factors which have an impact on why women offend.
> The intention is not to give women offenders preferential treatment but
> to achieve equality of treatment and access to provision. (Home Office
> 2004: 5)

Other positive developments followed. There was to be no new funding, but rather the aim was to embed a consideration of the needs of

women in existing systems and approaches. The Sentencing Guidelines Council[3] was also invited to produce guidance and instructions on how the new sentencing powers in the Criminal Justice Act 2003 might impact differently on women. The Women's Policy Team (2006) set up a cross-departmental liaison group, encouraged the development of guidance concerning services for women on probation, and lent support to existing initiatives to improve community-based responses to the mental health needs of women. Notwithstanding earlier commitment to change without new funding, the Policy Team also managed to obtain some £9.15 million to build on best practice developed by small-scale initiatives such as the 218 Centre in Scotland[4] (Loucks et al. 2006) and the Asha Centre in England and Wales[5] (Rumgay 2004) and support a demonstration project *Together Women* (five women's centres in two regions of England and Wales) which sought to provide holistic support for women who were either former or current offenders or whose social exclusion needs were thought to put them at risk of offending (Hedderman et al. 2008).

Recognising that women are often disempowered by their experiences of victimisation (e.g. Hollin and Palmer 2006), a key element of the *Together Women* approach was to involve service users in the design and review of their support plans, enabling them to take a degree of control over their lives. Criminal justice professionals and other practitioners (e.g. drug service providers) welcomed the development of Together Women (Hedderman et al. 2008). Most importantly, the way in which Together Women supported women to take control of their lives and to have the confidence to make life-changing decisions was seen as crucial in enabling them to reduce their chances of offending (Hedderman et al. 2011).

It was also a positive development that awareness of a rapid increase in the number of women in prison had set in train various investigations as to what was happening. Gelsthorpe and Morris (2002), for instance, linked the huge increase to a simultaneous change in the social and economic marginalisation of women and to legislative reform which encouraged a 'punitive turn'. Deakin and Spencer (2003) suggested that women's offending had become more serious and persistent in relation to burglary, for instance. Yet another explanation related to the harsher sentencing climate fueled by media demands for the courts to use custody (Hedderman 2004). There was also the idea that following improvements in prison regimes, women' prisons had become modern day 'social services' so to speak (Carlen and Worrall 2004). But broadly, women continued to commit less serious crime than men and they were less likely to persist in crime thus there was little foundation for the increase in the use of custody in terms of offending behaviour. Another immediate prompt for action followed the deaths of six women in one prison (HMP Styal) which drew attention to the high number of women being sent to prison and the negative effects this had on them. Douglas et al. (2009), for example, reported that the initial shock of imprisonment, separation from families, and enforced living with women experiencing drug withdrawal and sometimes serious mental ill-health issues, impacted on the wider of group of women in prison. All of this led the Labour Government to commission Baroness Corston to review women 'with particular vulnerabilities' in the criminal justice system. She interpreted her brief very broadly, seeing most women in prison as 'vulnerable':

> There are many women in prison, either on remand or serving sentences for minor, non-violent offences, for whom prison is both disproportionate and inappropriate. Many of them suffer poor physical and mental health or substance abuse or had chaotic childhoods. Many have been in care. (Corston 2007: i)

Whilst it is clear from the above that the push towards co-ordinated community services for women preceded the Corston Report, it was reinforced by the wide-ranging recommendations within the report (see Annison et al. 2015). Shortly after the publication of the report, the NOMS[6] issued a National Service Framework for Women Offenders (NOMS 2008) which set out the kinds of services which were to be provided (subsequently replaced by a NOMS Women and Equalities Group authored report: *A Distinct Approach: A Guide to Working with Women offenders* (NOMS 2012)). A *Short Study on Women Offenders* carried out by the Social Exclusion Unit within the Cabinet Office (Cabinet Office 2009) further reinforced movement towards holistic services for women in the community. Indeed, by 2010 there was a network of some 40 women's community centres across England and Wales. By 2016, Women's Breakout,[7] the national network of centres and programmes reported a membership of nearly 50 organisations. Other positive developments include the development of guidance on regimes and standards of care (HM Prison Service 2008) and, more recently, there has been receptiveness within prisons to trauma informed work (privately sponsored, but publicly supported by the Prison Service) to ensure that women offenders are not further brutalized and that their vulnerability is fully acknowledged.[8] We have witnessed parallel positive developments in probation with recognition that women are 'equal but different' (HM Inspectorate of Probation 2011).[9]

This city is a very positive one…it is even one in which there is consumer satisfaction. The evaluators of *Together Women* conducted two rounds of interviews with service users; 43 service users were interviewed shortly after their first contact with Together Women, and 14 of this number, three months after the first interview. One common theme to emerge was that key workers were perceived as 'being personally interested in their clients, with a long term commitment to seeing them through, rather than seeing them as 'cases' to be resolved as quickly as possible (Hedderman et al. 2011: 10). As the researchers described, there were benefits to the personal interest shown, some service users then felt that they 'owed' their key worker attendance when they would not otherwise have done so. Others described how they did not want to let their key worker down (Hedderman et al. 2011). Numerous evaluations of new initiatives and developments for criminalized women have received positive acclaim from women themselves—too many to mention. Holloway and Brookman's (2010) evaluation of the *Turnaround Project in Wales* and McCoy et al. (2013) evaluation of the Liverpool Women's Turnaround Project reveal positive experiences of non-judgmental support, improvements in the use of alcohol, physical and mental health, relationships, offending, and social skills, for instance.

The practice of women's centres across the country in creating non-authoritarian co-operative settings, where women might be empowered to engage in social and personal change (see Gelsthorpe 2011 for an overview) perhaps gave the impression that women were no longer the 'correctional afterthoughts' that they were once thought to be (Ross and Fabiano 1986).

Yet policy and practice are sometimes some distance apart. Whilst optimism abounds in this first tale, the realities on the ground are rather different and can tell a different tale.

Tale 2: A More Gloomy City

Where has the critical onslaught and the positive praxis taken us? This second tale is rather more gloomy. It focuses on the shadows of criminal justice reform which have benefited women in recent years. There are still nearly 4000 women in prison, with a high proportion of women being imprisoned for non-violent offences, and for short sentences at that. Some 84% of women entering prison under sentence in 2017 had committed a non-violent offence (Ministry of Justice 2017) and 70% of women entering prison in the year to December 2016 were serving six months or less. This figure has grown enormously since 1993 when only a third of women were given these very short sentences (Ministry of Justice 2017). We might expect the Sentencing Council's Definitive Guideline on the Imposition of Community and Custodial Sentences to help raise the custody threshold (Sentencing Council 2016), but past performance in ensuring that custodial sentences are used as a last resort does not inspire confidence. Turning to prison regimes themselves, at best, they have improved slightly in terms of access to education and training for employment, but the impact of staffing shortages and an emphasis on security combine to limit developments (Prison Reform Trust 2017).

Other examples of shadows on the ground include evidence to suggest that whereas the police previously referred women to Women's Centres on an informal basis, they began to refer them formally (via a Women's Specific Conditional Caution) (Easton et al. 2010) with concomitant concerns about net-widening. Notwithstanding positive feedback from users of Women's Centres referred in this way, there has been confusion about the requirements, services and support available at the centres (Easton and Matthews 2011). Alongside insufficient bail accommodation for women, mental health liaison schemes have been under great strain which has meant that women have not always been referred to the specialist services which they need. There is particular evidence of an absence of dual diagnosis resources (e.g. drug misuse and mental health, for instance), and the whole approach of commissioning means that services are competing against each other rather than trying to provide a holistic service for women (Page 2013; Grace et al. 2016). *Together Women* is widely perceived to have been successful in terms of consumer views yet it was not at all clear that magistrates fully understood (nor understand) the use of Women's Centre Services as a resource in sentencing, and that placing women offenders alongside other women (in challenging circumstances, but not necessarily involving crime) can be beneficial (Hedderman and Gunby 2011). Moreover, the analysis of re-offending following *Together Women* has highlighted the lack of standardized measures and systems for recording data, limiting evaluation (Jolliffe et al. 2011). With one or two exceptions (e.g. Brighton Women's Centre Inspire Programme, following up 44 women; Ministry of Justice 2017) there has been relatively little analysis in the direction of linking the benefits of Women's Centres and reductions in re-offending. Indeed, there have been missed opportunities for networks of community services for women to engage in meta-analytic approaches to make the best of research findings based on small numbers, but there has been neither government support nor funding for this kind of venture. Non-reconviction outcomes are harder to measure, and although there has been positive work towards the creation of interim outcome measures, impact evaluations are difficult because there is no 'counterfactual'. In other words, there is no way of estimating what could have happened for users of the Women's Centre services in the absence of an intervention. Some commentators (including myself) might argue that to judge from consumer views, the benefits of women's centres far outweigh challenges of this sort, but governments require hard evidence of impact (see Radcliffe and Hunter 2016; see also HM Inspectorate of Probation 2016).

One other shadow which merits attention concerns the ORA 2014 and what it has entailed in terms of the dissolution of Probation Trusts and the creation of a new National Probation Service (NPS) responsible for public sector duties and Community Rehabilitation Companies

(CRCs) commissioned by the NOMS to work in 21 'contract package areas'. The legislation has also extended statutory post-prison release supervision to short sentence prisoners (those serving less than 12 months in custody). ORA 2014 (implemented 1 February, 2015) states (in section 10) that 'in providing supervision or rehabilitation the Secretary of State must comply with the public sector equality duty under the Equality Act 2010 as it relates to female offenders and must also identify anything in the arrangements that is intended to meet the particular needs of this group.' From the outset there were concerns that these changes would not bring unalloyed benefits to women. In 2013, Clinks published an interim study of the experiences of initiatives and centres providing community support to women offenders (*Run Ragged*); there was then a follow-up study in 2014 (*Who Cares? Where next for women offender services?*) within which 89% of initiatives felt that their service was less secure or as insecure as 12 months earlier. Probation Trust funding stopped at the end of January 2015 when the CRCs took over responsibility. *Changing Lives*, the women's centre in Cardiff, for example, was told that its contract would not be renewed, despite having been named as a sub-contractor in the original bid submitted to NOMS by Working Links. That service has now closed, with the loss of experienced staff, although the CRC did retain the city centre premises as a women's hub. Thames Valley CRC withdrew funding for work delivered by Alana House, an award-winning centre in Reading, having worked with probation services to deliver a quality service to women offenders for a number of years. There are similar stories which have affected provision for women offenders in other areas (Prison Reform Trust 2015); some contracts were extended; some became part of complicated supply chains and funding was uncertain; some centres for women have had to close as a result of the new probation landscape. Women's Break Out, the national network of women's centres and initiatives has now been absorbed by Clinks, following recognition that there was insufficient sponsorship to continue, government support for the initiative previously having been curtailed.

The closure of the Asha Centre in Worcester (a forerunner to TW) in January 2017 because of difficulty in finding funding symbolizes the uncertainty and dismay now surrounding provision for women offenders in the community.

Protected commercial interests mean that it is difficult to gain a full picture of how different CRCs are addressing the need to give attention to women. We certainly know that community service providers have been struggling to engage with some CRCs; we also know that some CRCs have decided to create their own programmes for women rather than investing in existing community provision (London CRC, for example, has created a Structured Supervision Programme for women).

To sum up this sorry tale, the Justice Committee's follow-up on women offenders (House of Commons Justice Committee 2015: paras 3 and 4) noted:

> We are concerned that funding appears to be a recurring problem for women's centres and that future funding arrangements have not been put on a sound basis as we recommended…we reiterate our recommendation that sustainable funding of specialist women's services should be a priority.

But this is not quite the end of the tale. There is also evidence of a selective focus for reform.

A Selective Gaze

In 2011 Liz Hales and I interviewed a Vietnamese woman in an English prison (Hales and Gelsthorpe 2012). This was a bright, modern prison near London with a specially designed Mother and Baby Unit, gardens, and modern workshops. There was a prison singing group, and weekly visits from a group of Quaker women who brought in cakes and good cheer. A private (or privatized) prison as it happens. We had interviewed the woman six weeks previously too, but there was so much to cover in that interview, and the necessity of a translator made things slow, so a second interview was planned. *Lam* (not her real name) was in prison for working on a cannabis farm (the offence was to do with the cultivation of cannabis). She had been there for six months. Her young children, two boys of six and eight, were back in Vietnam, living with their grandmother. She had had very little contact with them for two years. We had wanted to talk with her to see if there might be a hidden story of trafficking. And indeed, that proved to be the case, although it had been very difficult to convey anything of her experiences to the police, court or prison authorities. At the conclusion of this second interview, we asked if there was anything she wanted to ask us; we waited for the translator to speak...but she stumbled in translating the response. The question that our interviewee, '*Lam*', wanted to put to us, it seemed, was 'When am I going to be shot'? How can this be, I wondered, in an era of unprecedented penal reform regarding the treatment of women? How could those working in the system be so inhumane so as not to realise her fears and not explain what was going to happen to her? How was it that this was the first opportunity to ask a question about her own life?

Between May 2010 and November 2011, our research on the criminalisation of migrant women[10] aimed to further our understanding of migrant women, that is, foreign national women who enter the UK from overseas to seek work or asylum, voluntarily or under coercion, and who end up in custody on criminal charges (Hales and Gelsthorpe 2012). We looked at this in the context of economic and political debates around migration and asylum and the increasing awareness of the scale of international crime that profits from the illegal movement of people across borders, their sale as commodities, and their exploitation and abuse within organised crime. Our first task was thus to identify whether there were potential victims of trafficking, smuggling and work under duress in custody and, in the context of national data, assess the nature of the problem. By identifying and monitoring cases of potential victims, our second task was to provide evidence on how such victims were being managed within the Criminal Justice System and by the UK Border Agency. From this, our intention was to identify compliance with the rights of victim protection in the context of the European Convention on Trafficking[11] and the Human Rights Convention.[12] This is not the place to elaborate on findings, suffice to say that from examination of the cases of women in prisons in the South East of England, and Yarls Wood, an Immigration Removal Centre, we found 103 migrant women charged or sentenced for offences potentially linked with illegal entry or exit from the UK or work under the control of others. Following screening interviews, evidence emerged that 43 were victims of trafficking,[13] of whom two were formally re-assessed as children whilst in the adult estate.[14] An additional 5 women had entered the country independently but had then worked in slavery or servitude-like conditions and 10 had entered the UK in the hands of agents and had been arrested resultant on the theft of their documents by their smugglers. With their consent, the progress of these 58 women within this 'target group' was then monitored in terms of their management within the criminal justice and immigration systems. This was carried out by 49 follow up interviews in prison, 10 in Yarl's Wood Immigration Removal Centre and 15 more in the community for those who were not immediately deported. We tracked their progress through the courts, observing 33 appearances and gathered additional information by communication by letter and examination of relevant paper documents held by those interviewed, their legal representatives and relevant others, wherever this was feasible.[15]

Twenty of the women trafficked were forced to work in prostitution and 15 in cannabis production. Eight worked in domestic servitude, 2 were acting as drug mules and 8 were involved in street robberies and the sale of fake goods. An additional 5 women were forced into these areas of work after entering the country independently of those who controlled them in the work. The common experience of all the women within this target group was seemingly one of disempowerment, and for those trafficked or smuggled this process started from the point of recruitment. All of those interviewed indicated that they had been victims of physical and/or emotional abuse. Twenty-four women disclosed in interview that they had experienced multiple rapes and for an additional two women this had been an ongoing threat. For those who migrated to seek asylum, disclosures indicated that these experiences started prior to their move and were the key reasons for migration. For others, disclosures in interview indicated that it was integral to the relationship they had with those who brought them to the UK, who worked them under duress and to whom they were sold. For many the hold and threats made by those who had recruited, moved and controlled them did not disappear on arrest. The women's experiences led to them reporting to us that they felt socially isolated, vulnerable, traumatised, subject to flashbacks, ashamed to tell others what had happened and finding it difficult to know whom to trust. One of the key threats imposed by those who held them was that they would inform the police or immigration and this, combined with their experiences of multiple trauma, impacted on their ability to cope with arrest, imprisonment and detention.

Of those 43 who were identified as victims of trafficking by the researchers only 11 were processed through the National Referral Mechanism (NRM) and this did not happen for two of these women until their sentence was completed. Four other women were advised that this option was open to them but declined to go through this process.[16] Even where referrals were made to the NRM that resulted in a positive decision and non-prosecution, the victims spent on average 4 months in custody.[17] For the remaining women there was no formal recognition of their victim status and no access to appropriate support or protection from deportation other than applying for asylum. Of equal significance is the fact that in only one of the cases did victim disclosures result in a full police investigation in relation to the actions of the perpetrators. In two other cases, where the women stated they had been held in sex work, there was only one follow-up interview in custody by two male officers. In both cases the women, who were still on remand, declined to disclose all that they had experienced without legal support. In none of the five cases of criminalisation resultant on work under duress, or in slavery like conditions, was this formally presented to the court in terms of a not guilty plea and only one of the women whose smuggler had stolen her documents was encouraged to plead not guilty to intentionally entering the country without legal documentation.[18]

A key question of this research therefore was why so few of the women offenders, whose disclosures at interview with the researchers exemplified the key indicators of being a victim of trafficking, had been identified as such within the criminal justice system?

We identified a wide range of key policy and practice implications from the research and, noting several breaches of the Convention on Trafficking, the Human Rights Convention and the Bangkok Rules approved in 2010,[19] we urged reforms via discussions with policy-makers and via a Parliamentary seminar facilitated by the Prison

Reform Trust. This ultimately fed into the government's review of the national referral mechanism for victims of human trafficking (including 'offender' victims) (Home Office 2014). The main recommendations of the Review of the NRM were to: extend the NRM to cover all adult victims of modern slavery (including those who are seemingly 'offenders'); and strengthen the first responder role—the point when potential victims are first identified and referred—by creating new Anti-Slavery Safeguarding Leads, allowing direct referral to specialist support. A report concerned with an evaluation of a pilot study to check implementation was published in 2017 (Home Office 2017) and showed some improvement in the speed at which decisions are made, but revealed critical issues in regard to both the consistency in decision-making, resourcing of the Anti-Slavery Safeguarding Leads, and the building up of expertise.

In addition, a review of immigration carried out by Shaw (2016), recommended that government should reduce its use of immigration detention 'without delay'. Faced with evidence regarding appalling treatment of this category of women 'offenders' (against immigration law), Shaw (2016) indicated that pregnant women should never be locked up in detention, and that survivors of sexual and gender-based violence should not be detained. However, a recent research report from the charity Women for Refugee Women 'We are still here' (Lousley and Cope 2017) suggests that government policy to protect vulnerable people in regard to detention in immigration centres is not working in practice. The report, based on interviews with 26 women in Yarl's Wood detention centre in Bedfordshire, where the majority of women are held, shows that the promised new approach to safeguard and protect women who are vulnerable and prevent them from being detained, has not been properly implemented, with little evidence of active screening to discern whether someone is vulnerable or 'at risk', and survivors of sexual and gender-based violence are being detained before any attempt has been made to find out about their previous experiences (Lousley and Cope 2017). These research studies illustrate omissions in the gaze of academics, policy makers and penal reformers alike.

Concluding Reflections

Women may no longer be 'correctional afterthoughts' but these contrasting tales suggest that there is more work to do in ensuring consistency in provision of women's centres, facilitating proper evaluation of the work within, promoting scrutiny of net-widening potential in initiatives and promoting the use of imprisonment as a last resort, to name but a few areas requiring further attention. Whilst some women offenders are now being recognized as victims, there is criminalization of other women right under our noses. In other words, all the so-called reforms have been selective. Of course, we can turn to the politics of cultural difference for an explanation. The women in the second city, in prison as victims of human trafficking and women in detention centres, are not seen as *real women*,[20] they are 'other' women. Evidence here reminds us of the need to avoid an exclusive focus on the criminal justice system and to think about the panoply of control across society, in different forms and guises.

Recent debate has focused on various strategies to reduce women's imprisonment, including: recognition of women's vulnerabilities and the inappropriateness of imprisonment, diversion from the courts altogether (where there are mental health problems), limiting magistrates' sentencing powers, raising the custody threshold, deferred sentences for structured interventions and perhaps even establishing a presumption against short custodial sentences (Gelsthorpe and Sharpe 2015; Scottish Government 2017). There has also been discussion about the scope for 'specialist women's courts' (Gelsthorpe 2017). Such courts have often been described in terms of 'therapeutic jurisprudence'. The twenty-first century model of a problem-solving court focuses on discussion about the underlying reasons why a crime might have been committed and what an offender needs by way of strategy and support. The key features of problem-solving courts are thus specialisation around a target group (e.g. women, drug misusers), collaborative intervention and supervision, accountability through judicial monitoring, procedural fairness (including the offender in discussions), with a focus on outcomes. In December 2015, the British Government expressed enthusiasm for problem-solving courts and pilot schemes were set up, with the ultimate hope that this would reduce the prison population, though scepticism had set in by August 2016 and it is not clear what has happened since then in terms of evaluation (Guardian Newspaper 2016).

The potential impact of problem-solving courts should not be overstated. There is promise, but they are never going to be a complete solution to the over-use of custodial sentences in England and Wales However, in the context of other measures there may be scope for problem-solving courts to play a part in the panoply of holistic provision for women. Alongside this, we need a holistic approach to understand and respond to concerns beyond criminal justice in order to correct the recent selective gaze.

Notes

1. For the purposes of comparison, in Northern Ireland the number of women in prison has increased over time (56 in 2017; 23 in 2000), whereas in Scotland, following a peak of 443 women in prison in 2010, there has been a reduction to 360 women in prison in 2017 (Walmsley 2017).
2. Not even radical thinking about pathways into crime, which marked a movement away from individualist positivistic approaches to recognize structural oppression and inequalities in power, encompassed recognition of women. Interestingly, neither *The New Criminology* (Taylor, Walton, and Young 1973) or *Critical Criminology* (Taylor, Walton, and Young 1976), much lauded for posing questions about state definitions of crime, capitalist economies producing crime as a result of oppression and state controlled responses to crime, gave much attention to women.
3. The Sentencing Guidelines Council and Sentencing Advisory Panel were replaced by the Sentencing Council in 2010.
4. Centre 218 in Glasgow had its origins in reviews and consultation processes following a series of suicides in Cornton Vale Prison—Scotland's only prison for women. The creation of the centre was based on the idea that women should be able to 'get out of' their normal (chaotic and stressful) environments without resorting to custody.

5. Asha in West Mercia owed its origins to the pioneering work of Jenny Roberts—former Chief Probation Officer in that area. It was a community based centre offering holistic support for all women, but women offenders in particular—child care, transport, health, debt, and employment advice, for example.

6. From April 2017 renamed as Her Majesty's Prison and Probation Service (HMPPS).

7. Women's Breakout: http://womensbreakout.org.uk. The organisation merged with Clinks, a national umbrella organisation for third sector parties involved in criminal justice, in September, 2017.

8. See One Small Thing: http://www.onesmallthing.org.uk/about/. One Small Thing is an initiative sponsored by Lady Edwina Grosvenor to ensure trauma informed practices in women's prisons. The training is now being rolled out in men's prisons too.

9. For a more elaborate account of the early development of policy initiatives, see: Gelsthorpe, L. (2011). 'Working with women offenders in the community: A View from England and Wales.' In R. Sheehan, G. McIvor, & C. Trotter (Eds.), *Working with Women Offenders in the Community*. Devon: Willan Publishing.

10. ESRC funded: RES-062-23-2348.

11. Council of Europe. (2005). *Council of Europe convention on action against trafficking in human beings: Explanatory report*. Available at: http://www.coe.int/trafficking.

12. Of equal relevance are the United Nations General *Bangkok Rules for the Treatment of Female Prisoners* approved in October 2010, after commencement of this research.

13. Conclusions as to victimisation in relation to trafficking were drawn from accounts of recruitment, transportation, exploitation and evidence of physical and emotional abuse as outlined in the section on Identifying Victims in SOCA (2012) NRM www.soca.gov.uk/about-soca/ukhtc/national-referral-mechanism.

14. Within this report the term 'women' includes these two children.

15. Formal consent was sought from all interviewees for engagement in this research and before accessing additional information from relevant others.

16. This was due to desire to return home and/or fear of the repercussions of making full disclosures.

17. See the new Legal Guidance on how the CPS should manage these cases: section on Statutory defence for slavery or trafficking victims who commit an offence, Crown Prosecution Service Legal Guidance

(2017) *Human trafficking and Smuggling*: http://www.cps.gov.uk/legal/h_to_k/human_trafficking_and_smuggling/ (replacing the 2011 guidance which was in operation at the time of the research).
18. This resulted in a finding of not guilty.
19. UN General Assembly A/C.3/65/l/5. (2010). *Bangkok Rules for the treatment of women prisoners*. (Of particular relevance are rules 5, 10, 11, 12, 13, 25 and 26).
20. Foreign national women as a group make up nearly one in five of the female prison population (Women in Prison (2017) *Corston+10*).

References

Annison, J., Brayford, J., & Deering, J. (Eds.). (2015). *Women and criminal justice*. Bristol: Policy Press.

A Prison Matron. (1862). *Female life in prison by a prison matron* [F. W. Robinson]. London: Hurst and Blackett.

Barbaret, R. (2014). *Women, crime and criminal justice. A global enquiry*. London: Routledge.

Burman, M., & Gelsthorpe, L. (2017). Feminist criminology: Inequalities, powerlessness, and justice. In A. Liebling, S. Maruna, & L. McCara (Eds.), *The Oxford handbook of criminology* (6th ed.). Oxford: Oxford University Press.

Cabinet Office. (2009). *Short study on women offenders. Report conducted by social exclusion task force 2009*. London: Cabinet Office and Ministry of Justice.

Cain, M. (Ed.). (1989). *Growing up good: Policing the behaviour of girls in Europe*. London: Sage.

Carlen, P. (1990). *Alternatives to women's imprisonment*. Buckingham: Open University Press.

Carlen, P., & Worrall, A. (2004). *Analysing women's imprisonment*. Cullompton: Willan.

Clinks. (2013). *Run ragged*. London: Clinks.

Clinks. (2014). *Who cares? Where next for women offender services?* London: Clinks.

Corston, B. J. (2007). *The Corston Report: A review of women with particular vulnerabilities in the criminal justice system*. London: Home Office.

Deakin, J., & Spencer, J. (2003). Women behind bars: Explanations and implications. *Howard Journal of Crime and Justice, 42*(2), 123–136.

Dickens, C. (1859). *A tale of two cities*. London: Chapman & Hall.

Douglas, N., Plugge, E., & Fitzpatrick, R. (2009). The impact of imprisonment on health—What do women prisoners say? *Journal of Epidemiology and Community Health, 63*(9), 749–754.

Easton, H., & Matthews, R. (2011). *Evaluation of the inspire women's project.* London: London South Bank University.

Easton, H., Silvestri, M., Evans, K., Matthews, R., & Walklate, S. (2010). *Conditional cautions: Evaluation of the women's specific condition pilot* (Research Series 14/10). London: Ministry of Justice.

Gelsthorpe, L. (2011). Working with women offenders in the community: A view from England and Wales. In R. Sheehan, G. McIvor, & C. Trotter (Eds.), *Working with women offenders in the community.* Devon: Willan.

Gelsthorpe, L. (2017, July). The potential and pitfalls of problem-solving courts for women. *Howard League for Penal Reform, Early Careers Academic Network Bulletin,* (33), 4–8.

Gelsthorpe, L., & Morris, A. (2002). Women's imprisonment in England and Wales. A penal paradox. *Criminology & Criminal Justice, 2*(3), 277–301.

Gelsthorpe, L., & Sharpe, G. (2015). Women and sentencing. In J. Roberts (Ed.), *Exploring sentencing practice in England and Wales.* Basingstoke: Palgrave Macmillan.

Grace, S., Page, G., Lloyd, C., Templeton, L., Kougali, Z., McKeganey, N., et al. (2016). Establishing a 'Corstonian' continuous care package for drug using female prisoners: Linking drug recovery wings and women's community services. *Criminology and Criminal Justice, 16*(5), 602–621.

Guardian Newspaper. (2016). Available at: https://www.theguardian.com/law/2016/aug/20/liz-truss-abandons-michael-gove-plan-for-problem-solving-courts (Accessed 1 October 2017).

Hales, E., & Gelsthorpe, L. (2012). *The criminalisation of migrant women.* University of Cambridge: Institute of Criminology. (Accessed 17 December 2017). ESRC Grant: 062–23-2348.

Hedderman, C. (2004). Why are more women being sentenced to custody? In G. McIvor (Ed.), *Women who offend.* London: Jessica Kingsley.

Hedderman, C., & Gunby, C. (2011). Diverting women from custody: The importance of understanding sentencers' perspectives. *Probation Journal, 60*(4), 425–438.

Hedderman, C., Gunby, C., & Shelton, N. (2011). What women want: The importance of qualitative approaches in evaluating work with women offenders. *Criminology and Criminal Justice, 11*(1), 3–19.

Hedderman, C., Palmer, E., Hollin, C., Gunby, C., Shelton, N., & Askari, M. (2008). *Implementing services for women offenders and those 'at risk' of offending: Action research with together women* (Research Series 12/08). London: Ministry of Justice.

Heidensohn, F. (1968). The deviance of women: A critique and an enquiry. *British Journal of Sociology, 19*(2), 160–175.

Heidensohn, F., & Silvestri, M. (2012). Gender and crime. In M. Maguire, R. Morgan, & R. Reiner (Eds.), *The Oxford handbook of criminology* (5th ed.). Oxford: Oxford University Press.

HM Prison Service. (2008). *Women prisoners, prison service order number 4800.* Available at: www.justice.gov.uk/offenders/types-of-offender/women. (Accessed 1 December 2017).

HM Inspectorate of Probation. (2011). *Thematic inspection report: Equal but different? An inspection of alternatives to custody for women offenders.* Manchester: HM Inspectorate of Probation. Available at: http://www.justiceinspectorates.gov.uk/probation/wp-content/uploads/sites/5/2014/03/womens-thematic-alternatives-to-custody-2011.pdf.

HM Inspectorate of Probation. (2016). *A thematic inspection of the provision and quality of services in the community for women who offend.* Manchester: HM Inspectorate of Probation. Available at: https://www.justiceinspectorates.gov.uk/hmiprobation/wp-content/uploads/sites/5/2016/09/A-thematic-inspection-of-the-provision-and-quality-of-services-in-the-community-for-women-who-offend.pdf.

Hollin, C., & Palmer, E. (2006). Criminogenic need and women offenders: A critique of the literature. *Legal and Criminological Psychology, 11*(2), 179–195.

Holloway, K., & Brookman, F. (2010). *An evaluation of the women's turnaround project.* NOMS Cymru.

Home Office. (2004). *Women's Offending Reduction Programme (WORP) action plan.* London: Home Office.

Home Office. (2014). *Review of the national referral mechanism for victims of human trafficking.* London: Home Office. Available at: https://www.gov.uk/government/uploads/system/uploads/attachment_data/file/467434/review_of_the_National_Referral_Mechanism_for_victims_of_human_trafficking.pdf (Accessed 1 December 2017).

Home Office. (2017). *An Evaluation of the national referral mechanism pilot.* Research Report 94. N. Ellis, C. Cooper & S. Roe. London: Home Office.

House of Commons Justice Committee Justice—Thirteenth Report. Women offenders. Follow-up. (2015). http://www.publications.parliament.uk/pa/cm201415/cmselect/cmjust/314/31407.htm.

Hutter, B., & Williams, G. (1981). *Controlling women: The normal and the deviant*. London: Croom Helm.

Jolliffe D., Hedderman C., Palmer E., & Hollin C. (2011). *Re-offending analysis of women offenders referred to Together Women (TW) and the scope to divert from custody* (Ministry of Justice Research Series 11/11). London: Ministry of Justice.

Loucks, N., Malloch, M., McIvor, G., & Gelsthorpe, L. (2006). *Evaluation of the 218 centre*. Edinburgh: Scottish Executive.

Lousley, G., & Cope, S. (2017). *We are still here. The continued detention of women seeking asylum in Yarl's Wood*. London: Women for Refugee Women.

McCoy, E., Jones, L., & McVeigh, J. (2013). *Evaluation of the Liverpool women's turnaround project*. Liverpool: Centre for Public Health, John Moore's University.

Ministry of Justice. (2015). *Justice data lab reoffending analysis: Women's centres throughout England*. London: Ministry of Justice.

Ministry of Justice. (2016). *Statistics on women and the criminal justice system 2015. A Ministry of Justice publication under Section 95 of the Criminal Justice Act 1991*. London: Ministry of Justice.

Ministry of Justice. (2017). Offender management statistics quarterly July–September 2016. London: Ministry of Justice.

Ministry of Justice. (2017, April). Justice data lab analysis: Re-offending behaviour after participation in the Brighton Women's Centre Inspire Progamme.

National Offender Management Service (NOMS). (2012). *A distinct approach: A guide for working with women offenders*.

National Offender Management Service (NOMS). (2015). *Better outcomes for women offenders*. London: NOMS.

Page, G. (2013). *Risks, needs and emotional rewards: Complexity and crisis in the drug interventions programme*. Unpublished PhD, University of Cambridge.

Prison Reform Trust. (2015, September 23). *Prison reform trust response to HM Inspectorate of Probation's call for evidence on work with women offenders*. Available at http://www.prisonreformtrust.org.uk/Portals/0/Documents/Consultation%20responses/HMI%20Probation%20women%20offenders.pdf.

Prison Reform Trust. (2017). *Why focus on reducing women's imprisonment? Briefing*. London: Prison Reform Trust.

Radcliffe, P., & Hunter, G. (2016). 'It was a safe place for me to be': Accounts of attending women's community service and moving beyond the offender identity. *British Journal of Criminology, 56*(5), 976–994.

Ross, R., & Fabiano, E. (1986). *Female offenders: Correctional afterthoughts.* Jefferson, NC: McFarland.

Rumgay, J. (2004). *The Asha Centre: Report of an evaluation.* Worcester: Asha Centre.

Scottish Government. (2017). Consultation on proposals to strengthen the presumption against short periods of imprisonment: An analysis of responses. Available at: http://www.gov.scot/Publications/2016/03/8624/3.

Sentencing Council. (2016). *Imposition of community and custodial sentences.* Definitive Guideline. London: Sentencing Council.

Shaw, S. (2016). *Review into the welfare in detention of vulnerable persons: A Report to the Home Office.* Available at: https://www.gov.uk/government/uploads/system/uploads/attachment_data/file490782/52532_Shaw_Review_Accessible/pdf (Accessed 1 December 2017).

Social Exclusion Unit. (2002). *Reducing re-offending by ex-prisoners.* London: Office of the Deputy Prime Minister.

Smart, C. (1976). *Women, crime and criminology.* London: Routledge and Kegan Paul.

Smith, A. (1962). *Women in prison. A study in penal methods.* London: Stevens & Sons.

Walmsley, R. (2017). *Women and girls in penal institutions, including pre-trial detainees/remand prisoners.* World Prison Brief. Birkbeck, University of London: Institute for Criminal Policy Research.

Women in Prison. (2017). *Corston+10. The Corston report 10 years on.* London: Women in Prison.

Women's Policy Team. (2006). *Women's offending reduction programme: 2006 review of progress.* London: Home Office.

Erratum to: Women and the Criminal Justice System

Emma Milne, Karen Brennan, Nigel South
and Jackie Turton

Erratum to:
E. Milne et al. (eds.), *Women and the Criminal Justice System*,
https://doi.org/10.1007/978-3-319-76774-1

The original version of this book was inadvertently published with an outdated editor affiliation. The affiliation of the book editor, Emma Milne, has been corrected as follows:

Emma Milne
Middlesex University
London, UK

The updated online version of this book can be found at
https://doi.org/10.1007/978-3-319-76774-1

© The Author(s) 2018
E. Milne et al. (eds.), *Women and the Criminal Justice System*,
https://doi.org/10.1007/978-3-319-76774-1_11

Index

© The Editor(s) (if applicable) and The Author(s) 2018
E. Milne et al. (eds.), *Women and the Criminal Justice System*,
https://doi.org/10.1007/978-3-319-76774-1